THE BOOK OF
new FAMILY TRADITIONS

How to Create Great Rituals for Holidays and Every Day

Meg Cox

Illustrations by Trina Dalziel

RUNNING PRESS
PHILADELPHIA · LONDON

A man becomes the song he sings.

—*Irish proverb*

Published by Running Press,
A Member of the Perseus Books Group

Books published by Running Press are available at special discounts for bulk purchases in the United States by corporations, institutions, and other organizations. For more information, please contact the Special Markets Department at the Perseus Books Group, 2300 Chestnut Street, Suite 200, Philadelphia, PA 19103, or call (800) 810-4145, ext. 5000, or e-mail special.markets@perseusbooks.com.

Excerpt from *The Family Dinner: Great Ways to Connect With Your Kids One Meal at a Time* by Laurie David, with recipes by Kirstin Uhrenholdt, is reprinted with permission from Hachette Book Group (Grand Central Life & Style imprint).

ISBN 978-0-7624-4318-5
Library of Congress Control Number: 2012931454

E-book ISBN 978-0-7624-4494-6

9   8   7   6   5   4   3   2   1
Digit on the right indicates the number of this printing

Cover and Interior design by Corinda Cook
Illustrations by Trina Dalziel
Edited by Jennifer Kasius
Typography: Franklin Gothic and Sinclair

Running Press Book Publishers
2300 Chestnut Street
Philadelphia, PA 19103-4371

Visit us on the web!
www.runningpress.com

Parents Praise *The Book of New Family Traditions*

"I bought this book and read it cover-to-cover with a highlighter and a package of Post-it flags so I could refer to it again and again when "that" holiday/event/ritual/chance arose. I have given it as a gift as well several times and recommended it, and it is always cherished. A beautiful, innovative book that helps you establish your own family traditions."
　—*Susan Wagoner*

"When I got together with my husband, his daughter was ten years old. Your book helped make the three of us into a family. Before the book, recommended by friends, there were no rituals for the three of us. But this book opened doors for us. You helped me create relevant, fun, meaningful, and fresh rituals."
　—*Linda McKittrick*

"Since your talk and reading the book, I've been able to incorporate many of your ideas like half birthdays, painting rocks on the first day of spring, and on and on. I've also noticed how rich our lives were already with ritual. Little ones, like my sons touching my husband's freshly shaved face in the morning to take some 'good smell' for their own faces when he leaves for work. Thanks for the fresh ideas!"
　—*Alexandra Barcohen*

"My entire playgroup of moms went to the bookstore together and purchased a copy of your book some years ago. It is my number one recommended book for parents to this day. My copy is getting worn because I continue to refer to it. This book has had a life-changing impact on our family."
　—*Jane L. Pierce*

"Some parenting books are great but abstract. This one is so practical, and not intimidating. This has given me actual ideas of things to do with my family that will create meaningful memories."
　—*Wendy Patterson*

"I don't know of a more unique book for families and significant family rituals out there than this one. One example of inspiration is that every Christmas, my family sat down and wrote out answers to a question about what each of us means to one another. Our sons are in their twenties, but I discovered they kept the questions and answers from those times. This has been a very special ritual for us, and it would not have happened without me reading your fantastic suggestions."
　—*Mary Jane Mitchell*

Contents

Chapter 4: Holidays . . . 201

Preface

Author's Note on the New Edition of
The Book of New Family Traditions

For those who are not familiar with the original edition of this book, let me be clear about what it is, and what it is not. This is not the book of an expert. It is the book of a passionate journalist, a well-trained and credentialed reporter who interviewed dozens of experts and hundreds of families.

I've been researching family traditions ever since writing the proposal for my first book, *The Heart of a Family*, while I was pregnant with my son in 1994. I've worked hard all these years to check facts and provide reliable information, but my main job is to search for all sorts of families with powerful, memorable rituals and organize their amazing stories into useful tools for families.

Since its publication in 2003, thousands of parents have used *The Book of New Family Traditions* to help them create fresh, fun, and memorable family rituals and gatherings. I've heard from countless mothers and fathers who tell me it's a well-thumbed resource they keep going back to as the seasons and years progress, using it to spice up existing rituals and add new ones as needed.

As the years have gone by, I have continued to write a newsletter on family traditions and magazine articles on the topic, and I still lecture and teach about ritual creation. I keep collecting additional great ideas for celebrations from the families I meet, the readers who contact me, and the traditions I create for my own family.

When *The Book of New Family Traditions* was first published in 2003, my son, Max, was nine. Now he is seventeen, so I've learned a lot from personal experience about how family traditions evolve and grow—and sometimes fall away. I also became a grandmother when my stepdaughter, Kate, gave birth to her daughter, Lucy, in 2008, opening a new window onto family celebrations.

I wanted to share all these resources and gather fresh research and family stories to make this book an even more valuable tool. Fans of the original will find that virtually all the previous content is still here, but nearly every category and section has been expanded with new examples and suggestions of ways to make holidays memorable and find little, practical rituals to smooth out the rough patches in a child's day.

What's different this time?

This book has always stood out from the pack by covering such wide ground, running the gamut from major holidays to everyday rituals like bedtime and dinnertime, and for including the quirky practices of creative families that live outside the box. But the 2003 edition was organized with holidays and major celebrations first, pushing everyday rituals into the second half. I have long believed that although most parents focus on the big events when they start creating traditions for their kids, what really matters most to the quality of a kid's life is the everyday stuff. To a toddler, next Christmas is farther away than the next millennium, but if he has a bedtime ritual that makes him feel safe and loved, his life today is golden.

So I decided to reverse the book's priorities in that direction, not only starting the book with everyday rituals, but also weighting the new material heavily toward daily, weekly, and monthly practices. Although there are awesome new ideas here for Christmas, Thanksgiving, birthdays, family reunions, and other big moments, I've really focused my search on powerful and practical day-to-day rituals. You will find a lot more ideas than before on how to use ritual to solve all the routine tensions of daily family life, like sibling fights, supermarket "gimme" tantrums, and bedtime meltdowns. I've especially ramped up the section on dinners, because I'm such a believer in the value of eating together daily. Solid scientific research continues to back up the anecdotal evidence that regular family meals are one of the best predictors that kids will grow up centered, confident, and resilient.

I also asked myself as I prepared the new edition: What has affected family life the most in the nine years since the original? Clearly, the answer is technology, which has swept through both our daily and our ritual lives. In 2010, I was startled by an article in the *New York Times* about how some Jewish kids were preparing for their bar/bat mitzvahs by studying online. There are multiple websites with names like MyBarMitzvahTeacher.com, where kids utilize up-to-the-moment tools like Skype and YouTube and iPods to learn their passage of the Torah in Hebrew.

Which is a good thing. Technology opens up all sorts of wisdom, ancient and modern, and allows for new ways of learning and sharing and connecting. But there are definitely downsides, when it comes to keeping families close.

Everyone in this culture is relentlessly peppered with electronic messages, surrounded by enticing screens everywhere we go. The number of personal electronic devices has multiplied astronomically, and it's way more fun to play a game or watch your favorite TV cartoon than learn how to share toys with your sister or have a real conversation at the dinner table when everyone is tired and hungry.

These are very seductive devices, because while everyone is engrossed in their own video game or TV show, there may be fewer fights among brothers and sisters. But what have we lost? When you stop and think about it, sibling fights are a type of ritual, too, ones that teach kids how to get along with other people. The idea isn't to eliminate conflict but to use ritual as a tool to dissipate crises so your kids learn how to react in a positive way.

Certainly, technology isn't going away, and I think the only real solution is for parents to figure out how to use it wisely. This edition explores the many ways in which they can harness these devices to actually bring their families closer by both creating and recording great memories. Whether it's through a family blog or secret texting codes, or silly themed movies made on smart phones, families can create new traditions using technology to *unite* rather than divide them.

Truly, Americans are a nation of tradition lovers, people who cherish their roots. As before, I've included a very diverse group of families, from all sorts of ethnic backgrounds and religions and domestic arrangements, and if anything, the variety is even greater this time.

Here's an important point: When it comes to ritual (and loads of other things), parents should feel free to borrow from good ideas that are already circulating, no matter that another family's tree was planted in a different country or type of soil. I mean, whether it's an apple tree or a fig tree or some other type of tree, there are certain principles of good stewardship that apply to virtually *all* trees. Am I right?

So, before you turn the page and skip some family's ritual in the book because they are Christians and you are Jewish or Buddhist or Hindu or Muslim or agnostic, do yourself a favor and check it out anyway. You might stumble across a kernel of an idea that will inspire your next family celebration. Just because you didn't grow up celebrating Kwanzaa or Passover or Arbor Day doesn't mean you couldn't start now. Maybe you've been celebrating Easter for years but would like to add something new for the kids: Why not try the ritual of *cascarones,* confetti-filled eggs, so popular with Mexican Americans?

There are surely many traditions in this book that won't fit your family, but my goal was not to present these hundreds of rituals just to be copied—I hope they will inspire. If you know additional creative ways to mark big occasions and deepen simple daily rituals, I hope you'll share them with me, because I'll never stop looking for more. Send me an e-mail at meg@megcox.com, or write a letter to me through my publisher.

I dedicate this book to parents in families everywhere who know that their kids' childhoods will zoom by in a flash and are determined to break those years down into memorable moments and deeply shared experiences.

Introduction

Why Does It Matter So Much?

Kissing a boo-boo is both a ritual and a metaphor.

If your child takes a tumble, you scoop her up, dust her off, and check for cuts, bruises, or breaks. Even before any necessary medical attention, it's time for hugs and kisses. Likely, there are certain words you always use at these times. "That's my strong, brave girl!" or "Mommy's here, and you're fine." Or whatever sounds right to you.

This is a ritual because it's a series of actions we parents perform intentionally, in a particular order with prescribed words and actions. The holding and comforting of the child is as vital as the disinfectant and Band-Aid in keeping her safe, because it also works as a kind of long-term psychological talisman. The reassurance that loving arms will always be there to pick her up and keep her safe is a lot of what makes it possible for your child to keep taking one more leap into the big, unknown world out there.

And that's where the metaphor part comes in. Ritual in general, all the little and big things we do together as families, works as a safety net, a security blanket, and an ongoing promise of protection.

I knew a family that actually had something they called the "Poor Sweet Baby Blanket," a worn blanket they kept in a closet. When any member of the family had an atrocious day, they took the blanket out at day's end and wrapped it around that person, while hugging him or her and saying the soothing words, "Poor Sweet Baby!"

Most parents already have a life laced with ritual and tradition, but they don't always realize it. The dozens of small, often idiosyncratic actions and responses that occur every day just come pouring out of them from love and habit. These are things as simple as a catchphrase you say when you pull out of the driveway, or the precise way your toddler's stuffed animals must be lined up at bedtime. Parents don't glorify these things with words like "ritual" or "tradition." But they should.

In my work, I start by trying to get parents to realize the supreme importance of these small gestures and how they fit alongside the bigger, more dramatic events and celebrations that constitute a family's ritual life.

Let's start with a definition. I sometimes use the words *ritual* and *tradition* interchangeably, but I prefer the word *ritual* because it covers more ground. It's a stretchy word that covers everything from saying grace at the table to big ceremonies like weddings and funerals.

The dictionary says a ritual is an action repeated. Ritual is something you do in the same way over and over, on purpose. To me, family ritual is practically any activity you purposely repeat together as a family that includes a heightened attentiveness, and something extra that lifts it above the ordinary ruts. A habit isn't the same at all. It's something you do like brushing your teeth—without thinking, on automatic pilot.

Another difference between rituals and habits is the nature of your purpose. You brush your teeth so they stay clean and won't fall out. You don't have family dinners just for the purpose of putting food in your bellies: You gather together because you want to build a deep, satisfying sense of belonging for your tribe.

Here's another way to describe the difference between ritual and routine, and it comes from an unexpected source, a California-based fitness trainer named Chip Conrad. I found this quote on his website:

There is a great difference between routine and ritual. Routines are obligatory activities that require little or no thought. Rituals encompass spirit, magic, and that overused word, empowerment, to transform you to new levels of accomplishment and being.

Now, Conrad is talking about taking people to transformative, new levels of physical fitness. But he's really made the distinction brilliantly, and I think families that work to achieve memorable, personal rituals will very likely tap into something magical. And they will definitely empower their children.

But what's the extra pizzazz that makes an activity a ritual, not a routine? You need to create a splash, throw some metaphorical sprinkles on top. Repeated words or actions, special food or music, and a heightened sense of attention can provide the juice you need. I wouldn't call it a ritual if you sometimes sit on the front steps of your house, blowing bubbles with your kids. But if you do it every Friday while consuming cookies and lemonade and call it your "Welcome to the Weekend Party," then it's definitely a family ritual.

Many of my favorite rituals are extremely simple. There's the mother who writes inspiring messages in colored chalk on her driveway and street for her daughters to find on the first day of school. Or the father who provides "monster spray" in a spritz bottle so his son can fall asleep every night feeling protected.

Ten Good Things Rituals Do for Children

1. Impart a sense of identity
2. Provide comfort and security
3. Help to navigate change
4. Teach values
5. Pass on ethnic or religious heritage
6. Teach practical skills
7. Solve problems
8. Keep alive a sense of departed family members
9. Help heal from loss or trauma
10. Generate wonderful memories

Ritual is a package deal. It's everything we do to celebrate our families, not just on special occasions, but also every day, every meal, every bath, and every bedtime story. In ritual, little is big: Although dress-up holidays with lavish feasts are fun, it's the everyday traditions that determine how we experience our families and demonstrate hands-on love for our children.

Intuitively, we know this is good, and we consciously pass down beloved traditions from our own childhoods. But the power of ritual and the need for it are far stronger than we realize. Anthropologists have never found a human culture without ritual!

Even the most bewildered new mom quickly realizes that her baby gets calmer with a settled routine for sleeping, eating, and other activities. And if you start singing a funny little song every time you get ready to dip her in the baby tub, she starts cooing in anticipation: The two of you are in a private sorority, and she loves knowing the secret handshake. Through rituals and traditions as simple as this, you are building the bond of your joined identity, defining your relationship by acting it out.

There's no question that creating and sustaining family traditions takes effort. But if you enter into ritual making with an understanding of its awesome, multiple benefits, you will never want to stop.

Comfort and security are two of the most important benefits of early ritual, and these are not just things we need as babies.

Rituals also provide a sense of identity: Religious families build their beliefs into every tradition from high holidays to bedtime prayers. Sports-crazed families often have sports-related rituals, whereas musical families sing together. Children grow up feeling Mexican or Chinese partly because of ethnic celebrations and ritual foods. Kids who grow up feeling close to their extended families are those who regularly attend family reunions, or go to "cousins camp" at Grandma's every summer.

Next to rituals of celebration, which include birthdays and holidays, the biggest category is probably rituals that help children handle transitions. Bedtime rituals, for one, are all about helping infants and children to switch gears from activity and togetherness to stillness and solitude.

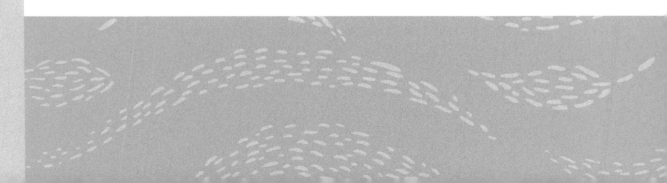

But there is so much more going on. Rituals need to be conscious because they also pass on our values. That's why many families add rituals of philanthropy to their holiday festivities and don't just focus on gift giving. I interviewed members of one Jewish family that was so wedded to living their values about donating 10 percent of income to charity that they actually had a ritual of donating 10 percent of their Monopoly money when they passed Go in the game. No, that pretend money didn't heal a sick person or feed a hungry one, but it was a ritual reminder of what mattered to them, threaded through their family lives.

Rituals can also be designed to teach practical skills, as in families where the kids take turns making Sunday dinner—even if they start off serving peanut butter sandwiches.

Savvy parents realize early that one of the most practical uses of ritual is in problem solving. Do the kids bicker constantly? Create a tension-diffusion ritual. Having a crisis every time you drop your toddler off at day care? Design a good-bye ritual that helps him feel loved but independent, ready to explore new grounds.

Ritual is also an important tool in helping families heal in times of stress or loss, whether it's the backyard funeral for a beloved pet or the loss of the Little League championship. Looking back on the aftermath of the 9/11 terrorism, there was a constant focus, not just on the loss, but also on the rituals of mourning and healing, from New York City Fire Department bagpipes to the planting of a million daffodils around New York City. Victims' families handled grief with their own private rituals, as with the little boy who ran around in his backyard every night waving a burning sparkler for his dad in heaven to see.

Ellen Galinsky, cofounder of the Families and Work Institute and the author of such books as *Ask the Children*, has done groundbreaking research on what kids really think of their lives and their parents. When she asked kids what they would remember most from their childhoods, Ms. Galinsky learned that it wasn't big gifts or fancy celebrations, but simple rituals and everyday traditions; modest but personal gestures of love, like made-up bedtime stories, that left the children feeling safe and cherished.

Three Studies That Prove the Power of Family Traditions

Study 1

Teenagers who have dinner with their families infrequently (less than three times a week) are three and a half times more likely to abuse prescription drugs than teens who have frequent family dinners (five times or more weekly). Teens who rarely have family dinners are also two and a half times more likely to smoke cigarettes, and one and a half times likelier to use alcohol.

Source: A 2007 study, "The Importance of Family Dinner," conducted by The National Center on Addiction and Substance Abuse at Columbia University (www.casacolumbia .org). Further, the center released a study in 2011 saying that 90 percent of adults who fit the criteria of being addicts began smoking, drinking, or using drugs as teenagers.

Study 2

Studies of families with alcoholic parents have shown that if the parents continue to perform the family's established rituals and traditions, including the celebrations of major holidays, the children are much less likely to become alcoholics themselves. In a study group in which the parents were extremely scrupulous about continuing family rituals, only 25 percent of the children grew up to be alcoholic. Among those families in which ritual practice was haphazard, more than 75 percent of the children suffered from alcoholism as adults.

Source: Dr. Steven J. Wolin, psychiatrist and professor at George Washington University Medical School. Dr. Wolin said in an interview with the author that he has long been fascinated by cases in which children from extremely troubled backgrounds still manage to grow up well-adjusted. With colleagues, he conducted a series of studies of families of alcoholics during the 1970s and 1980s, writing many papers on the results. In the *Journal of Studies on Alcohol 41* (1988), he and several colleagues published a paper, "Disrupted Family Rituals: A Factor in the Intergenerational Transmission of Alcoholism."

Study 3

Children who grow up with solid, satisfying family rituals, including such traditions as dinnertimes, weekend outings, vacations, and holidays, adjust much more easily and happily to college life.

Source: Dr. Barbara Fiese, a professor at the University of Illinois and director of the Family Resiliency Center there, has written often about the importance of meaningful family traditions in such publications as the 2006 book, *Family Routines and Rituals* (Yale University Press). Her many reports on the topic include "Reclaiming the Family Table: Mealtimes and Child Health and Well-Being," published by the Society for Research in *Child Development Social Policy Report 22* (4) (2008). The professor discussed her overall findings in an interview with the author.

These and other studies confirm what we know intuitively: Rituals and celebrations help kids feel connected and valued. This is where the rubber meets the road in terms of "quality time." If parents make an effort to create traditions, and then routinely, reliably practice those traditions, they are sending a message very loudly that their kids aren't just a bothersome distraction from plowing through the to-do list but are the central focus of life.

So we all want memorable, meaningful family traditions. But when do families need rituals and celebrations? And where do they come from?

CHAPTER 1

Ritual Recipes: Getting Started

Many families start with holidays, a natural place to begin. There are also the rituals that just creep up on us: You serve pancakes with chocolate chips one Sunday, and then the next Sunday, the kids wonder, "Why aren't we having the special Sunday pancakes?" A ritual is born.

But where else do rituals belong? What is enough? Can there be too many? What is the recipe for ritual?

There is no minimum daily requirement of ritual prescribed by the US Department of Agriculture or child psychologists, but if I had to reduce ritual life to a formula, I'd give families three goals to meet.

First, research and experience suggest that families should have one solid ritual of connection daily, and I'll explain in a minute what that might look like. Second, I recommend they also plan a modest weekly family ritual. In addition, all major milestones, accomplishments, and relevant holidays deserve to be celebrated, leaving enormous leeway to individual families about which occasions they mark, and how. Third, but just as vital, I suggest applying rituals as a corrective whenever there's a bumpy spot in the regular routine. Transitions are always tough for young children: Substituting a fun or silly ritual for a ritual of tantrums and fussing can miraculously smooth over rough patches.

If you follow the simple guidelines above, you'll have all the major bases covered, and anything else will be gravy. You will soon find yourself and your kids becoming attuned to ritual, to the point that when some major event occurs or is coming soon, at least one family member will pipe up to say, "We need a ritual for this!"

Daily and Weekly Rituals of Connection

Daily rituals of connection don't have to take up much time and can take many forms. The important thing is that every family member gets to act or speak. Some families have breakfast together and compare their thoughts about the day ahead. Other families find it easier to connect after school each day, or at dinner or bedtime.

The Kyger family in Virginia saves its connection ritual for dinner. After a simple Quaker grace, during which family members briefly hold hands and pray silently, each person around the table has to share something "new and good" about their day, even the teenagers. Another family has a bedtime ritual called "gratefuls and grumbles," when the children have to come up with one of each but must end on the positive note of something for which they are grateful.

Bobbi Conner, longtime host of the National Public Radio (NPR) program *The Parent's Journal,* created her daily ritual of connection when her kids were small. It occurred right after she got home from work each evening. She writes about it in her excellent book *Unplugged Play,* noting that before she started doing this, her reentry time at home was extremely stressful. The kids were hungry and cranky and wanted to tell her things, but she felt pressure to put down her purse and immediately make dinner, and the tension escalated. So instead, she decided to really connect with them right after walking in the door. She would make a simple healthy snack, like apples and cheese, sit down with her children right away, and get caught up on their moods and news. Then, after everyone was reconnected, the kids happily ran off to play and Bobbi could calmly prepare a meal.

One of my favorite family rituals of all time, and a good simple template, was created by Suzy Kellett, a divorced mother of quadruplets. Starting when the quads were in grade school, she started having a relaxed "teatime" with her kids in the evening. As they got older, teatime would move a little later, until it eventually reached 9:00 PM or so. But every night, at the designated time, her four kids would stop doing homework, hang up the phone, and gather in the family room for twenty or thirty minutes. In addition to drinking cinnamon herbal tea, the Kelletts were drinking in each other's stories. All of us change continually, and such "check-in circles" allow us to witness one another's transformations, while also celebrating what stays constant in our connection.

Weekly rituals also vary widely, including weekly meetings or a designated "family night." One family has a weekly "pizza night" at home but structures the meal to include family business. Family members may tell jokes and rate their favorite sports teams while eating pizza, but over dessert, they always discuss current family issues, anything from behavior concerns to vacation ideas. It's also fine if the weekly get-together is "movie night" in your family room. But in that case, it's even more important to build in a conversational give-and-take component. Saying "please pass the popcorn" doesn't qualify as a ritual of connection.

Many religious families use a weekly family night to help pass on their faith, devoting part of the evening to prayer. Some families have a meeting format, maybe half an hour that includes a review of everyone's schedule that week and a discussion of chores. To make it fun, this is also a good time to pay the kids their allowances or designate a family "winner

Five Signs You Need a Family Ritual

1. A big occasion is coming: holiday, birthday, new driver's license, graduation, and so on.
2. A family member gets hit with major news, good or bad: a sports victory, hugely improved report card, death of a grandparent or a pet, big promotion.
3. A recurring rough spot clouds the family routine, a time when the kids always whine, such as during transitions. This rough patch could be bath time, getting dressed for school, starting homework, or bedtime.
4. The whole family, especially the kids, displays a general sense of boredom or malaise. Maybe it's the winter doldrums or an economic downturn, but people need a lift.
5. You want to make "teachable moments" both fun and unforgettable. Among the lessons you seek to teach could be your values, the family's history, or practical life skills.

of the week," based on attitude and accomplishments, and end with a special snack.

In the following pages, this book will offer detailed ideas for holidays and celebrations, but families should also be on the lookout for unconventional milestones. Maybe your child isn't ever going to be an Olympic swimmer but finally conquered a long-standing fear of getting his face wet or completed his first real dive. To celebrate such spontaneous triumphs, keep a package of instant brownie mix in your pantry. Make a brownie sundae, or use a star-shaped cookie cutter on the brownies to properly celebrate his stardom.

One of the most rewarding but under-appreciated uses of ritual is to smooth over rough spots in a family's regular routine. Take the mother who had trouble getting her kids out of bed after weekends—she invented "Monday sundaes" for breakfast (frozen yogurt, fresh fruit, and sprinkles), which only get served to kids who are dressed and downstairs inside her time limit.

Ingredients:

The Three Parts of a Ritual

But once you know you want a ritual, how do you make one?

There is no "Joy of Rituals" cookbook, but after interviewing hundreds of families across the country and trying lots of rituals with my own family, I've developed some basic "recipes" for making memorable traditions.

A satisfying and thorough ritual has three parts: It has a beginning, a middle (the central action), and an end. Even a simple grace before supper has those elements: a nod or verbal cue that grace is to be said, the grace itself, and "Amen" at the end. Although extremely basic, these are similar to the three stages anthropologists observe in tribal rites of passage: First comes preparation, then action (and often transformation, say, from boyhood to manhood), and finally the stage of integration and celebration.

The reason you need some sort of beginning is that ritual is human life in capital letters: It needs to be punctuated, capitalized, elevated. Ritual is *not* normal life. It isn't bland or boring but is vivid, whether by virtue of blaring noisemakers or solemn silence. Ritual requires intense focus, and a good ritual beginning gets the participants engaged. It tells people a ritual is starting, like the rising curtain before a theater performance.

A common way to signal a ritual's start is by sound: a verbal cue, or special music, or tapping a fork against the side of a glass. Visual cues work, too.

If you think about a simple birthday celebration, the "beginning" is as basic as turning out the lights before presenting the cake. The "action" stage is when the child blows out candles and makes a wish while everybody sings "Happy Birthday." In the final or celebration stage, everyone eats cake and the child opens gifts.

Ritual beginnings make us aware that something special is about to happen, functioning like the verbal "Once upon a time" cue of a fairy tale. But special doesn't have to mean complicated.

How to Start and End a Ritual

You will find detailed advice later in the chapter about the central action in a ritual, but here are some quick ideas about how to signal when a ritual, of whatever size, is about to start or end.

Beginning

Sounds: Clapping, bells, whistles, gongs, a drum roll, or other musical cues (play a fitting song on whatever device is handy). Or the absence of sound, a moment of silence.

Verbal cues: A prayer, a simple group chant, or a direct declarative sentence, such as "Let us begin."

Visual cues: Lighting of a candle (or candles), lights turned out or flicked on and off, a curtain lifted, the dramatic entrance of a leader.

Ending

Choose from among the sound and visual cues from the Beginning section: You may want to bookend your ritual with something similar. If you turned out the lights, turn them back on. If you lit candles, blow them out. If you are doing musical cues, choose something that comes to a crescendo or fades to silence.

Possible physical cues for ending include bowing heads, holding hands (with a squeeze at the end), hugging.

Verbal cues: Silence. Simple words such as "Amen" or "Blessed be." Or a pop culture or literary reference that suits the tone of your ritual, like "Mischief managed," a nod to Harry Potter.

Keep in mind that the three-part format applies generally to more weighty or lengthy rituals. But it's a good rubric to keep in the back of your mind when you set out to create a new tradition for your family.

This isn't meant to denigrate simple rituals at all, because some of the simplest can be incredibly powerful. These often just happen spontaneously and should be treasured.

Two examples: I once interviewed a woman whose family had a simple ritual from her childhood of squeezing one another's hands three times, to signal the three words *I love you*. On the day she got married and her father walked her down the aisle in church, he squeezed her hand three times. Only she knew that this was happening, a tiny personal ritual lodged invisibly within one of the grandest and most public, and she says it was one of the most moving moments of her life.

Another incredibly simple ritual, also between a father and daughter, was called "Gimme Skins," and it simply consisted of the dad giving his little girl "high fives" with his palms before heading off to work. I met this woman years later, when she was running a day care center for a major corporation. She told me that one day when she was about three years old, she woke up late because she had been sick. Her dad had left for work without doing their little ritual, and she was so alarmed, without thinking, she lit-erally ran into the street in front of her house naked! To an adult, this might be a tiny ritual, but its absence left a big hole in her day.

Whether your rituals are small and spontaneous or complicated and planned out, giving some thought to their structure and the signals that you send to family members and they send to you will make these shared moments more memorable.

The Two P's:

Find Your Purpose, and Make It Personal

The seed for a ritual's form, the central action of a ritual, grows directly from its purpose. That includes everything from holidays to problem-solving rituals. Figure out your purpose, and then you can imagine creative ways to achieve it that suit your family.

Take this problem-solving ritual: After they were in a minor car accident, the Suttons vowed they would never again forget to buckle their seatbelts, so they decided to invent a seatbelt ritual. The purpose, of course, is buckling, which becomes the ritual "action," but this has to be preceded by a simple beginning to cue the behavior, which turns out to be Mary Sutton, the mother, saying, "Buckle up, everyone!" After they buckle, Mary asks her three kids why they do this, and they all chorus back, "Because we love each other!" This qualifies as a "celebration" ending: The kids may not get cake or cookies, but there is an emotional payoff.

The first year my son went trick-or-treating, I invented the Good Witch of Halloween. My purpose was this: I was afraid he'd want to eat that huge candy hoard and I wanted to find a fun reason for it to disappear. Because Max's birthday was two weeks later, I told him to put his plastic pumpkin full of candy outside his bedroom door the night before he turned three. The Good Witch of Halloween would come and take the candy for poor children and replace it with a small birthday gift, which he would find when he awoke. Not surprisingly, my son loved this ritual, and it achieved my goal.

For a Thanksgiving ritual, the purpose is to give thanks. But when it comes to narrowing down the millions of possible ways to do that ritual-wise, it's helpful to focus on another P—make it personal. Take something from your family's history or passions to create a ritual of thankfulness that will be much more meaningful than a generic ritual because it is specific to you.

One family I know loves to camp, so all of them dress up like pilgrims and Indians each Thanksgiving and canoe out to an island where they put on a rather primitive outdoor feast (they precook the turkey). Another family of avid needleworkers started a special tablecloth ritual for Thanksgiving: Every person at the table signs his or her name in pen on the cloth, and the family matriarch later embroiders over the signatures, a different color each year. Then there's the family whose ancestors nearly starved out west, surviving one bad year only on turnips; they include a turnip dish every Thanksgiving, thankful they have so much else to eat now.

Ritual Actions

The bigger and more ceremonial the occasion, the more elaborate the ritual, and the more attention must be devoted to the ritual's central action. But what is the right action for a ritual? One that powerfully expresses the core emotional truth of the ceremony.

Think of the actions within a wedding and the way in which the ceremony combines speaking with doing. It isn't just the vows that make us feel married, it's also the action of placing rings on each other's fingers. The circle is a powerful symbol of eternity, and we are placing this physical object around a part of another person's body. A designer wedding dress, elegant flowers, and a string quartet will add to the atmosphere, but this simple act is the emotional core of the ritual.

But sometimes, there is no ritual pattern to follow. I decided, for example, to invent a ritual when I legally changed my last name to that of my husband and changed my first name to Meg, instead of my birth name, Margaret. To me, this seemed to require a sort of baptism. I decided I needed to submerge myself and asked my friend if I could dive into her swimming pool before witnesses—in a dress. She is such a dear and understanding friend that she didn't even blink (though my husband was a little dubious when I first suggested my plan).

I spoke to the group before I dived, explaining why I was doing this. I dove in and swam to the shallow end, where my husband stood waiting for me with a glass of champagne. We toasted, and kissed. And afterward, we celebrated with our friends, eating cake. I changed into a new T-shirt, on which my new name was painted.

I've thought a lot about what constitutes a major milestone in a child's life, and how each can be marked. One way, borrowed from tribal rites of passage, is to create a threshold or gateway, an actual barrier that the child must cross through as he or she acts out this important transition.

There are lots of ways this can be done. Lynn Rosen and her husband tape streamers and newspaper comics across their kids' bedroom doors each year on the night before their birthdays, and when they wake up (after alerting their parents to grab the camera), they burst through the paper, into their new age. I know of a private preschool where the kids "graduate" by walking across a bridge made of wooden blocks: They are literally embraced by the kindergartners waiting on the other side.

You could expand on this idea by organizing a "love gauntlet"—two parallel rows of people—and gently push and hug the celebrated one down the line.

In the case of my son, I've created thresholds using painted bedsheets, which are taped to the entrance over the family room. I cut a slit up from the floor, and Max has to cross through the sheet to get to his presents. (See Birthday section for details.)

Simple actions become profound when placed in a context of ritual focus and meaning: When I wanted to create a womanhood ritual for my niece on her thirteenth birthday, it was mostly about the words I spoke, but they carried extra weight because we were standing inside a circle of sparklers on the beach, in the dark.

If a ritual is about letting go, than the action of burying something in the ground is a possibility, as is releasing helium balloons. We did the latter after scattering my father's ashes on the golf course. Tied to each balloon was a farewell message to my dad, and seeing those bright balloons swept out of sight by the wind provoked a visceral feeling of release.

If you can't think of a ritual action, a great place to start is by mentally going through the list of four elements (earth, air, fire, and water) and asking if any of them fit the core emotional truth. A ritual of remembrance, for example, could include lighting a candle (fire) and talking about a deceased person or pet, or planting a tree for that person (earth).

Starter Ideas for Using the Four Elements in Rituals

Earth

Earth is used for burying things in ceremonies of mourning or remembrance, such as pet funerals, or writing down a list of bad experiences or habits you want to get past and literally burying them in a box underground. Conversely, earth is symbolic of new life, new beginnings. To mark the beginning of a new baby, home, venture, or relationship, plant something. This could be in a pot or your yard. It could be seeds or baby trees, wildflowers, or flowering shrubs. Plant sunflower seeds every year with your kids to welcome spring. Months before turning fifty (a spring birthday), I planted fifty daffodil bulbs outside my kitchen window. Search online for an old-fashioned list of what different flowers and plants "mean," such as red tulips to declare love and ivy as a symbol of fidelity.

Air

Air suggests wind and balloons, a ritual staple. There is an intimation of buoyancy and breeziness, which is hopeful. Kites are good, too: When my father turned seventy-five, my sister and I surprised him by flying down to the North Carolina shore, where my parents lived. We bought him a kite, then flew it together on the beach. The kite was frisky and brightly colored, and we passed the string from hand to hand. Other props for air rituals include pinwheels, streamers, or bubbles. Adults should blow bubbles more often: The

New York Times wedding column was once about a playful couple that was surrounded by family and friends blowing bubbles right after they were declared husband and wife.

Fire

Fire calls to mind everything from bonfires to the hearth at home. Fire can warm or destroy, making it apt for rituals of paradox: The phoenix arises from the ashes. The greatest ritual staple is a simple candle, which is portable fire. A candle isn't as much a symbol of burning or purging as it is one of illumination, and the forces of light and good. Candles are also good for focus: Turn out all the lights (and shut off all screens), and look deeply into the candle flame for a family meditation session. There are many winter holiday traditions in this book centered around candles and fire, but fire can be used in more daily or weekly ways, to make dinner feel special. Have an annual fireplace dinner: Don't forget to toast marshmallows! And if you are creating a ritual that calls for fire to purify, consider using that ancient Native American tool, a smudge stick. Some people make their own, but there are lots of online stores that sell these dried, tied bundles of grasses and herbs in various sizes. Sage is commonly used. A smudge stick is touched on the tip with fire and then the fire is blown out, leaving a smoking edge. Rituals should engage as many senses as possible, and smudge sticks tend to be quite aromatic, sort of a rustic incense.

Water

Water purifies, renews, and makes life possible, so it is suited to rituals of both baptism and cleansing. It can make a powerful statement: After a police corruption scandal in Harlem, local black leaders were seen literally scrubbing the sidewalk in front of the station with sponges and cleanser. Water can be solemn and soothing. When having a ritual near any body of water, from pond or pool on up, consider beforehand how to inter-act with that water: Dip a toe, splash your face, full immersion? Water can also be mischievous and playful: Think squirt guns and water balloons. One family I know had a silly ritual of dunking the father in the bathtub on Thanksgiving: It got started as a joke when he was bathing the kids before the feast one year and got very wet. Now, he and the kids put their bathing suits on, then get soaked together.

Just remember this: Start with your ritual's purpose and let that guide you to a central ritual action. Your best chance of success is to keep it simple, and be playful. If you set a tone of having fun, of everybody having a say, then family members won't feel awkward or too embarrassed to participate.

And please, do *not* feel you have to reinvent the wheel with your rituals. If there is any kind of remotely logical template already practiced in the world that works for you, grab it with both hands and tweak it a little to fit your family. My friend Amy Milne remembers that when she grew up, her artist father would invent variations on the old Pin the Tail on the Donkey birthday game that suited her. Like "Pin the Heart on Raggedy Ann." And she does the same with her kids. Her son, Clark, was especially excited about playing "Pin the Light Saber on the Jedi."

Another tip: When it comes to starting a new ritual, it's vital to announce your plans in advance, so everybody knows what's coming. Kids love routine, so the first time you try a new ritual, they might be wary, and adjustments may be needed before the family embraces this new tradition wholeheartedly. (And family rituals often need tweaking over the years, giving kids a bigger role as they age.)

Don't worry about finding good ideas for new traditions. There are hundreds of them in the pages that follow. You can adopt these rituals and celebrations just as they are, or use them as the germ of a new idea.

Celebrate wherever you are right now, with whatever gifts you possess, as creatively as you possibly can. There is much talk about teaching children "life skills." In my view, you shouldn't just teach them manners, how to drive, how to cook, and all of that. You should also teach them how to celebrate. Food feeds the body, but ritual feeds the soul.

I'm not a Pollyanna about ritual: I don't think it's the only tool parents need to build a cohesive tribe, but I do think it's a lot more powerful than most people believe, and the lessons for our children run deep.

Children raised with tradition, especially those who have watched their parents invent new rituals as occasions and milestones occur, learn that their own response to life can be active and creative and extremely personal. They're going to be resilient children, confident they are loved and that they know how to express that love to others.

Some Lessons Learned:
A Note on Humor and Letting It Rip

Being a sometimes bossy and rather earnest person, it took me a while as a parent to learn the supreme importance of a sense of humor in creating family traditions—along with the necessity of just rolling with the punches, whatever happens.

In family ritual, perfection is the enemy. This is a very hard thing for a controlling person to accept, but I have learned the hard way. The goal is to have your family traditions be more like a wildly original, outside-the-lines crayon drawing than a formally posed studio photograph in which nobody cracks a smile. Rituals are homemade and hand-crafted, not something made by factory robots, and they should look and taste and feel DIY (do-it-yourself), with everything that implies.

It turns out that the more outrageously imperfect a ritual is, the more kids love it and remember it. The family party your children never stop talking about is the one when the dog ate the cake. In one family I interviewed, in which the mom always hides treats before the weekly family meeting (the kids have to hunt them as part of the meeting ritual), the kids are still laughing about the time she forgot that she hid the cupcakes in the washing machine–and threw the clothes in on top of them.

I will never forget when my yoga teacher from the YWCA invited me to a simple coming-into-womanhood ritual for her teenage daughter. It was a potluck lunch, and we brought small gifts for the girl. Flowers that people brought were woven into a garland for her hair. Later, family and friends waited in the backyard for my friend and her daughter to come out onto the deck and say a few words. It was clear they were both nervous, especially the girl, who was shy by nature. I believe she was afraid to make a mistake, awkward partly because they were improvising as they went.

Suddenly, one of the two let loose with a very loud fart (they won't say who was responsible). Instantly, everyone present broke out laughing and the girl and her mother just leaned into each other, laughing hysterically. The tension was broken, and we could all let go and fully appreciate the moment and each other.

I hope you'll remember many of the principles from this book, but especially, I hope you won't forget the fart story. Anytime you find yourself getting all pompous about your big occasion or snapping at your kids because you are getting stressed about whether the turkey will be done at the same moment as the trimmings, do something just for laughs. I mean it! Break an egg on the floor, if you have to. Get everyone to bang pots with spoons to release tension, sing the silliest song you know in the loudest voice you've got. Get goofy.

Mischief managed.

CHAPTER 2

Everyday Rituals

Daily Rituals

The most vitally important rituals you can practice with your family are the ones you perform every single day. This consistency is especially important for infants and young toddlers: One day is endless for them, and the world is vast and unfamiliar. Being able to trust that certain things will happen each day at regular times in a certain order provides them with immense comfort. Ritual is an anchor, a home base.

But daily connections also keep older children, even teenagers, connected to their comfort zones, bringing them back to the safe haven that stays familiar as they change beyond all recognition. These rituals must grow and change to accommodate their new schedules and tastes, but I'm far from the first parent to notice that when you create a calm, steady zone inside a hectic life, kids are able to share all sorts of unexpected things. As they mature, they bring new things to the table—both literally and figuratively.

Mealtimes

Let's start with the ritual of daily meals. In some cultures, the simple ceremony of sharing a meal with someone makes you part of the tribe, and it's impossible to overstate the importance of regular meals together as a family.

Obviously, conflicting work and school schedules can make this difficult, but do whatever you can to sit down and eat together as often as possible—even if that means that your "together meal" is a snack before bedtime.

To be effective as ritual, family meals need to focus on quality as well as quantity. Michael Lewis, a psychologist who has spent years researching American family dinners, discovered most families spend between fifteen and twenty minutes at the table, and a good amount of that time is spent nagging and whining. When people don't have a mouth too full of food to speak, many of the comments run along the lines of: "Please pass the butter," and "Stop kicking your sister under the table."

So, getting everyone to sit around the table together is just the first step. As I said in the previous section on the parts of a ritual, it helps set the mood if you do something to signal the start of a ritual and the transition from ordinary time.

There is a good reason the stretch of time before dinner in households with children is known as "arsenic hour": Early evening is the time when tired, hungry kids (and often grown-ups) can become button-pushing cranky. Even if sibling battles aren't escalating at this time, every family member has his or her head somewhere else entirely: on the easy hit missed at baseball practice, the train wreck of a meeting at work, the daunting homework ahead, or that text message that just *has* to be sent to a BFF (best friends forever) right this second, or the world will come to an end.

Creating a dinner-is-starting signal is a great way to get everyone to change gears and refocus on the home team. This can be something incredibly simple such as ringing a bell or chime, turning the lights down, lighting a candle, putting on the local jazz radio station. You can say grace, hold hands, or say a one-sentence phrase in unison (even better if it's a silly nonsense phrase that only means something to your brood).

Once the actual ritual of the meal begins, you'll want some strategies to liven up the event, get the conversational juice flowing, and make sure the meal doesn't devolve into a nag-fest on table manners. But first, some helpful ideas about getting started, for families that begin the meal with a blessing of some sort.

Grace

Even for families that aren't religious, saying grace before a meal can be a wonderful ritual of transition. It functions like a call to reconnection after a day of separation.

Simple and Good

Some of the most profound graces are the simplest, such as the lovely Quaker grace "Us and this: God bless." I also like: "Now my plate is full, but soon it will be gone. Thank you for my food, and please help those with none."

Simplest of All: A Collective Pause

Amanda Soule, a mother of five who homeschools in Maine and writes the hugely popular SouleMama blog, says her family's mealtime blessing is extremely important. "Once everyone gets to the table, we just pause and hold hands and take a breath together. It's a really simple tiny thing that feels huge. This pause before the chaos resumes makes us all fully present and aware in the moment we are sharing together."

Sing for Your Supper

The Hodge family sings together often, including for grace. A favorite is the Johnny Appleseed song that goes: "The Lord is good to me, and so I thank the Lord / For giving me the things I need / like the sun and the rain and the appleseed / The Lord is good to me. Amen."

Holding Hands

The Michaels of Minneapolis say a simple grace, and then all squeeze hands before they eat.

Taking Turns

The Mowbrays take turns saying grace. Often they improvise, but in a pinch they keep returning to a traditional Christian blessing, "Bless us, O Lord, and these thy gifts, which we are about to receive from your bounty. Through Christ our Lord, Amen."

Buddhist Blessing

Karly Randolph Pitman, a mother of four in Bozeman, Montana, often does a variation on a Buddhist loving kindness blessing. It has three parts, and the Pitmans say each line together: "May I be happy, may I be healthy, may I be peaceful, may I be true." The second time through, they substitute "you" and look at the others while saying it: "May *you* be happy. . . ." The third time, they all chime in: "May everyone be happy," and so on, extending their blessing to the whole world.

Choosing a Grace

Two terrific books are *A Grateful Heart: Daily Blessings for the Evening Meal from Buddha to the Beatles*, edited by M. J. Ryan, and *Bless This Food: Ancient and Contemporary Graces from Around the World*, by Adrian Butash. Both provide many blessings and draw from a wide range of religions and regions.

Tip Box for New Parents: Rituals and Rules Are Sometimes the Same

When it comes to setting rules and rituals for every day, make this your mantra: It is far easier to turn a long-standing No into a once-in-a-blue moon Yes, than the other way around. Make strict rules about no screens at the table, no watching TV while eating, no staying up late, homework first after school, and so forth. Kids quickly get used to the limits you set, even find them comforting (but don't expect them to say so). Then when you bend those rules for a meal or a day, it will be a *huge* treat. Just eating finger foods on a picnic blanket in front of the TV will be a major occasion. Think about it: If they can do anything they want, all the time, nothing is special and everything is chaos. Then, if you try to push back and set limits later, they will fight you every inch of the way.

Dinner Family Traditions

With a little planning and prodding, even hungry, preoccupied kids can make sparkling conversation.

Family News

Patrice Kyger insists that her children each share a "new and good" that happened to them during the day. Complaints and bad news are allowed, but never without the compensating good news. The Kygers are also on the lookout for what they call "blurbs," random comments that strike everyone but the speaker as out of context and hilarious: These are written down in a special book.

Dinner Toasts

Amy Milne and her family clink glasses and make a toast at every dinner. "Sometimes it's as simple as saying 'To us,' while other times we are honoring a special occasion," says Amy, whose family lives in Asheville, North Carolina. "My parents always had a ritual to light the candles at dinner every night when I was growing up, and we had a candelabra on the table. The idea is to have something we do over and over, at home or in a restaurant, to celebrate that we are together. We taught the kids to always have eye contact while clinking."

One, Two, Three . . . Whine!

Courtney Andelman got tired of complaints about the menu and such. When the moaning begins, she simply calls for communal whining so everyone can get it off their chests. She says, "Let's all whine at the same time, here we go! One, two, three . . . waaaaaaaah!" Then everyone at the table laughs—and eats her food.

Current Events

Gloria Uhler's kids had to come to the dinner table nightly with one topic of conversation related to current events. The rule was that all the children introduced their subject and shared some information they had heard or read. Everyone else in the family had to ask at least one question to keep the conversation going. If every night won't work for you, try this as a weekly event.

Thankfuls and Unthankfuls

At dinner, Elizabeth Elkin always goes around the table and has everyone share a "thankful," which means something simple like a good grade or a sunny day. Often her two boys have three or four thankfuls to share. In cases where they are especially glum and can't think of any, she will do a round of "unthankfuls," but she refuses to leave it at that. "I start asking them: Do you have a roof over your head? Do you have food to eat? Do you have a family that loves you? They quickly get the point. As a breast cancer survivor, I often give thanks for health." Sometimes kids need both a good model, and a pointed prompt.

Conversation Basket

This was a real help in getting fun conversations going at my house. I decorated a small basket with ribbons and bought beads with letters on them. I spelled out the word *talk* and strung it on three ribbons, and then attached them across the handle of the basket, so they dangled down. When the basket is placed on the table at dinner, the ribbons ripple and sway, so it seems as if they are speaking the words to us, inviting us: "Talk, talk, talk" they say.

I cut pastel-colored paper into strips about two inches wide and wrote fifty different comments, questions, or instructions on them. Then I folded each one and piled them all in the basket, so we could take turns at dinner picking one. Often, we all wanted to respond to the query one person got, so we would each chime in on such questions as: "If a holiday were named after you, how would people celebrate?" and "Make up a nickname for everyone at the table, including yourself (nothing mean)." Another favorite was: "Tell us something you can do better than your parents."

There are many variations on this ritual: decide if you want to do this every night, every other night, or once a week.

One thing we learned is the importance of refreshing the questions. We would take out the papers we had just chosen and keep them in a kitchen drawer for a while. Always keep blank papers and some pencils in the basket, and invite family members to add their own questions. Kids who can't read or write yet will love this tradition, too, though they will need someone to help them with their contributions.

Sampling of Dinner-Table Conversation Starters

What would your personal robot do for you?

What can you do now that you couldn't do a year ago?

What scares you?

What is your favorite movie pet?

Which character in *Lord of the Rings* (insert favorite movie or book) is most like you?

Describe your dream house.

What do you like to smell?

What cheers you up when you are sad?

What is the best game ever invented?

If you could have dinner with any person in history, who would it be?

What or who makes you laugh?

Tell us about a dream you remember.

You just won the lottery—$1 million a year for life. What will change in your life?

    What will stay the same?

What is the single best thing about you?

How would you make the world better?

What do you love enough to save for your own children?

If you could relive any day of your life, which day would it be?

What bad habit do you wish you could break?

What stories do they tell about you as a baby?

What was the worst day of your life?

What is your definition of friendship?

If you could possess a talent or gift that you weren't born with, what would it be?

Who inspires you?

(See the rest of this list in Appendix 1 at the end of the book.)

Family Feast at 4:00 PM

Marla Michele Must is a mother with three kids, and for her family, the best time to eat the big meal of the day happens to be at 4:00 PM, after school and before rushing around to various activities. "Later, they have ice skating or martial arts, or whatever, and it's too hectic to sit down and eat a real meal at 6:00 PM or 7:00 PM. I realized they were starving when they come home from school, so why have them load up on snacks that are a waste of calories? Instead, at that point, we all sit down together and eat something healthy. Each of us has to share one thing that was unique or different that happened that day. They'll be hungry again around 7:30 PM, and that's when they have their weekday snack."

Daily Family Almanac

When her four kids were little, Letitia Suk of Evanston, Illinois, used to read an Almanac

Terrific Online Resource for Family Meals

Dr. Grace R. Freedman, a national expert in public health and public policy with three children of her own, is fascinated by how deeply the simple ritual of shared meals strengthens families. In 2007, she started a website called www.eatdinner.org, to encourage families to eat together more often, providing them with support in the way of fresh resources, practical ideas, and the latest related research.

This isn't a recipe site, but it is full of good information and is frequently updated. The site does suggest great cookbooks for families, including for kids learning to cook, and it links to a whole bunch of other sites and blogs that are getting parents jazzed to make memorable—as well as healthy—regular family dinners.

item from the *Chicago Tribune* called "What Happened on This Day in History?" at dinnertime. She got the idea to start a "Family Almanac" project and purchased multiple packs of three-by-five cards. She counted out 365 cards and wrote a date on each card, and started by entering birthdays and anniversaries and other important family dates.

Then, as the days and weeks went by, she would write down anything notable for that day as it happened. The cards became rich resources for documenting the past, so that as she pulled out a card on a particular day, she could remind her kids what had happened on that day in previous years. Every July 26, she would say, "On this day in 1993, we were at Old Faithful together. Remember that trip?" She kept this card deck of memories in the kitchen for easy access. It does require a bit of work to set up the Almanac deck, but once begun, this Family Almanac is easy to maintain and provides a big payoff!

tech tip

Mama's Monday Update and Almanac

Flash forward, and these days, all the Suk kids are out of the nest. Except for the son living in China, the others still live near their parents. But the usual phone texts back and forth are pretty mundane and businesslike. So Letitia started a weekly ritual e-mail she calls "Mama's Monday Update and Almanac," in which she updates the kids on any current family news but also checks out the Family Almanac cards for the entire week ahead. "Remember that time in 1990 when our car died and we had to take a cab to church?" was one of the events she reminded them about. She comments, "It's been so great to remind them of the bond we have together. Usually there will be a flurry of Reply All responses where the kids will chime in and say, 'Yeah, I remember,' or 'No, that's not how it was, Mom!'"

Unconventional Meals

Don't be afraid to break some rules about family dinners if it works for your family. Tailor meal traditions to your schedules, passions, and personalities. Paper plates are fine; distractions like television aren't, as a rule.

Indoor Picnics

Moving the meal from the table to the floor can make the same old carryout Chinese food or pizza feel like a special treat. If you don't have a picnic blanket, an old sheet works just fine and goes right into the wash afterward.

No Reason Family Dinner Parties

In the book *New Traditions: Redefining Celebrations for Today's Family,* Susan Abel Lieberman wrote about the Singleton family and the "no-reason" dinner parties they have from time to time. The Singletons set the table with their best china and flowers, dress everyone up, and march the kids out the back door. The children walk around to the front, where their parents usher them in as honored guests. Sally Singleton told Susan that her kids get to practice their company manners, and they love these special nights.

King Henry VIII Dinners

When Ellie Just was growing up, her mom would declare a meal from time to time where table manners *were not allowed.* "We would eat outside, throw our chicken bones and corn cobs on the ground. There was plenty of smacking of lips, burping and elbows on the table," she recalls. Ellie could invite friends. (Origin story: Ellie's mom started the ritual because her own mother was very strict about table manners, and they ate at Grandma's house once a week. This was her antidote.)

Opera Meals

One family I know occasionally declares an Opera Meal, and everybody sings instead of speaking, even to ask, "Please, pass the butter." Being in tune isn't a requirement, and they all get pretty silly. An alternative is to try a silent meal and see if everyone can communicate entirely with hand signals.

Finger Food Only

Once a week, serve a meal that requires absolutely no utensils and let the kids eat with their hands. Even salad and vegetables taste better that way. This could be an all-appetizer meal (be sure to include veggies and dip as one way to keep it nutritious), or an ethnic dinner, for instance, Chinese dumplings and ribs.

Friday Night Special

When her three kids were younger, Patricia Gray had a Friday night ritual of "pizza with a video on a picnic blanket with all the junk food I won't serve at all during the week—chips, soda, topped off by hot-fudge sundaes. My kids looked forward to that every week for years."

Making It Special

Seat of Honor

Some families have a special plate that a person gets to use to celebrate a major triumph or their birthday. Sue Eaves has something different, a way to dress up the chair itself when someone is celebrated. She saw a blog post about making a simple fabric slipcover for a chair and embellishing it, so she added the words "My Special Day" to the slipcover she made. It gets used on big days like birthdays, but also, Sue says, "It's a great way to recognize the smaller things that often go unnoticed, like the first day our son put his head under the water in swimming class, and the day my husband signed a contract for a new job. It has become very important to us. Everybody asks if they can have it when they feel that something significant is going on."

Spotlight Dinners

Sydney Gines has these surprise dinners once or twice a year for each of her four kids. Some dinners celebrate an accomplishment such as "learning a complicated piano piece or breaking a bad habit," whereas others are scheduled for "a self-esteem boost." Sydney pretends company is coming, so the kids dress up a bit and expect a special dinner. When the kids come to the table, Sydney and her husband announce that the "special guest" is one of the children and throw confetti at him or her. A small gift is given, and the whole family lauds the spotlighted child.

Sunday Kids' Choice

Teacher Anne Hodge wanted her kids to share the kitchen chores and make Sunday dinners special. She started Kids' Choice, and though her three children have to take turns cooking and cleaning up on that night, they also take turns making up funny rules for the meal. On Lego Night, the table was decorated with Legos, and then there was Changing Seats Night, and another time they could eat only with spoons.

Toast Night

Barb Brock, a professor in Spokane, Washington, decided to make one dinner a week special, so on Thursdays, the family uses fancy dishes even for carryout. Also on that night, each member of the family makes a toast. Making a toast is something kids love, as it seems like such a grown-up gesture. Eating by candlelight once a week is also a treat for kids.

Soup Nights

Children's book author Martha Freeman and her family host Soup Night every Thursday from October through March. Every September, Martha sends out a standing invitation to about sixty people, friends and neighbors, to come any Thursday they want after 5:30 PM, provided they bring bread or wine, or both. Martha makes huge pots of soup and provides paper bowls and spoons, plus apple juice for the kids. Her three children love the casual party atmosphere and seeing all their friends.

Family Dinner Rules

An Excerpt from *The Family Dinner: Great Ways to Connect with Your Kids, One Meal at a Time*, by Laurie David, with recipes by Kirstin Uhrenholdt (Grand Central, 2010)

This book is a treasure box for any parent who ever wanted to get the most mileage out of family dinners. In addition to clever and doable recipes by Kirstin Uhrenholdt, a young Danish woman hired to help cook meals for the David household in Los Angeles, there is a great deal of practical information about getting family members to truly connect around the dinner table. An essential element of what has made family dinners so satisfying for Laurie David's family is the list of ten rules by which everyone abides. Here is a streamlined version of that list from her book. I was already doing many of these, but I have adopted her suggestion to always have a pitcher of water on the table and am delighted to see my son reaching for that rather than pulling juice or milk from the fridge.

"Ten Simple Steps to Successful Family Dinners"

Step One: It's a Date!

Laurie David (yes, she is the former wife of TV writer-star Larry David) is a big believer in having a set time for dinner. It saves a lot of nagging and reminding, and just gets built into everyone's schedule.

Step Two: Everyone Comes to the Table at the Same Time

"Even if you don't eat, you still have to participate (in my experience, the nonhungry participants usually forget they weren't hungry and end up eating the whole meal," says Laurie. (You can tell she has two daughters and no sons!)

Step Three: No Phones

"No ringing, vibrating, answering, or texting allowed."

Step Four: One Meal, No Substitutions

"Be prepared for initial stubbornness and a few uneaten meals, but the phase won't last long."

Step Five: Everyone Tries Everything

"The rigid insistence in the old days on eating all of your vegetables only accomplished one thing—it turned kids into stealth veggie Houdinis. . . .

Tasting everything is an important rule. It shows respect to whomever prepared the food and respect for yourself. Why not give your taste buds an opportunity to be pleasantly surprised?"

Step Six: No Television

"Your kids will argue with you that they can do three things at the same time (watch TV, eat, and listen closely to your every word, maybe even IM [instant messaging], too!), but it doesn't matter. Here's the good news: On special occasions, the television is invited to dinner and as a result of the novelty, it is a really fun treat."

Step Seven: Tap Water Only, Filtered If Needed

"Serve it cold and preferably from a filtered tap in a clear glass pitcher. Garnish with slices of lemon, lime, cucumber, oranges, apples or sprigs of mint. Adding whole fresh or frozen strawberries, raspberries or blueberries to their glasses makes kids want to drink even more water in their attempts to reach the berry treasure at the bottom!"

Step Eight: Friends and Family Welcome

"I always encourage my kids to invite their friends and even their friends' parents to dinner. 'The more the merrier' really puts everyone in a happy mood at the table, and everyone is on their best behavior, too."

Step Nine: You're Excused

At the David's house, no one leaves the table until after dessert. Laurie says she believes that having a final little segment to the meal resolves unfinished business and brings a second act to the meal. She says she doesn't do a big dessert every night, but that the end of her meals can mean sharing orange slices, or even just cups of tea.

Step Ten: Everyone Helps Clean Up

"No exceptions. It's more fun and cleanup is faster when everyone chips in."

Hello and Good-Bye Rituals

Looking up and suddenly realizing that Mommy and Daddy have simply disappeared can be traumatic for a toddler. Are they gone forever? Although it can take a little extra time to act out a small ritual of leave-taking when you go to work or drop your kids off at day care or school, it's worthwhile to help them work through those moments and realize that though you are gone, your love remains behind.

Some of the best of these little rituals give your children a tiny bit of power in deciding the exact moment of departure, and it's amazing how little they abuse that, because you've made it playful and given them a feeling of confidence. They have seen this movie before and they know the ending: You always come back.

At the other end of things, it's also helpful to have a greeting ritual to reengage with your children after you've been apart for hours or days. Simple hugs and kisses are great, perhaps some silly nicknames and endearments, a special handshake, or a reunion song if you feel like it. Don't forget to also take the time to hear about their day. If you get them in the habit of sharing the details when they're really young, maybe they won't stop once they become self-conscious teens.

Surprise Daily Drawing

Lisa Coughlin's husband, Sean, knows that when his daughter, Stella, wakes up on a weekday morning, he will already have left for work. So every weekday night, after she goes to bed, he makes a quick drawing about something that happened that day and leaves it on the kitchen table for her to find the next morning. "The drawings are very simple with stick-figure people," says Sean. "I have drawn her with her friends at the park or her cousins dancing, or she and I playing [the card game] Uno. It just takes me a minute or two to make the drawing and add a caption. The goal is to remember the little moments that may be forgotten in the crush of everyday life." Some of the drawings have been framed, but many remain in the various notebooks Sean has used over the years.

Good-Bye Car Song

Mary Routh, a mail carrier in Iowa, knew her daughter worried about her parents while she was in preschool. So she used to make up a little song to sing on the way to the school, with a prayer element, such as, "I pray that Daddy works hard and Mommy won't get wet in the rain, and help us to remember to pick up milk on the way home." It was a window into their day, and being able to sing about it and bless them made her feel like she had an active part: It became familiar, knowable, hers.

Day-Care Drop-off Magic Words

Elinor Craig, a California mom, was having trouble getting her son, Mose, to separate at preschool, so she created a ritual in which he would pick a secret code word on the way, based on something he had seen. When they arrived, he would hang up his jacket, play a little with some toys, and then when he said the code word, such as "snowman" or "fire engine," that would mean he was ready for her to leave. This cemented a feeling of closeness and conspiracy with his mother, and his peers never had to know he had any qualms about being left.

A Token to Remember Mommy All Day

A couple of Karly Randolph Pitman's four kids had separation issues at school, and she says she didn't want them to feel guilty about that. "I was a sensitive child and grew up feeling like it was a character flaw. I have chosen to validate their sensitivity, and not make it wrong," she explains. For two of her sons, she had tangible objects she would give them representing her, "so we were still connected." Her youngest has a little aqua heart-shaped stone in a bag. "I usually kiss the heart and give it back to him," Karly says. Another son carried a little Hallmark angel charm with an inscription on the back: "My heart is with you always."

Special Handshakes

On an old episode of the *Oprah Winfrey* show, a father demonstrated the complicated handshakes he does with his son and daughter as part of a morning good-bye ritual. These were more like elaborate hand ballets than handshakes, but performing them before separating gives the kids a vivid reminder that their connection to Dad is close, and unique.

Circle Hugs

The members of one family I know take a moment each morning before they all head off to work and school to do a quick circle hug in the kitchen. They face the center, bow their heads, and ask God to "bless this day and our love for each other."

Daily Wishes

Along with good-bye morning hugs in our house, we try to say at least two things we hope for the person that day. My son might say to his father, "For today, I hope your commute is easy and your work is fun." Tailoring the wishes to the day proves we're paying attention to each other's lives: a comforting proof of love.

Special Kiss

The popular picture book *The Kissing Hand,* by Audrey Penn, has inspired many a parent to create a special good-bye kiss for an anxious child. Leah Whigham Grendall is one of those parents. With the guidance of her two-year-old son, she and her husband invented a series of moves they do for good-byes, whether it's at the morning school bus, or at bedtimes or other leave-takings. Leah or her husband kiss the boy in each hand and once on the lips, then follow up with a hug. At the age of five, he sometimes added other things, like literally pushing her out the door at preschool. "The push is always kid-size," says Leah, "But I overexaggerate and leap through the door. " Sometimes he wants lipstick kisses from his mom, so when he walks by a mirror, he will see them: love made visible. These again are powerful rituals of comfort, partly because the boy feels like he's in charge of them.

Stuffed Animals in the Trees

Right before meeting my son's bus when he was in grade school, I used to grab a handful of his favorite stuffed animals and perch them on tree branches, rocks, and the swing set. He would get off the bus to find them and always walk in the front door grinning.

Homecoming Blessing

To really feel conscious of resuming the family connection, some people devise simple rituals of homecoming at day's end. Kathleen O'Connell Chesto, a writer on Catholic family ritual, suggests hugging the kids when they return from school and saying this simple prayer: "Lord, help us to be present to you in one another. Amen."

Hello and Good-Bye
for Divorced Families

Children of divorced parents who share custody often have serious issues of transition between households. No matter the ages of the children or how often they switch households, it's very helpful to give some thought to creating comforting rituals for both departures and arrivals.

Keep things calm and predictable. If the kids have to travel a long distance and only make the switch a couple times a year, consider things like always having the same last-night meal, or always eating at the same pizza place, or going out for sundaes at Dairy Queen. Have a ritual for saying good-bye to the house itself, and any pets. Suzy Kellett has quadruplets who fly out to see their dad for part of every summer. The night before they leave, the kids bring sleeping bags into her room and they all "camp out" on her bedroom floor. That was their departure ritual for years, before they all grew up and left for college.

Of course, it also makes sense to create rituals for returning, whether related to food or activities. Take a walk together and discuss how the visit was, or sit around the table and have a snack, or play a favorite game.

Another idea is to practice something like the text in *Goodnight, Moon* only in reverse: have the kid(s) say "Hello" to various rooms, their toys, any pets and the house itself.

This is also a time when all the various smart phones and laptops can help the kids stay in touch with the household they just left. Once they get home, they can send a quick text message or short video to the parent whose house they just left, reporting any new and sharing "I love yous."

Waving at the Window

Louise Witonsky and her children used to rush to the window every morning as Daddy went to work, and wave. If it was dark and guests were leaving, they would flick the house lights off and on to say good-bye, and if the person leaving knew about the ritual, he or she would blink back with the car lights. Very simple rituals, but if they didn't happen, Louise says, family members would miss them.

Reconnection Ritual at Day's End

Bobbi Conner, longtime host of NPR's show *The Parent's Journal,* had to learn some things the hard way while raising her own kids. She used to come home from work and try to prepare dinner right away but was confronted by cranky, hungry kids who wanted her attention. So she created a pause, a reconnection ritual, in which she would serve them a healthy snack like apples and cheese, grab a cuddle, read a story, and learn about their day. Once they got their "Mommy dose," her kids drifted off to play and she was able to fix dinner in a more relaxed way.

"When things just feel rushed and out of whack with your daily family routine, in most cases the best fix is just a small shift in routine or a new ritual that lets you enjoy time with your kids," says Bobbi. "Instead of thinking, 'Our life is too hectic, let's quit our jobs, sell the house, and move to Alaska,' parents can make a new routine. Turn off the TV, play some new game for twenty minutes."

Note: Bobbi's excellent book, *Unplugged Play* is full of fresh, fun (non-electronic) games to re-engage with your kids.

Mom and Dad
Away-from-Home Rituals

Stuffed Animal Traveling Pals

Every time I go on a trip, for years now, I pack a small stuffed animal named Gus in my carry-on bag. He's an adventurous alligator who loves to travel, check out swimming pools, and drink beer. In every city I visit, I find somewhere to photograph Gus, even if it's only in the hotel room, though sometimes it's at a meeting or restaurant. I know that this is not uncommon: I remember spending time on a delayed flight comparing stuffed

animals with the male engineer sitting next to me—I believe his son's proxy was a plush lobster.

Becky Romph says her kids pack "sleeping buddies" in her husband's suitcase when he is getting ready for a business trip. One time, she reports, when her husband was in Ireland, the hotel left an extra chocolate candy each night for the sleeping buddy.

Coin by Coin to Count the Days

When Elaine Mellon had to accompany her older son abroad for a boy-choir festival, she had to leave his five-year-old brother behind with Dad. Partly to make the absence visual and tactile, Elaine taped twelve quarters to a low table in their home. Every day, her young son would peel off one quarter, and his father would take him to church: He would donate the quarter at church to pay to light a candle and say a prayer for the safe return of mother and brother.

Message-Each-Day Calendar

Suzy Happ sometimes has to attend conferences, and she has made special calendars for her son and daughter covering the exact number of days she would be gone. For every day of absence, there is a window (like an Advent calendar) that they can fold back and get a message from Mom. (This can be done quite simply: Draw the proper number of squares on a page, write a message or draw a little picture inside each, then cut out papers slightly larger than the size of the squares and tape or glue them on one side so they can be lifted up to reveal their secrets.) She might just write where she will be at that point, or wish them luck on a test or sports outing. Once she wrote, "At 8:00 PM, look up at the moon and think of me. I'll be doing the same!" Each kid got one of these mini-calendars, and it was personalized for each of them.

tech tip

In a sentimental and popular commercial a few years back for Cingular (now AT&T), a father on a business trip finds his daughter's stuffed animal monkey packed in his suitcase. He uses his phone's camera to photograph the monkey on his travels and sends the pictures to his little girl at home. This is a great use of the tech tools many of us carry around: reminding our kids that we're thinking of them. I'm also planning on making a book about Gus the Gator's travel, using Shutterfly.com or iPhoto's services for compiling digital photos into a personal, one-of-a-kind book. I've used both services before and they are excellent: I've made multiple copies of photo books for major birthdays and reunions, but I think there will only be a single copy of the Gus book, for my son.

Problem-Solving Rituals

If there were one thing I could do to help parents most, it would probably be helping them to understand the immense power of ritual to ease the bumpy transitions of everyday family life.

The two most important secrets to problem-solving rituals are distraction and humor. This may seem simpleminded, but it has a sound basis in human psychology. Therapist Aaron Horowitz says that rituals sometimes work as a kind of "hypnotic distraction." The distraction is helpful whether you are trying to coax a child to end a meltdown or use the potty.

We all love that kids live so fully in the moment, but sometimes they get stuck in that moment and they need help pulling out of it. Also, little kids don't have the experience yet to know that they can be other than they are: If your son has never used the potty or gone without a pacifier, part of the problem is he can't imagine being that kid. He can't make that leap. By promising a reward or giving him a tiny ritual to perform or making him laugh (or all three), you are giving him something to focus on other than his fear or intransigence. Next thing you know, he's used the potty or stopped hitting his brother, and you can celebrate and congratulate.

Humor is also an important part of the equation. One way to get kids unstuck is to just crack them up. If you can think up something goofy for family members to do whenever tensions soar, you'll spend a lot less of your life organizing time-outs.

Friday Night Bubble Baths

When my son was a toddler, he couldn't get enough bubble baths, but the pediatrician frowned on that (some experts say chemicals in the bath products irritate little bottoms). I wanted to end the whining, so we started the tradition of Friday Night Bubble Baths. If Max would say, "Mommy, I want a bubble bath now!" then I could explain, "Well, it's only Wednesday, honey. We have to wait for Friday. Tomorrow is Thursday, and the next day, it will be Friday Night Bubble Bath time." A lot of problem-solving rituals are about turning a permanent "No" into a special-occasion "Yes"—and usually, it works like a charm.

Silly Soothing Songs

A little ditty that announces a transitional activity works like magic. Karly Randolph Pitman, the mother of four from Montana, says, "I learned from the preschool teacher, if I am struggling, I create a song. They hated to wash their hands when they were little. So I invented the silly potty song, and the words go, "We always wash hands when we go potty!"

Kissing/Wishing Ritual to Defuse "Gimmes"

Courtney Andelman is a stay-at-home mom with twin daughters, and very savvy at problem-solving rituals. One of my favorites is the one she invented when her girls get the "gimmes" in a store. "When I am out with the girls and they want things, I say, 'Make a wish!'" Courtney explains. "So we whisper the wish into cupped hands, kiss the wish [kiss into the cupped hands], give it a big hug [the child hugs herself] and then throw it up to the North Pole. I try to stand close enough to hear the whisper!"

Seatbelt-Buckling Ritual

Mary Sutton started this after her family was in a car accident. Luckily, there were no major injuries, but none of them was wearing a seatbelt, so it could have been bad. In their ritual, they pile into the car, Mary says "Buckle up!" and the three kids say "Why do we buckle up?" Then they all chorus the reply: "Because we love each other."

Grocery Store Math Distracter

Doni Boyd's two kids, like most, nagged their way through shopping trips. So Doni came up with a savvy idea. "We gave them each a $2 credit for every supermarket trip, which really stopped them from begging to buy this and that," says Doni. "The credit part was because we didn't want to have to check them out separately. If they spent less than $2, they didn't get paid the change until we got home and put groceries away. It worked great because they had to do some math to make it work, and if they wanted something worth more than $2 they had to negotiate with siblings and pool their money."

Reward for Detested but Necessary Hygiene Tasks

After clipping nails, Courtney Andelman gives her two girls temporary tattoos. She says that because they are so thrilled at the prospect of tattoos, they don't stop to whine about the actual clipping part. And here is her advice on the topic of temporary tats: "The big trick with temporary tattoos is to use lots of water. The paper needs to get very soft to transfer the image well. We count together while we do this, which is probably how my girls learned to count to thirty at such a young age!"

Eight Common Rough Spots That Rituals Can Smooth Over

1. Daycare or school drop-off
2. Naptimes and bedtimes
3. Grocery shopping and other errands
4. Waiting (in lines, for restaurant food, etc.)
5. Bathtime
6. Hair brushing or other grooming
7. Departure of a friend or family member
8. Taking turns/Sharing during playtime

Problem-Solving Rituals Basics

- Silly songs or rhymes, either about what is happening, or something wildly different that distracts
- Visual games, such as "The person who sees the most people dressed in red before our food comes wins!"
- Always bring and read books (This one saved our lives, waiting in long lines at Disneyworld to take Max, at four, on rides.)
- Comic choreography: Make-up goofy dance moves, even for sitting down

Rituals to Keep the Peace

Kids will bicker and fight, especially siblings. But sometimes a brief ritual can calm the combatants. Teaching young kids to avoid violence is a powerful life lesson.

Family Huddle

When the two Abbe kids have been fighting, especially in the car, their mother hollers out, "Family huddle time." Even in a parking lot, they stop and huddle like teammates, stack their hands up in the center of the circle, yell out the family cheer ("Let's go, Abbes!"), and punch their fists to the sky. Afterward, they go on their way as a united force.

Crazy Dance Party

Members of the Pfeiffer family say that unity is always restored if they can laugh together. So when any of them feels it's needed, he or she calls out, "Crazy Dance Party," and starts a countdown from ten to one. By the time one is reached, someone has found a rock oldies radio station to listen to, and they dance like lunatics till everybody is laughing.

Shakespearean Insults

This is one of those problem-solving rituals in which humor is the magic ingredient. Liz Hawkins, mother of four, had some fridge magnets on hand that were decorated with colorful insults taken from William Shakespeare's writings. When her kids were little, she used to say, "If you're going to fight, then you have to hug," but when they got to be teenagers, she needed a new defense-against-the-dark-arts ritual. She got the idea to tell her warring children that if they were going to insult one another, they could *only* do it using one of these Shakespearean taunts. "They looked at me like I was nuts," she says, but they soon rose to the occasion and discovered it was impossible to keep a straight face after calling their sibling "Thou crusty batch of nature!" (usually with their best British accent).

If your kids are too young for the bard, there are variations on this concept: I know one mom who announced to her kids that they could only call each other names in a foreign tongue. Because they don't speak any languages other than English, they would quickly crack themselves up by inventing outrageous insults in pretend languages.

Three Tips on Handling Anger from Expert Naomi Drew

1. Create a cooling-off ritual for yourself:

Breathe deeply three times, then get a drink of water, go into another room, and listen to quiet music; or light a candle and calm your thoughts.

2. Help your children to create their own cooling-off rituals.

Some kids pet their dog, run around the yard, wash their face, write in a journal, or take their frustration out by making something out of clay.

3. Peace shield ritual:

Put a drop or two of essential oil of lavender in a spray bottle full of water. During a calm moment, have your children close their eyes and imagine a shield of light, protecting them from hurt and anger. Spray some lavender water in their direction to "lock in" the shield's power. Next time they get upset, have them imagine the peace shield protecting them from hurt and anger.

Naomi Drew's many books include *No Kidding About Bullying: 125 Ready-to-Use Activities to Help Kids Manage Anger, Resolve Conflicts, Build Empathy,* and *Get Along* (Free Spirit Publishing). Find out more at her website, www.LearningPeace.com.

School Rituals

Preparing First-Timers

The beginning of preschool is one of the biggest transitions your children will ever go through, at an age when change is especially scary. Preparing them well and making the send-off a joyful ritual will equip them well for all the transitions ahead.

Meet the Teacher/Playground Picnic

Most preschools arrange a tour of the school to acclimate the new kids. Take advantage of it, and try to engage your child in a conversation with the teacher. Take your camera and take a photo of the teacher, so she becomes even more familiar in coming days. On another day right before school starts, take your child for a special picnic at the school playground: Having had fun there and knowing her way around the swings will make her more comfortable on the first day.

Drop-Off Rituals

Saying "good-bye" is terribly hard, especially at the beginning, so think beforehand about a ritual that might ease the transition for your child. Elinor Craig found her son settled in quickly after she let him choose a secret code word on the way: When he said, "It's *fire engines,* Mom," it meant he was ready for her to leave. One mother kisses her daughter's hand before she goes, and tells her it's a magic, all-day kiss: If she gets lonely and holds the hand to her lips, she'll get a "love buzz." Create a secret "big boy" or "big girl" handshake and hug combination, express your love in words, then if possible, get your child engaged with some toys on a table or a book on the floor before leaving. Never sneak out!

Pretend School

Before school starts, begin the practice of "playing school" for a week, with your child's stuffed animals filling in as some of the students. Engage in some of the activities you know are standard at your child's new school, such as blocks or story hour. If you can get the names of a few other children who will be in the class, invite one or two over to join the pretend, and make sure to include a fun snack.

tech tip

Instant Book on First Day of Kindergarten

When each of her three kids started kindergarten, Kim Inglee of Albany, New York, took digital photos of every thing that child did to get ready for the big day: waking up, dressing, brushing teeth, combing hair, waiting for the bus. Being a reading teacher, she also wrote captions underneath: "Ben woke up on the first day of kindergarten," "Ben made his bed on the first of kindergarten," and so on. For each child's book, she printed the photos on paper using her home printer, glued the pictures and captions onto card stock, made a front cover, and had the instant book laminated and bound at Staples or Office Depot that same day. "Just as they get off the bus that first day, they get this special book," says Kim. "And the best part is that I write a mushy letter to them and place it on the back cover. I find them re-reading these books every now and again, though they are now eleven years old, nine, and seven."

Celebrating Back-to-School Days

Even for older kids, the first day of a new school year is a big deal. Thoughtfully celebrating these days is one way to convey a sense that learning is a joy.

Think Harry Potter

Muggles don't get school supplies as nifty as pet owls and magic wands, but make your school shopping into a fun outing including lunch, and let your kids pick as many items as possible, even if their taste appalls you. Harry loves going back to Hogwarts partly because he had such memorable experiences there, so on the night before school starts, go around the table and talk about the most memorable events from the previous school year. Talk about the school play, a favorite teacher, the science experiment that blew up. The Giehl family of Colorado has a feast in the dining room on the night before and each kid receives a school-related present, such as a fancy pencil box or a globe.

First Week of School

Erica Rawson, a mother of four in New Mexico, plans and cooks elaborate breakfasts for the whole first week of school. Her menus include pancakes, burritos, and the kids' favorite, Breakfast Lasagna, in which the layers that are usually pasta are items like waffles and pound cake, the filling is berries and custard. Like many families, the kids pose for a first-day photo, but Erica got the brilliant idea of having her kids each hold up a handmade sign declaring which year of school they are about to enter.

Front-Step Photos

Many parents take photos of their kids dressed up in new clothes, carrying new backpacks and lunchboxes, but posed in the same spot on the front steps. It's wonderful to look at these photos over the years, and maybe even combine them in one collage.

Sweet Beginning

On the first day of a new school year, Pam Skripak serves her kids homemade hot apple pie and ice cream for breakfast. Yum. (They get this on the last day of the year as well.)

Pep Talk in Chalk

In Maryland, Kunni Biener used to wake up extra early on the first day, so she could write messages to her daughters on the sidewalk that led to their school. They giggled as they walked along reading "Good Luck!" and "Have Fun!" and when they reached high school, they started writing messages to each other in the street on the first day.

Bus-Stop Party

Gail Spencer always starts out the year by providing juice and bagels to the ten or so kids who wait at the bus stop with her kids.

Drop-Off Blessing

Cheryl Maner started doing this when her son had to adjust to a first-grade teacher who was a good educator, but not cuddly like the kindergarten teacher. There were a few behavior issues, and she thought a ritual like this would help focus him: "May God bless you, may He smile his shining face on you, may He guide you and direct you in everything you do today [and she would insert particulars like "including the spelling test"], and most of all, may God give you peace." Her son, Parker, usually joins in and says, "Peace," at the end.

Rewarding Good Work

Basically, I agree with Alfie Kohn, author of *Punished by Rewards: The Trouble with Gold Stars, Incentive Plans, A's, Praise, and Other Bribes*, that it's better (and more effective) to instill a love of learning than to try bribing a kid to succeed. Here are some rituals I think offer positive encouragement.

Report Card Dinners

The Suttons of Casper, Wyoming, don't eat out that often, but they have a ritual of a restaurant dinner for the whole family every time report cards come out. "They mostly get straight A's, but we have the dinners no matter what," says Mary Sutton. "We feel it's important to reward the effort." Even more important, she says, she and her husband feel like they really get caught up with their kids' school lives at these relaxed meals. Thus, these dinners are more about celebrating their children as students than they are about tying certain rewards to specific achievements.

Book Rewards

Books should be treasured, and one way to reinforce that is to make books the reward for good work. When my son was learning to read, we had "reading treasure hunts," in which he had to read clues all over the house. After each hunt, he put a sticker on a sheet taped to the fridge and, after ten stickers, I took him to the bookstore and let him pick out a book.

Ms. Frizzle Awards

One of the problems with rewarding good grades is that it encourages kids to take easy courses and avoid challenges. My favorite teaching philosophy is that of the fictional teacher Ms. Frizzle, from the *Magic School Bus* series on public TV. "Take chances, make mistakes, get messy!" is her motto, and such behavior leads to learning. Every month during the school year, give the Ms. Frizzle Award (a piece of white paper with fancy writing) to the family member who follows her advice and learns the most—parents included.

Homework Rituals

If kids learn early to set aside specific times for homework, they'll develop the discipline they will need all the way through school and beyond. Establish the time for homework the first day of school, and dedicate a special "Homework Zone" in a bedroom, kitchen, or den. Ideally, this should be a quiet place, with no television or other distractions. Our son used to use the kitchen table, but as he worked his way up through high school, he gravitated to the bigger table in the dining room. It's very easy to tell if he's goofing off, when he's stationed in such a visible place. We've also made sure his computer is downstairs rather than in his bedroom.

Brain Food

It's good to develop a transition ritual from school to home, with a snack and some goof-off time to start. Physical activity could be included, a quick phone call to a best friend, or fifteen minutes of a favorite computer game, but limit the time. Some kids like to take off their shoes or change clothes.

Q/A Partners

It can get pretty boring sitting in your room staring at a textbook. Parents can help make it more lively, partly by drilling their kids on material that requires rote memorization. My friend Jean Donaldson used to toss a koosh ball back and forth with her kids while they recited math tables or spelling test words: The physical activity kept them from getting too lethargic, and I suspect the rhythm worked like a mnemonic device, helping to anchor the data in their brains.

Sentenced to Laughter

It's good to develop family rituals related to learning apart from the school curriculum. By regularly including games in which you play with words and use your brains for fun, you show that creative thinking is a lifelong form of play. There are plenty of great word games, including Scrabble®, but it's also fun to buy a set of words to stick on your fridge. Magnetic Poetry® has an early reader version, small words in big print, and you can keep them in an empty coffee can in the kitchen. Try to get every family member to invent a sentence a day—the more absurd the better—and read them aloud at dinner.

Lesson of the Week

Once a week, during a family meeting or Sunday dinner, have each person in the family share something valuable or fascinating he or she learned that week. Again, you reinforce that learning is a lifelong activity. At the same time, this exercise works as a lesson review for kids and may actually make them realize they learned something useful.

Country of the Week

Once a week, on Sunday night or Monday morning, announce a country the family will focus on that week. Pick a country that's in the news at that time, and start by looking up its location on a map or globe. Talk about why it's newsworthy, and help the kids look up its language, history, and customs on the Internet or at the library.

Show and Tell

Part of the daily homework ritual should include a parental review of what's been done. Some kids feel a sense of accomplishment if they can make a checkmark on the calendar when they finish, or add a sticker. Compliment perseverance as well as creativity. You might create a winding-down ritual of a warm bath, or a back rub, or end the day by reading aloud from a book your kids enjoy.

Sunday Sundaes

It's important to set specific homework rituals for the weekends as well, so everything doesn't get left till the last minute. One family gets together in the kitchen on Sunday nights for "make-your-own sundaes," but only those with finished homework can come. You might have special treat food for weekend homework sessions: Instead of serving popcorn when you watch videos, save it for homework period.

tech tip

Best Study Websites

Kids today have no idea how lucky they are to have such great online resources to help them study and do homework. But as we all know, not all web-based resources are reliable. Presumably, your kids' teachers are warning them about trusting Wikipedia and other sites as authoritative, but it's also good to know about some study sites you can rely on.

One good resource is on the Microsoft website, the "Top 14 Websites for Students," compiled by journalist and tech expert Marc Saltzman. Here you will find overall homework help sites he recommends like RefDesk.com and Fact Monster. But he also singles out specific sites for help in English, history, math, and science, such as Shakespeare-Online.com and Project Gutenberg. The latter is an archive of more than 36,000 free downloadable books, including most of the classic novels your kids will be assigned to read. Ulysses, anyone?

Find this master list at: www.Microsoft.com/athome/students/student sites.aspx.

Playing Hooky

In general, I don't advocate teaching kids to skip school. However, I know many families who allow it for one or two special days a year, and their kids haven't turned into habitual truants.

A Day with Mom

Julie Stockler was allowed to play hooky one day a year when she was young and has passed that tradition on to her daughters. When she was young, she would use her day off to go shopping with her mother at a department store and eat lunch in the ladies' tearoom. Her girls prefer to go to the movies or skiing, but they also treasure the one-on-one time with her as much as the forbidden pleasure of skipping out on school.

Surprise Kidnap

One mother I know surprises her kids by "kidnapping" them from school one day a year. She pays attention to when tests and school field trips are scheduled and picks a day when they won't miss much. The kids go off to school, their mother takes a shower and dresses, then shows up at school and surprises them. Once they get in the car, the lucky kid gets to decide how to spend the day.

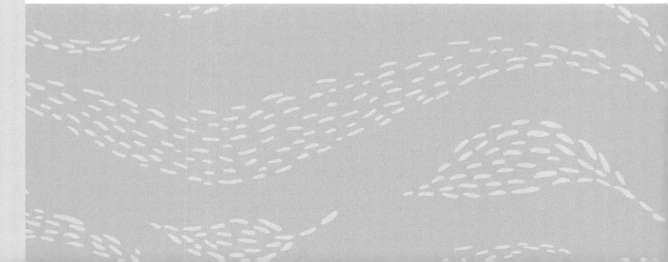

Sty Day

A friend of mine used to skip work and take one mental health day a year with her daughter, when they would never get out of their pajamas. They watched television and ate junk food all day, never taking showers or washing the dishes. (This explains the name of their annual frolic, taken from the farm structure typically occupied by pigs.) No one would argue that this is educational, but it sure was a fun contrast to work and school, and it didn't hurt the daughter, who later graduated from one of the country's top law schools.

Museum Days

If you've ever been to a major museum like the American Museum of Natural History in New York City, which has one of the greatest dinosaur collections anywhere, you know how crowded it gets on weekends and school holidays. I started taking my son there when he was two years old, and it's probably his happiest place on the planet. He's learned so much and seen so many amazing exhibits, and I wanted to plant the idea early that this was a treat. Throughout grade school, I used to pick one day a year to pull him out of school so we could see the *T. rex* up close and eat dino-shaped chicken nuggets in the museum cafeteria. I always worked with his teachers to pick a day when he wouldn't miss a test, major event, or field trip, and they were always cool with it. Starting with middle school, we stopped museum days, but he has such good memories of this annual tradition!

End-of-School-Year Rituals

Teacher Tribute

To encourage gratitude and practice writing, have your children write and decorate thank-you notes to their teachers. Encourage them to list specific areas in which they learned a lot, or an area where the teacher provided crucial, extra assistance. They might also bring a small gift, such as flowers.

Kid's Choice Dinner

Food isn't the only thing kids choose when the Fitches of Columbus, Ohio, celebrate the last day of school. They not only pick the menu but also where and when to eat it. When Corey Fitch was nine, the year the ritual began, he decided he wanted to eat carryout Chinese food on the steps of his elementary school—at midnight. "We sat there eating noodles and talking about the past year," says Sally Fitch. "It was wild and crazy, and he loved it."

Ending the School Year with a Bang

No matter how well he did in school, there were always a few obligations and events during the year in grade school that really annoyed my son. Our ritual for the last day of school started out with buying ice cream cones and signing up for the library's summer reading program. But when we got home, there would be three or four brightly colored helium-filled balloons on strings, which I had tied to a drawer handle in the kitchen. Max would take a black marker and write things on the balloons he was joyful to be done with, like having to learn colonial dance, then he would gleefully stab each balloon with a pin. Not particularly edifying, I admit, but extremely satisfying, and it produced a real sense of liberation, a great way to start the summer.

Library Payback

When Patrice Kyger's kids graduate from elementary school, they are allowed to pick out a book and have her buy it for the school library, an act that makes them feel very grown-up.

Welcome Summer Party

Carolyn Hecht's son, now grown, always celebrated the last day of school by hosting a huge watermelon fight in the backyard. "There were always seven or eight boys, and it was a big, messy fight that lasted all afternoon," says Carolyn. There are other activities and foods for welcoming summer in the backyard: You can serve lemonade or ice cream cones, and if it's sunny, start the summer off with a squirt gun and water-balloon battle.

Crystal Ball

When Sandy Graham's daughter, Jaime, finished elementary school in Denver, local teacher Barb Herman had students in the class write a letter predicting their own future: Where will they go to college? What will their major be? Future profession? Will they marry? Have kids? She saves all the letters and mails them to the kids in the spring of their senior year in high school. She has to track down a few who left the local school district, but her track record is good. And kids *love* seeing what they predicted for themselves seven or eight years before. Sandy suggests that any parent could execute this ritual and present the predictions list to their kids when they graduate from high school. Perhaps you could build a whole evening around filling in the form, complete with candle-light, robes, and a crystal ball. And parents might talk about what they expected for themselves at that age—versus the reality that emerged.

End-of-School Awards Dinner

The Giehls of Colorado, who always have a fancy family dinner on the night before school begins, also have a feast on the day it ends, but with more fanfare.

The meal is served in the dining room, the food is festive, and the dessert is always spectacular. But the main ritual is the presentation of special posters Nancy has made for each child. The point is not to praise grades, but to applaud what each one learned and is still learning. After second grade, for example, Nancy described her daughter Julie on the poster as "reader, writer, pianist." After the meal, each child is given a letter Nancy has written about the year's highlights and the parents' pride in his or her hard work. And they have their pictures taken next to their special posters.

Another highlight of the meal: a family survey about what special activities and trips they should plan for the summer, ranked by level of enthusiasm.

How to Make an End-of-Year Award Poster

Materials

Sturdy poster board from office supply or crafts store

Markers

Ribbon

Scissors

Class photo of the child that year or a photocopy of same

Pictures of your child at school (if you have them)

Magazine photos

Instructions

Cut the school photo into a round or oval shape and glue it into the center of the poster. Color around the photograph, making an elaborate border. Write across the top in marker: Star Student (child's name) and the year. In an oval pattern around the central photo, place photos either of your child engaged in different activities, such as sports or studying, or drawings of such, or magazine photos that suggest these things. Write underneath each image something your child did or learned. Glue one end of a piece of ribbon next to the central photo, and glue the other end near the image of an accomplishment. Repeat the process, attaching additional ribbons to the central photograph and the surrounding images, so the ribbons radiate out like spokes of a wheel.

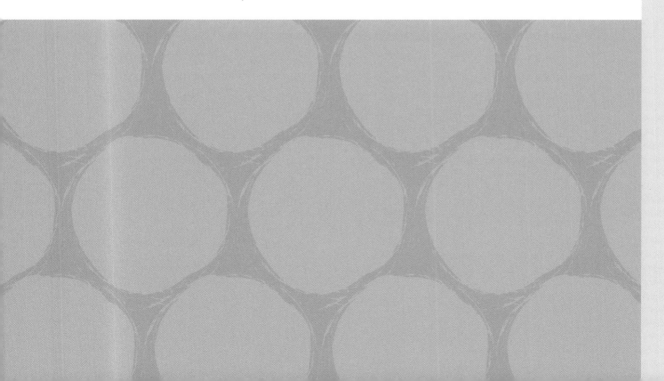

Pet Rituals

I know a guy who sends postcards to his parrot when he goes on vacation (he mails them to the pet store where he boards the parrot), and a woman who sings a different lullaby for each of her two dogs at bedtime: She swears they recognize the tune. Many of the rituals we enact with our pets are more for ourselves, but routine comforts animals of all kinds. And rituals can help young kids relish the regular duties of pet ownership.

Walking the Dog

Dogs demand ritual and respond to it as devotedly as children, and this is especially true with the all-important routine of daily walks. Dog owners tend to have pre-walk rituals that include verbal cues and flourishes, such as having the dog carry his leash to the door. Adding on silly songs or other fun antics makes this more enjoyable for kids, too. Whenever my son visits Auntie Na (a.k.a., my husband's ex-wife, Anita), he loves to walk her dog, Luna, and when he was younger, they always got ready for walking her with a special song. ("Get the poop papers, Peggy, we're going for a walk, these dogs will poop so much, the neighbors will all talk. . . .")

Mealtimes

Never tease a hungry dog about food, but many owners like to have their dog sit first and give him or her a pat on the head before placing the bowl on the floor. If your child wants to sing a special song or even say grace before the cat gets supper, why not? It will help a kid remember to feed his or her pet because the routine is spiced with fun.

Baths

For most dogs, a bath is not a treat. Try to make it fun by having the kids put on their bathing suits and climb right into the bathtub with the dog. Pretend that you're preparing the dog for a big dog show, while drying and combing your pet, adding embellishments like ribbons and maybe taking silly photographs.

Birthdays

The Pompi family celebrates the birthdays of all seven of their cats, and their dog. The cats get a can of tuna decorated with a candle stuck in it, and the dog gets a meaty bone from the butcher, also with a candle. The dog gets the biggest party, because he's the oldest. Naturally, the Pompis sing "Happy Birthday" before helping their pets blow out candles.

Dog-Friendly Errands

Gretchen Zimmer, who owns the Rocky Top Dog Park in New Jersey, engages in many regular rituals with her dogs. She goes so far as to frequent establishments that provide dog treats. "They love to ride in the car with me," says Gretchen, so she always fills her gas tank at a station that provides free dog treats. She even goes to a drive-through bank where the teller puts money in the plastic tube—and sticks in a biscuit for each of Gretchen's dogs. And get this, in warm weather, Gretchen takes her pets to an ice-cream kiosk called Lickit that always reserves cracked cones for dogs. If you have dogs, make your errands more fun by finding local businesses that welcome them, too: For little kids, errands can sometimes be fun, but often they make them restless. This adds an element of playfulness.

Pet Funerals

The death of a pet is a big hurt for a young child. Ritualizing that death helps children work through a painful loss and teaches them to value all living things.

Goldfish Burial

In the book *How to Bury a Goldfish: And 113 Other Family Rituals for Everyday Life*, Virginia Lang recalls the time she almost flushed her two-year-old daughter's dead fish down the toilet. Instead, she and her daughter dug a little hole together in the backyard, put the fish in the hole, and planted a flower on the spot. Her daughter invented a song about her pet. Ms. Lang recommends marking the calendar on the day a pet dies, as well as marking the ground where the pet is buried, either with a painted rock or by planting something.

Rats and Gerbils, Too

My friend Sandy Graham has found that her kids grieve greatly even when a pet rat dies. Her son and daughter make a gravestone with a piece of flagstone or brick and a permanent marker. The pet is put in a metal cookie tin, resting on a scrap of fabric that is soft and pretty (often satin or velvet). All the pets are buried by a special tree, a big cottonwood, and during the burial ceremony, all four family members reminisce about the pet's exploits and character. Sandy says a prayer asking God to welcome the critter into pet heaven with all the family's previous pets.

Memorial Garden

If yours is a critter-loving family, chances are, pet funerals will become a more regular ritual than you bargained for, and you may want to create a special garden for this purpose. You might consider planting specific plants for different animals, such as catnip for your favorite cats, or bright yellow sunflowers for a pet with a sunny disposition. You can paint a special marker for each animal, or place special garden decorations here, such as wind chimes or a birdbath. When my son's beloved pet gecko, Dart, died, I found a brightly painted twirling garden marker for sale online that included a lizard. When Max's pet frogs departed, they were buried under a big rock, upon which sits a small metal frog wearing a crown.

Celebration of a Pet's Life

My friend Anita had a cat named Madness (she was allergic, but this stray cat captured the attention of her daughter, my step-daughter, Kate), who lived a long life and was a beloved family member. When the cat became frail and was approaching an age that translated into 100 human years, Anita threw a "Century of Madness" party. All the guests got an apron and a baseball cap decorated with the party's theme and a drawing of a cat. There was an enormous cake, great food, and Madness himself was carried around the room atop an ornate pillow, so he could be petted and admired. Later, this cat's death left a hole for sure, but the tribute (and all the leftover commemorative gear and photos) keeps his memory alive to this day.

Chore Rituals

Mary Poppins was right about that spoonful of sugar; we all have duties and chores, but rituals can liven them up. That applies to chores we assign our kids, and chores we must do ourselves, when they'd rather we play. If all else fails, invent specific silly songs for different chores; this works well with toddlers. Whistle while you work!

Laundry

One of our babysitters started this ritual of letting my son "ride" the bulging laundry bag as it was pulled across the floor to the laundry room, and for years I performed this weekly. "Oh my goodness, my laundry is heavy!" I would moan as I tugged him along. Then, I'd pretend I was going to throw my son in the washer and set him down on top of it. One mother I know does laundry with her daughters on Friday night, creating "intermissions" in their video watching to go change loads. The girls bring their own dirty clothes to the washer in a baby carriage.

Charts and Stickers

My mother had four kids and went back to work when I was in grade school. We all had to do our own ironing, strip and make our beds each week, and so forth. But it helped that she was an artist and provided very explicit directions in colorful ways: I remember a painted chart in the upstairs bathroom that even indicated what types of clothing to throw in the hamper, according to the day of the week. For today's kids, it's always good to create charts so that they get a certain type of favorite sticker every time they do their chores without nagging, and these can add up to a treat at week's end, while providing a visual daily reminder of what's expected.

Yard Work

You'll get a lot more work done if your kids can help. Get smaller copies of some of your tools, and give them their own part of the yard to tend. Have a regular routine such as always checking under certain rocks to look for insects, always climbing a certain tree, always leaving seeds or bread crumbs in the backyard for the birds.

Freeze Rest

Elizabeth Elkin's two boys, Noah and Eli, hate cleaning up as much as the next kid. So she decided to make it more entertaining with the "Freeze Game." "I would play fun, upbeat music and they had to clean up as fast as they could while the music played." When their mom stopped the music, everyone had to freeze, generally in silly and awkward postures, which got everyone laughing.

Mix a Privilege with a Duty

Amanda Soule, a mother of five, assigns each kid a certain duty for the week: laundry helper, bathroom helper, dish dryer after meals, etc. One of the things that has helped compliance for the kid who has to be chief dishwasher, is that he or she gets to pick the music that the whole family listens to during meals.

Grocery Shopping

Little kids can become very cranky sitting in those cramped metal carts. In addition to bringing a snack like a baggy full of Goldfish crackers, I always told my son stories when we went on errands. My invented polar bear, Pete, would be in the grocery store with us getting into trouble, usually by climbing into the freezers and eating all the Klondike bars. We had brief but fun rituals for different sections of the market: When we came to the seafood section, Max always said "hello" to the live lobsters in the tank.

TV Rituals

There are many good arguments against giving children too much television and screen time generally. Although I watched a great deal of television throughout my childhood, after college I lived without owning a television for at least a decade and I rarely felt that I missed anything. When I wanted to watch something special like a dance concert on PBS (Public Broadcasting Service), or the Oscars, I'd find a friend with a television who was watching and invite myself over. And bring food.

I know a good number of families that still don't own a television, or limit their kids' tube consumption drastically. Farther along in this section, you'll find information and resources on how to limit overexposure to all types of screens in your household. But I did want to cover TV-centric rituals in this edition because television watching is so deeply ingrained in American life, and I believe that can be a positive thing if parents are disciplined about using it.

Let's face facts: The vast majority of families already have daily and weekly traditions around watching certain shows, whether they religiously watch the evening news or their favorite sitcoms and reality shows, or wouldn't miss kid faves like *Sesame Street, The Backyardigans,* or *American Idol.*

Another indisputable fact: Most Americans watch too much TV for their own good, which is one cause of our obesity epidemic. By the time the average American turns sixty-five, he or she will have spent twelve years watching television! Yikes.

What the Experts Say

The **American Academy of Pediatrics** recommends that children under two have no screen time whatsoever, and that kids over two watch no more than one to two hours of quality programming per day.

Although there is a heap of mind-numbing junk on television, there are also amazingly educational, artistic, and powerfully thoughtful programs worth watching. Families that love football, baseball, tennis, and other sports have wonderful traditions of sitting around cheering on their favorite teams and booing their historic rivals, while eating special snacks.

Even the silliest comedy shows and their characters can become part of a family's shared cultural references, the source of everything from family jokes to pet names. When Max was little, he loved every type of animal show, and we all learned a lot about exotic animals by watching with him. Our shared love of *The Simpsons* has led to all sorts of conversations about everything from what makes a family to chasing down the plentiful movie references in the animated show.

So-called "must-see TV" events truly bring us together as families. As we watch the Olympics together or the president's State of the Union address, we have a chance to talk about current events and watch history unfold.

When it comes to creating family rituals around television, here are a couple of general principles that will work for most families:

Limit screen time: Be very intentional and direct about how much television time you allow. You don't want to have to spend every moment working as a TV cop, so set very clear guidelines. Limit your kids to the amount of time they can spend each day, especially on school days, or just let them watch on weekends. In many households, the television does not get turned on until homework is complete.

Turn the activity from passive to active: Teach your kids to be media critics by discussing what you see during and after a program. Whether it is a science show or a sitcom, you can challenge assumptions, and talk about whether it is realistic. Keep a family TV diary so that after you watch a program, every family member can decide how many stars to award it and write a one-sentence review. Tell your kids to find a book at home that covers the same topic, and spend some time reading it together. Or make art based on what you saw: Draw your favorite characters from a show, or get a book from the library about how to draw cartoons. If it's a game show, like *Jeopardy*, play the game yourself. If it's a cooking show, head into the kitchen and make a snack together. Watch the latest episode of *American Idol*, then let every family member perform one song, whether dancing, singing, or playing an instrument.

Bring everyone together: Especially if your kids are older or far apart in ages, they won't all want to watch the same programs. You may want to let each watch one or two favorite programs alone, but TV watching doesn't qualify as a family ritual unless everyone is having a shared experience. And there should be an activity that follows, even if it's just a short discussion of what you all just watched.

Curate your own programming: With built-in video recorders, on-demand programming, and rental services like Netflix, families have a great opportunity to personalize and control their viewing experiences. So think of yourself as the curator of your family's TV time and pick and choose thoughtfully. Perhaps you can program Friday Night Videos and pick a different theme each month: One month, you watch only animal shows or movies, and the next month it's World Travel Month, and you learn about different countries. Have a double or triple feature. Serve popcorn or cookies and milk at "intermission" or during the shows. Let the kids help shape the programming.

tech
tip

Shoot Your Own Show

One way to keep your family active and creative is to turn the camera on yourselves. The tools for doing this are everywhere, and not terribly expensive or hard to operate. One of my absolute favorite things to do as a kid was to perform "shows" in the basement with my siblings. We might have a variety show or I'd write a short play; everyone would dress up, and we'd make paper tickets and invite our parents and neighbors to watch. Many families today have a digital movie camera of some sort or a video camera built into their smart phone. So why not get creative? There are endless options: Write a sitcom with five- or ten-minute episodes, film it yourselves, then post it on YouTube if everyone is okay with that. Or do a "reality show" about your own family, with everyone taking turns as cameraman and narrator.

This all just scratches the surface, but you get the idea. In addition, here are a few rituals shaped around television watching.

Dance to the Music

Gail Prince says her family always used to dance like maniacs to the theme music at the end of a program they all watched together "It was the '80s, and the music was always happy and upbeat and fun to dance to," says Gail. Now that she is a mother, she does that with her kids, including during the credits for a movie.

Because television watching is generally sedentary, it's not a bad idea to create some sort of action ritual to get the whole family off the couch after every show they watch. Create a "playlist" of favorite pop songs—from any era—that make you want to move, and get everybody shaking and jumping and grooving for at least one entire song before sitting back down for more TV.

Mom's Oldies: A Crash Course in TV Classics

Michelle Olson lives in Minnesota, where the winter nights are cold and long. A few years back, she started a ritual of watching one episode at a time of an old sitcom with her daughters. This is always done after homework is finished, with everyone gathered in their favorite spot on the couch. "We have watched every single episode of *I Love Lucy,* in order," says Michelle. "And now we are in the middle of *The Brady Bunch.*" I can relate: One of my family's summer vacation rituals is finding a lauded TV series we missed and watching every episode in order. We especially love sci-fi shows like the short-lived *Firefly*.

Oscar Night Fun

One woman I know, a single mom with a teenage son, loves to make a big deal out of the Academy Awards telecast. They eat a fancy dinner in front of the TV, using silver, fine china, and crystal. Another family tries to make up a menu that is themed to the movies in the running for best picture.

Other ideas: Dress up for the show like movie stars, cast your own ballot to predict the winners in major categories, then give a prize to the family member who got the most predictions right.

Technology and Traditions

Double-edged sword is what comes to mind when I think about the high-tech times we live in today. What parent of a child far from home isn't hugely grateful for the existence of cell phones? What grandparent doesn't give thanks for Skype and other chat services that provide the chance to have a conversation with the grandkids while getting to see them at the same time, to watch as they play with the toy just sent, or observe their newfound skills in acrobatics or reading? Because of her daughter-in-law's blog (theDailyLil.blogspot.com) my friend Janell Byrne got to see a video of her grandbaby, Lil, crawling—on the first day she reached that milestone.

Kids born today will never know what life was like before all the information in the world was at one's fingertips. They're experiencing a form of instant gratification that we are not wrong in thinking could be detrimental to maturity and discipline. And they are becoming accustomed to a form of multitasking that makes it harder for them to focus deeply.

Although he's not allowed to do this while completing homework, my teenage son rarely has just one screen going when he's on his own. He likes to watch a TV show on the computer's screen while playing a video game in his lap on a handheld gaming device. When he's sitting on the sofa watching TV with us, he's often still playing a game with his hands. We were always adamant that Max couldn't have either a television set or a computer in his bedroom. Ironically, now that he has an iPhone, he's taking a mini-TV and computer everywhere he goes.

More and more, the multiplying and captivating screens in our lives are keeping people disengaged from one another, even when they are in the same room. It bothers me when I see a young couple eating dinner in a nice restaurant while staring into their laps instead of each other's eyes.

If anything, that disconnection gets worse on the home front. We love our families, but we also argue with them, ignore them, and often take them for granted. Kids who have a screen in their hands are usually paying more attention to that than their siblings and parents. The addiction starts earlier and earlier: Toddlers are handed smart phones with videos playing to distract them from meltdowns. Teenagers, well, you do the math. The average teenager, studies show, sends more than 100 text messages a day.

What's a Parent to Do?

First off, don't panic. There are pluses as well as minuses for families when it comes to this technology explosion. Just ask Anne Collier, a tech expert who chaired an Obama task force on online safety and serves on Facebook's safety advisory board. The mother of two teenage boys, Collier founded the website NetFamilyNews.org to provide "kid tech news for parents."

"The Internet is neutral: it's how we use it that counts," says Anne Collier. "You know your family's values and rules and those need to extend into technology and cyberspace."

Exactly. Parents need to have a strong sense of what they value and translate that into a clear and consistent policy about tech devices. Sometimes, I believe, it's important to declare screen-free times and places, such as the family dinner table and during homework hours. On the other hand, it's worthwhile exploring the very positive ways in which tech tools can be woven into existing family traditions, and even help start new ones.

Two Trusted Websites for Keeping Your Family Safe While Connected

To get specific details about how to control your kids' use of all types of screen technology, you will find lots of resources at www.NetSmartz.org/Parents (run by the National Center for Missing and Exploited Children) and www.PTA.org/mediasafety.

As stated earlier, it's much easier to start out with very strict limits on tech use with small children, and then relent only gradually.

Picking and Choosing Which Screens and When

Theresa Routh Chapman and her husband are both teachers and made the joint decision not to allow their sons, at seven and four, to own any video game devices. They also strictly limit the amount of time their sons can watch television, sticking to family fare like *Nature* on PBS, which the whole family watches together.

The family isn't opposed to technology per se: The boys join in for video chats to grandparents and send e-mails to cousins, aunts, and uncles. The ban on video gaming is getting tougher now that the older boy is in school, but the parents have clearly explained their priorities. "We would rather have him playing outdoors, or with his brother, or creating, reading or imagining," says Theresa.

Setting Weekday and Weekend Time Limits

Julie Buehler, a mother of two in Yardley, Pennsylvania, has a baby and a nine-year-old, and the older child is allowed just thirty minutes of screen time on weekdays, and that covers television, computer, and iPod. On the weekends, her maximum time to be on-screen is two hours per day. Like many parents, Julie worries about how hard it will be to keep these limits as her daughter ages.

Choosing for Interactivity

In a *Wall Street Journal* column titled "Baby's First App Store Download," technology reporter Michael Hsu wrote about checking out some Montessori-themed iPhone apps. He says he didn't like them as much as some simple apps that inspired his three-year-old daughter to explore the world by taking simple photos with the phone's camera. He said they also liked to view family photos together that are stored on his phone and talk about the people. And, she loves a free Apple app called Voice Memos that allows her to record her own voice and then play it back.

Michael says he plans to restrict his children's use of the devices but admits it's hard to strictly ration cell phone use when kids see their parents with the devices constantly.

Discriminating among the endless offerings available is very important, especially for really young children.

Finding the Right Software

The tech tools we have today are just the baby steps in a revolution, and they are drastically changing how children learn and interact with the world and other people. There is no denying that among a vast amount of commercial dreck, there are some compelling and very educational games and apps coming out constantly. Find some local resources and gatekeepers to help you sort the good from the bad, including tech-savvy local librarians and teachers at your children's school.

To name just a few outstanding examples, iPad games like Monkey Preschool Lunchbox teach kids their colors and numbers by counting out fruit and other items for a monkey's lunch. A software firm launched by parents in 2010 called Montessorium is creating groundbreaking math and reading apps based on lauded Montessori educational principles.

Another very popular app helps families to play a game called "Geocaching," a global treasure hunt that encourages kids to be both physically active and curious about the real world. Hidden containers called geocaches can be found by following clues to outdoor locations: Once a container is found, the person who discovered it takes out the tiny prize inside and places another token item inside for the next person, perpetuating the game. To find out more about the sport of geocaching and the app, go to www.geocaching.com.

Some Tech Tools for Creating New Family Traditions

By necessity, this can only scratch the surface and the technology keeps changing, but the idea is to bend these devices to your family's needs and values.

Family Blogs

A family blog can become a virtual scrapbook that is also a source of creativity and fun for the whole tribe, getting your kids more involved in contributing text, photos, and videos as they age. It's a great and not expensive way to keep your far-flung family and friends on top of your news.

Before starting a blog, browse around online and look at other family blogs to get an idea how varied they can be. There is a difference between a blog that is someone's home-based business (Soulemama.typepad .com), and a blog that's meant to be a virtual bulletin board for extended family, like the Crumley Family Blog, "a blog for the whole fam damily" (crumleyblog.com). A blog whose purpose is to generate income requires a different focus, high-quality photos, constant postings, and negotiation of business relationships, whereas a blog that is for simple family enjoyment and memory preservation can be extremely simple and casual.

Crumley Family Fun Blog

As the Crumley family of four from Chattanooga, Tennessee, explains on the blog, "Our intent in keeping this blog is to keep family and friends up to date on our lives." The postings, mostly by Alli Crumley, the mother, consist of a bit of description of family outings and events, plus photos and short videos. Alli posted about a St. Patrick's Day ritual, for example, with a short video showing how she created a "rainbow" using streamers, which she stretched and taped all through the house and down the stairs: They ended by dangling over the dining room table, and underneath she left a "pot of gold" (a gold-painted pot with candy inside).

Visitors to the blog can type in a comment after a posting, and there is one from the boys' grandmother saying she hasn't been feeling too well lately and is happy the family had a fun holiday.

Spring Break Blog

You may be thinking a blog is a huge commitment that needs to spotlight every meal and moment in your family life. But some blogs are created to mark a single event or experience, like the Miller Keithley family's blog from 2009, which mostly covers the adventures of the family of five on a vacation to the Grand Canyon. The kids got to post their own comments on the trip, saying what they liked most, and there are inserted short videos. You'll find it at MillerKeithley .blogspot.com.

Living Abroad Blog

Wags Party of 6: Trying to Get Beyond Status Updates is the name of the ongoing blog kept by Susan Wagoner about her husband, who serves in the military, and their four daughters and their daily life in Japan. Living so far away from extended family, she uses the blog to share holiday celebrations, the first day of school, or her daughter Claire's first ballet lesson. It certainly comforted everyone to

see postings right after the earthquake and tsunami in 2011.

As a working (telecommuting) mom, Susan Wagoner is way too busy to keep up her scrapbooking, but she finds it much easier to maintain the blog. "It's great to be able to share our life with family back home, but I confess my primary motivation is to get these cute stories and pictures down on 'paper,'" she explains. "I'm planning on exporting the blog into a book each year or so." Also, the blog exists as a reminder of different major happenings. Although Susan posts only a few of the photos from each day, she carefully saves all her digital photos on her computer, organizing them into monthly folders, so they can be appreciated and shared later when her daughters grow up.

One of the features included in the Wags Party of 6 blog, which is common to blog services, is that when you go to the Wagoners' blog, not only does it display the most recent post first, but it also displays a list of other blogs they like. In this case, the list shows blogs kept by other members of the extended family. These are automatically updated whenever a new post is added, so that Susan can go to her own blog and get an instant update on what else is going on within her tribe: After the name of each blog, there is the title of the latest post and the time it was posted.

Family Blogging 101

The most popular free blogging platforms include Blogger, TypePad, and WordPress. All three of them have fans, though many say Blogger is the easiest to use for the technophobe, whereas WordPress and TypePad have more flexibility.

Go to Blogger.com (a Google product), TypePad.com, and WordPress.com to get specifics on how their formats work, and tour some existing blogs. Resources like these will also keep you updated about all legal requirements. For one thing, the Federal Trade Commission requires that bloggers declare any free products or paid advertising they receive on the blog or face heavy fines.

For a good step-by-step tutorial on what is involved in starting a blog for WordPress, try HowToStartABlog.org. There is a good explanation of how the various blog services differ at the website DigitalFamily.com, though Janine Warner's website is mostly for professionals.

Memory Makers: Photos and Videos

There has been an explosion of services online that allow families to save, organize, and share their digital photographs and videos. As both a mother and grandmother, I'm a regular user of these technologies and love the contrasting sense of immediacy and permanence they can provide. My stepdaughter regularly downloads digital photos of her daughter into Shutterfly.com, so my husband and I can easily view a couple of hundred recent photographs, then select a few to print out and save. She also uses the service to create beautiful hardcover keepsake books, including one I got for Mother's Day during her daughter's first year.

The Big Scrapbook in the Sky

There are a growing number of online photo-storage and printing services that allow parents to "park" their ballooning supply of digital photographs at a central location, where they can be organized into virtual or printed albums that friends and family can enjoy. Here is a rundown of just a few of the better-known services.

Popular sites include Shutterfly.com, Mixbook.com, Snapfish.com, and Kodak Gallery.com. Check them all out and compare both prices and ease of use. Shutterfly makes really beautiful books but requires sticking to its library of templates. Mixbook is gaining ground because it's more freestyle, allowing users to create their own designs easily. All of these sites allow you to turn your photographs into books, calendars, greeting cards, and other items that make good keepsakes (and family gifts.)

Another hugely popular site is Flickr.com, which allows you to create virtual albums of photographs and videos. The free Flickr service limits the number of photographs and videos you can upload monthly: If your photo and video stash is way bigger, you can pay the monthly fee for a Pro account. An important feature for families is that Flickr has privacy controls, so you can decide who views your material.

Games R Us

Nintendo, Sony, and the rest have changed the notion of games forever with their new devices. Video games have made it possible for people to enter virtual places and live out their fantasies via an alter ego called an avatar. Games have also migrated to cell phones and portable devices like iPads, making games both more portable and more addictive than ever.

As a mom who was dragged kicking and screaming into the gaming world by her teenage son, I can attest that there is no putting this genie back in the bottle. Again, parents must inform themselves about what is available, set realistic limits on what their kids play and for how long, and look for the ways the various gaming devices and websites can be used to spark family fun and connection.

Meet Me Online Next Week to Play

Playing games of all kinds was always a big tradition in Malinda McCormick's family. So she was fine with it when her son, Dillon, began spending a lot of time playing online role-playing games in high school. But she never anticipated that when Dillon went away to college, playing World of Warcraft every Sunday would become a cherished ritual between them.

"Although I knew I could call or text him anytime at college, it seemed like our conversations were becoming less meaningful and we were starting to disconnect," Malinda

explains. Her son had asked her before this if she wanted to play World of Warcraft with him, and when he came home from college in his junior year, she took up his offer. "Because he had played WoW a long time, he was a respected leader online in his guild [an online group that plays together]," his mother notes. "His guildmates were amused by the fact that I was his mom, but they took me in and seemed to watch their language when I was logged in!"

Rather sweetly, Dillon began helping his mother within the game world, helping her acquire gold and the best weapons, but the cool part is that they began talking to each other online while playing the game. "Between slaying monsters, he would mention something that happened in school, or ask how things were going at home," says Malinda. "It was how we started reconnecting in a very natural, comfortable way."

But the ultimate was when Dillon turned twenty-one while away at school, and Malida plotted with his guildmates to set up a surprise birthday party *within the game*! "We chose to gather at a certain time before a planned raid," says Dillon's mom. "When Dillon logged in, we were all in Ventrilo together (an Internet-based voiceover tool for multiple users, similar to a conference call). About twenty people logged in from all over the world and sang Happy Birthday along with me. These kids were belting out the song and shooting off virtual fireworks, while Dillon's WoW character danced around and did back flips. What can I say? It was a mother's duty to make his birthday special, and it was genuine regardless of it happening in a virtual place."

Two Family-Friendly Gaming Resources

The Nintendo Wii gaming system really captured attention as a great source of family-friendly games. With multiple controllers added on to the system, which you play on your television screen, families are having great game nights and playing non-violent, fun games. Wii bowling is a favorite at our house.

OhanaRama.com is a safe, private platform for families to play games together, even if they live far apart. Founded by tech industry veterans and targeted at kids between five and twelve, the OhanaRama games appeal to multiple generations by taking "old school" games like checkers and tic-tac-toe online. There are also educational games.

Diane Miller of California signed up for OhanaRama after her sister joined the service, then Diane's eight-year-old son got involved. Next, her parents started playing online, too. "What we like about Ohanarama is that it is by invitation, family only. So you don't have to worry about who is trying to communicate with your kid online, and you have a real family connection," says Diane. Her son plays turn-based games like checkers online with his grandparents, and there are other games, like Max Damage (which involves blowing things up), in which family members can go online and try to beat each other's records.

Want to see which video games are good for families?

The site FamilyFriendlyVideoGames.com rates video games for parents, by age group. Another good resource is GamerDad.com, written by Andrew Bub, a father who has played video games for decades and blogs on "Gaming with Children."

Facebook

Facebook is the technology tool that has had the biggest impact on my own family traditions. Because all my nieces and nephews have Facebook pages, as well as my sister, I'm so much more on top of their daily lives

Need to Unplug Your Kids? Celebrate Screen-Free Week

In the olden days, as American kids spent more and more time watching television and got fatter and fatter, a movement began to limit TV watching. A campaign was launched through schools and other organizations to get families to try a full week without watching the tube. Studies showed that a large majority of those families that tried the experiment made it through the full week. And even those that didn't tended to cut back on the hours their families spent watching afterward.

In 2010, the TV-Turnoff campaign changed its name to Screen-Free Week, encouraging families to cut out all screen entertainments for a full week each year in April. To find out more, and to get lots of strategies for keeping your kids busy and happy during that time of abstinence, go to CommercialFreeChildhood.org/ScreenFreeWeek.

and what matters to them. I can follow my nephew's ice hockey career and see who my niece is dating. It was largely because one of my brother's sons reached out to me on Facebook that we put together an in-person sibling reunion in the summer of 2011. My son isn't interested in Facebook right now, but I agree with all the experts and parents who say it's vital that you be on the "friend" list of your kids, so you can monitor what they're posting and who they're involved with.

One of the most popular apps on Facebook is called Family Tree, which provides families with a way to share messages and information within their families while also reaching out and tracking down relatives and plotting a family tree. See this at Facebook.com/FamilyTree, or FamilyBuilder.com, which designed the app.

The Christopher Family Tech Traditions

It's no surprise that the Christopher family has loads of tech-related traditions. After all, the family business, run by Stacy Louise Christopher and her husband, Scott, is technology related, a mobile service/consulting business called Mr. Pink Computer Shrink. They run the business out of their home. Both parents and their son, Cousteau, twelve

years old, each have a Facebook page and keep in touch that way, as well as by sending frequent, often joking texts on their cell phones. The Christophers, who live in Santa Barbara, are a family of free spirits. Stacy loves the sport of roller derby and continues to work as a referee for a local league. Her husband and son love skateboarding so much that they started their own YouTube channel (surprisingly easy to do), where they post videos of themselves and friends on their skateboards. Go to YouTube.com/Qwackpipe. Perhaps the oddest family ritual of all is one they call "Playing Dead," which Stacy started after she read an article that said this was a popular activity in Korea. They all try to outdo each other by taking goofy photos of themselves pretending to be dead, whether photographed on a rock in the park or on the doctor's examining table (while waiting for the doc to appear). They post the photos online and share them with friends.

Obviously, this is a family that totally embraces technology in daily life and as a way to celebrate together, and Stacy is currently working on a book about technology, parenting, and family values. Her basic take on the topic is this: "There are positive and negative ways families can use technology. But it has to be a managed relationship, with each family being clear about its personal family values."

Bedtime

I will readily admit that I've made many mistakes as a mother. But bedtime, that's something I did really well. Early on, I put together a regular bedtime ritual with my son that included prayers, reading or telling stories, and a kind of incantation in the dark in which we said "Good night" to everyone in the family, nuclear and extended. Bedtime was the same time every night (with rare exceptions), and I remember it as a blissful, reliably relaxing half hour. What I don't remember is ever having a single fight with Max—outspoken and argumentative since toddlerhood—over going to bed.

This is such a precious time of connection for parents and children that I'm including even more bedtime traditions than in the first edition.

Planting Good Dreams

Some parents draw a circle with their finger on their child's forehead at bedtime "to put the good dreams in," but Sue McCandless goes even further. At two, Sue's daughter started having terrifying nightmares, and Sue started inventing good dreams at bedtime to drive them away. The suggested dreams are vivid and action packed. "I'll say, 'Dream you're riding a two-wheeler without training wheels in a race and your helmet is pink,'" says Sue. The outcome of the dream is left for Taylor to finish in her sleep. The girl says she often dreams what her mother suggests.

Proud-Prouds

Tim Mullin wanted to end his daughters' days on a positive note and started the ritual of asking them at bedtime to share something they did that day that made them feel proud. Then, he and his wife add something else the girls did that the parents want to specially praise. Tim and his wife often learn things during Proud-Prouds that they didn't know about their kids' day at school, and they try to praise things that reflect their values. "We tell them we're proud of how hard they tried something and not just the successes," says Tricia. "I don't want them to think perfection is the goal."

Monster Spray

Matthew Pompi invented monster spray when his son complained that there were monsters in his bedroom at night. Matthew simply filled a plastic plant-spritz bottle with water and pasted a colorful label to the front. At bedtime, father and son spray under the bed, in the closet, and anywhere else monsters might lurk. Nathan takes the bottle to the bathroom during the night for extra protection and for overnights at Grandma's house.

Good-Night Family Tree

When my son was an infant, I started a bedtime ritual that includes good nights "to all the people Max loves." The circle of family and friends that were named changed as he aged, with friends and teachers included in the school years. I would go through all the aunts and uncles and cousins and babysitters, and we always ended with "good night to all the grandparents up in Heaven. Good night to *all* the people we love." My son would fall asleep feeling surrounded by love, and it was a great way to remind him of relatives he rarely saw.

Touch the Darkness

Some children respond well to rituals that ease them toward bedtime one step at a time. Allison Defferner performs a ritual with her infant daughter that her own mother began: They open the front door and literally reach out their palms to "touch" the night before bedtime. Kathy Schuessler always drops her kids off in their rooms by linking them all together in a trainlike file and "choo-chooing" down the hall.

What We Learned Today Journal

Liz Hawkins, a mother of four, began this when she and her husband were first married. In a hardbound journal, maybe six by nine inches, they would write daily something that they learned, often just one line, maybe sticking in a ticket stub from a museum or show they saw that day. The tradition continued and expanded once the kids arrived. The current journal, since 2002, is bigger, leather-bound, and was started when the family moved to Philadelphia. Jottings can be profound, or goofy. One day, one of Liz's girls wrote "chocolate syrup sinks in milk." Liz remembers writing once that shopping with her toddler daughter "was like shopping with a hand grenade without a pin." The family takes it on trips, too. They do the journal ritual typically around 9:00 PM, when someone yells, "Time to do the book!" If a parent is out of town, they have to put what they learned that day on their Facebook status, says Liz, or text it, and it gets written in the journal later. "Sometimes we are tired and cranky, but we do it. If someone can't come up with a thing they learned, we might check the Wikipedia app for the daily fact. But really, it takes only ten minutes for all of us to do this ritual, and you really do make a connection."

Rating the Day

The Eaves family ends the day by sharing the good things that happened that day, plus anything bad or sad, and then each person gives that day a rating. "It can be anything from excellent to blah. We don't try to force days into being good if they were not," explains Sue Eaves. "It teaches us that most of our days are at least good, and those that aren't, we get through them. Also, you can have a day that had some bad things in it, but that didn't make the whole day bad. This has resulted in some interesting conversations about life."

Bedtime Stories

Telling stories is a great tradition in many families and cultures, and one of the advantages over stories in books is that you can tell your own in the dark. Kyna Tabor tells elaborate bedtime stories about her family's pet cats, "an ever-growing cat nation." Kyna finds her kids hurry to get in their pajamas and brush their teeth at night because they can't wait to hear the day's installment about "our cat who was a princess in another land." I used to tell stories about an invented polar bear named Pete, and my husband specialized in the adventures of Jake, a blue bulldozer.

Hugs and Kisses for Sisters

Debbie House, a divorced mother of two girls, says she decided to strengthen the family's daily rituals after the divorce "because I wanted them to know that even though the family is divided by divorce, we are still a family. The nightly rituals remind us that no matter what, they will always be loved." The hugs and kisses for sisters happen every night, even if the girls have just been squabbling. "After that, we do a Girl Hug that is the three of us together," says Debbie.

Map Ritual

One father I know uses bedtime to teach geography. His son has an enormous world map on the wall of his bedroom, and at bedtime, he closes his eyes and points somewhere on it. He and his father sit quietly and talk about what it's like in that place: language, history, climate, and customs. At times, they get so intrigued that they look up additional information the next day.

Bedtime Countdown

To keep her kids from popping out of bed constantly because they forgot to brush their teeth or collect their stuffed animals, Cora Berry created a bedtime checklist that stays on the bedroom door. As they go through each item on the list, which includes a prayer and bedtime story, she calls out "check." After the last item, the lights are turned off.

In-Bed Massage

Comforting physical touch is a great way to relax and let go of the day. Some parents have a tradition of rubbing their children's backs or necks at bedtime and find that being relaxed sometimes helps normally reticent children share confidences. Others massage their children's feet (warning: if they are especially ticklish, this might un-relax them). Scalp massage can also be extremely soothing, and some girls love to have their hair brushed and smoothed last thing.

Beyond the Bedroom Wall

Novelist Larry Woiwode wrote a luminous novel by this name, and the title refers to a child's bedtime ritual. The boy would lie in bed and picture himself in the room, then roam in his mind past the walls to his street, then to the edge of his town, and on and on. It's a wonderful meditative exercise, like stretching one's mind out to infinity.

Blow Out the Light

Turning off the light can be a tough transition for small ones. Coming up with a ritual in which they "help blow out the light " and make a wish may help. Or let them tuck in favorite dolls or stuffed animals.

Bedtime Reading Rituals

For some busy parents, bedtime is the only time they get to read aloud to their kids, and they want to make the most of it. For children, the combination of snuggling and story is heaven on earth. To avoid whining, some parents set limits, such as three picture books for a toddler, or just one chapter a night.

Six Tips for Starting a Bedtime Reading Ritual:

1. Pick books at or below your child's current level, as your little one may be tired and able to take in less at this hour.
2. Start bedtime reading in infancy, and not just with cloth or board books. Simple picture books or rhyming books are great.
3. Steer away from anything scary: Even at seven, many fantasy books, including Harry Potter, gave my son scary dreams.
4. It's generally best to read in the same place each night, whether it's a comfy sofa in the den, your child's bed, or your own bed. The books will vary widely, but as in any ritual, it's more reassuring if some parts of the ritual stay the same.
5. Always say the name of the author and illustrator aloud along with the title, as this helps kids understand that books are created by people. They will soon spot similarities between an author's works, like those of Dr. Seuss.
6. Don't stop when your child learns to read. Share the reading, perhaps taking turns reading a page at a time.

Stories from Far Away

One of the best parts of many bedtime rituals is the story or stories that parents read aloud, or the retelling of classics like Cinderella and Goldilocks and the Three Bears. If you've got the time to do this and have a special story ritual for bedtime or naptime, it's great to pre-record one of these, so it can be played for your child while you are away. Maybe you always read *Goodnight Moon*, and then say good night to various pieces of furniture and toys in your child's room. How comforting it will be for your child to hear that familiar story, in your familiar voice.

Choosing Books

The whimsical Chinaberry catalog picks great books by age group and provides tips for reading to very young kids. Call 800–776–2242 for the free paper catalog, or go to www.chinaberry.com.

In *The Read-Aloud Handbook*, Jim Trelease explains why reading to kids matters so much. This book has sold over 1 million copies, and it certainly changed my life: It taught me there is no such thing as too much reading aloud, and I think it helps explain why my teenage son still loves books and reading so much. The book also includes detailed lists of recommended books for every age. Trelease has retired from speaking and touring in recent years, but he still maintains an incredibly helpful website that is packed with downloads, updated book recommendations, and the latest research on reading. Go to www.trelease-on-reading.com.

Some of our favorites for toddlers and preschoolers are: *The Velveteen Rabbit*, all the A. A. Milne works, and anything by Bill Peet. For grade-school kids, don't miss the Guardians of Ga'hoole series, all the Eva Ibbotson novels, and the Artemis Fowl series.

tech tip

Although I didn't have a digital audio recorder when my son was still getting bedtime stories, there is one model in particular I would recommend, because I've used it to do interviews for an oral history project. You can get a small, reliable, and easy-to-use digital recorder for a very reasonable price. Your spouse or babysitter can hit play if you cue up the story, or you can use the USB port to download your story onto an MP3 player such as an iPod . I've had very good experiences with the Sony IC Recorder, which costs about $40.

Bedtime Prayers

The idea that someone powerful is watching over them while they sleep (in addition to their sometimes fallible parents) is enormously comforting to children. Bedtime prayers are also a wonderful way to pass on religious traditions and beliefs, and help teach a child empathy and gratitude.

God Bless

One of the simplest and most enduring bedtime prayers is for the child to ask God to bless each and every person important to him or her.

Thankfulness

Even before we attended church together, I started saying a prayer in bed with my son every night. It was sort of a loose conversation with God, asking for help and guidance for our family and others, but the heart of it was gratitude. I always started by saying, "Thank you for this day, God," no matter how rocky it might have been, and ended with, "Thank you for all the good things in our lives," some of which I would list. At first my son was mystified that I seemed to speak to the ceiling, but later, he would insert his own pleas and thanks to God.

Widen the Circle

Author Esther Ilnisky suggests that parents get their children to pray for others using what she calls "identity prayers." They can pray for all the kids in the world who share their name, or are the same age. She also suggests children who are having problems at school should pray for God to help not just them but also all the other kids at the school having a hard time. Ilnisky is the author of the book *Let the Children Play*.

Prayer Search

Any house of worship can provide guidance in finding suitable religious prayers for bedtime. The multidenominational website www .beliefnet.com includes a prayer library, which you can search by denomination or "need" or by text search.

Sports Rituals

Although my bookworm son still hasn't met a single sport he likes, most kids today participate with some degree of passion in one or more sports. Also, many families are fans of teams, actively cheering on their favorite pro teams, alma mater teams, and watching major sporting events like the Kentucky Derby, Super Bowl, and Indy 500. Rituals can celebrate victory, ease defeat, and help us perform at our peak.

Let's face it, sports are primal and visceral and emotional. Every sport, and every team, even every stadium, has its own set of specific rituals: team mascots, songs, cheers, and the standard gear worn by hard-core fans. There are iconic traditions like baseball's seventh-inning stretch. Whole books could be written about this stuff, and have been.

For your household, especially if you have a sports-crazy kid, you can use ritual to help your child work through the highs and lows that come with competition. Sports help prepare kids for life because they can't always win, and rituals help us deal with whatever life hands out. Ritual is also a tool that helps us dig deeper into each experience, making it that much more memorable, so it's a perfect match for sports, whether you are playing or watching.

Play Like a Champion Today

These words have long appeared on a famous sign at the University of Notre Dame in Indiana: Players touch it for luck before they head out onto the field to play football. There is something simple but powerful about the statement, and maybe you could adopt it as your family sports slogan. It's a good message about focus. You could also create a short ritual to perform with your child athlete before every game or match that is similar to a huddle. Beware of inventing anything too elaborate or time-consuming, because if your kid or her team wins, you'll be doing it a lot.

Divine Guidance

Many great athletes ask for God's help before beginning a game or contest. Kathy Chesto, a Catholic writer, always said this prayer with her track-star son before he started a meet: "Those who wait for the Lord shall renew their strength / They shall mount up with wings like eagles / They shall run and not be weary / They shall walk and not be faint."

Celebrate Wins and Losses

I heard about a Little League coach who brought helium balloons to each game. The kids would release them to the skies if they won and puncture them with a pin if they lost. Some prefer to celebrate a game well played, regardless of the outcome. All the people in my family are fanatical Cleveland Browns fans, and we always eat sundaes after watching a game on TV, either to celebrate or to console ourselves. (To help them win, we always wear team gear when we watch, hold hands during crunch plays, and tear apart our Ref doll, whose arms are attached with Velcro, during bad calls.)

Team Colors

To cheer on any team, hang crepe paper around your kitchen in the team colors and try to serve food in those colors. Milk and mashed potatoes are among the foods easily dyed with food coloring. Or make big sugar cookies and ice them in two different colors, one on each half of the circle. Make small paper flags in team colors, glue them to toothpicks, and stick them in various foods or table decorations.

Personal Best Award

Store a few sports tokens such as key chains, mini-trophies, or posters to give to your children after they work especially hard in a game. Maybe they didn't score the winning goal but made a breakthrough in catching a tough pass: Show them you noticed.

Your Family Olympics

Once every year or two, throw your own family Olympics. Invite the cousins or friends and neighbors if you want. If you have a pool, make swimming one of the sports, and if there is a basketball hoop in the driveway, have a shooting competition. You can play it seriously and by the book, or make up silly games and invented sports that little kids can shine at. Don't forget to create a colorful opening ceremony, where you parade around the yard and down the street.

Fantasy Leagues

The practice of putting together a pretend sports team and then forecasting how your pretend team will do against others isn't new. But with today's tech tools, it's gone completely epic, and it's gone way past football to just about any sport with a decent fan base. Soccer. Golf. Surfing? There are loads of websites, books, and apps for picking your team, strategizing, and keeping up with the statistics of the players you pick. For extended families, across multiple generations, this has become an extremely popular family ritual. In the last couple of years, my husband's family has gotten swept up in fantasy football, and they e-mail and text one another endlessly to discuss what players to pick before games and see which family member is "winning" each week.

If you want to learn more, CBS Sports and ESPN both have excellent websites that track lots of different sports. An online guide that explains the basics is www.fftoolbox.com/how_to_play.cfm. Perhaps you can dream up some great rituals to celebrate the winners in your tribe, both virtually and in person. Those who play in my family have a trophy: The name of each season's winner is engraved on that trophy, and the winner gets to keep it until she or he is unseated the next year. Some families that have all the players in the fantasy league living nearby celebrate the season's end in person (while trash-talking the victor as colorfully as possible).

Weekly Rituals

Having a weekly ritual is like a family-time insurance policy: The payoffs are definitely worth the time invested.

Dates with Dad

When people say they despair of staying close to a teenager, I tell them about Jim McCandless. Jim worked seventy-hour weeks and felt he was growing distant from his son, just starting junior high. They started weekly outings, and Jim moves mountains to keep that special night open. The key: His son dictates the activity each week, whether it's playing catch, bowling, or visiting the local hobby store. Father and son were amazed at how much better they got to know, and enjoy, each other by keeping this weekly date.

Weekend Campout

Teresa Schultz-Jones lets her three kids "camp" in the family room on one weekend night, but only "if they behaved well the previous week and did their chores." The kids sleep in sleeping bags, watch videos, stay up late, and sometimes get pizza.

Kids Cook Night

When Suzy Kellett's quadruplets got old enough, she gave each one a cookbook and scheduled them to take turns cooking dinner on Sundays. (She calls it "Open Mic Night.") The rules are: "You must cook something you've never cooked before, and you must invite at least one guest." Her kids love it.

Wrestling Night

Yup, you read that right. Karly Randolph Pitman's husband had done some wrestling coaching with local schools, and for fun the family declared Thursday nights as Wrestling Night. This is not an elaborate thing. "It started when the kids were really little, and the rules are no pinching or biting. My husband would show them a few moves, but mostly it's just piling on, rough-housing." But it's parent authorized and supervised. And, at least one of her kids did go out for the sport later in school. The point here: Different parents

have different gifts and backgrounds, and sharing their special skills with the family can make for some memorable traditions kids will brag about for years.

Surprise Excursions

Many families reserve Saturdays for errands, athletic practices, and household chores, and try to set Sunday aside as a special family day. One family I know goes to church in the morning, then saves Sunday afternoon for a special family excursion. The mother and father take turns picking the outing, keeping it secret until the last minute. One Sunday they'll go apple picking at a local orchard, and the next week, it will be a visit to a museum or historical site. When the kids are a bit older, they will take turns picking, too.

Walking Talks

Every Sunday, take a one-hour walk in a beautiful park or nature preserve. Take turns picking a conversational topic that everyone in the family can enjoy. You might answer a question like: "If you had a time machine, where would you travel?" or you can take the plot of a popular movie, for example, *Toy Story*, and jointly spin a yarn about your own toys in an adventure while you sleep or go on vacation. My family's version when we were watching all the *Lord of the Rings* movies was to create our own add-on "fellowship," which would accompany J. R. R. Tolkien's characters on their adventures. My husband and I would often add a major historical figure, and our son would add Homer Simpson for comic effect.

Sunday Night Rewards: Guai Cards

The experts always say it's more powerful to "catch your kids being good" than it is to scold them for doing bad. So some parents create some type of weekly ceremony to praise and reward family members who live up to the family's stated values.

Marla Michele Must of Michigan was inspired to create her Sunday night ceremony partly after watching the TV reality show *Survivor*. She liked the solemnity of the ceremony in which the contestants sit in a circle, with candlelight, and then discover who is being thrown off the show. "We do it in my bedroom, with candles," says Marla. She sits in a circle with her three kids for what they call the "Guai Ceremony." The family has two older biological siblings and a younger daughter adopted from China, and the word *guai* is Chinese for "being obedient."

(Sometimes Marla also refers to them as "mensch cards," the Yiddish word for a decent, helpful person.)

"I call it a family-incentive program," says Marla. "To me it's all about their emotional intelligence: I'm attempting to raise my children to be mindful and compassionate."

Typically, the cards are awarded for doing something considerate for another family member or for something above and beyond one's chores, but the kids can't crow about their accomplishment: A sibling or their mother has to "catch them being Guai."

The Guai Cards are simple cards that Marla prints on her computer. Each is worth one dollar, and typically each child will earn at least four a week. If they win ten, they get a nice prize, like a Lego set. But when one of them has reached that level, the others also get a prize, something smaller.

Marla keeps a printed sheet on her refrigerator reminding her kids to do right and listing some of the things they can do to earn Guai Cards. Here are a few:

- **Taking a garbage bag out to the garage without Mom asking**
- **Showing extra kindness to a brother or sister**
- **Not making things into a contest (letting another go first, for example)**

Partly because they get to decide when a sibling gets a card, Marla says, they really do pay close attention to one another's behavior, but it goes beyond that. "They really notice how it feels when someone does something extra nice for them, and conversely, when a sibling upsets them."

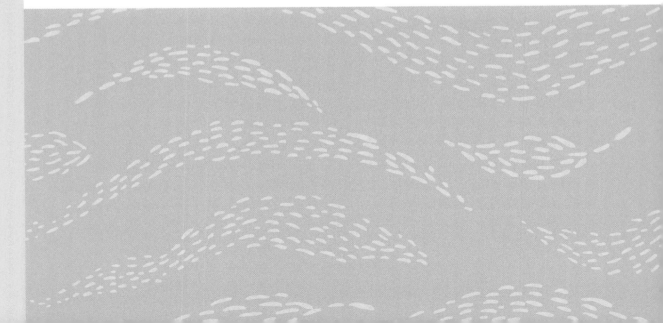

Weekly Family Nights

There are many ways to organize a weekly family night, including around religious traditions. Having even one hour to share, learn, and play together will do a lot to keep you close.

Prayer and More

The Suks of Evanston, Illinois, had family nights every Thursday for years, and they started with a kid-friendly dinner, "something like tacos that everybody loves," says Letitia Suk. The meal started with a hymn reserved for that occasion, and this was also the only time the family prayed together. "We would go around the table, offering prayers to everyone from the president to a favorite grandmother," says Letitia. After dinner, the family often went on a special outing, like a walk to the park.

Social Justice Night

The Vogts of Covington, Kentucky, started weekly family nights to pass on Catholic religious traditions and a passion for social justice to their four kids. Family night starts by lighting a candle; then the family sings "Jesus Christ is the light of the world." Each week is devoted to a single topic, often related to peace or social justice, that is explored with a Bible verse and then a related activity. The theme might be an upcoming holiday or the hurt of racism. One night the theme was blindness, and family members took turns being blindfolded.

Family Home Evenings

Like many Mormons, the Hilton family of Las Vegas, Nevada, has these weekly family get-togethers on Monday. The children are young, so they last only about twenty minutes, including a special treat. The kids take turns picking a song and a prayer, and Nanette Hilton or her husband chooses the lesson. "It might be a lesson about honesty, or if a grandparent has died, the topic might be death," says Nanette.

Great Resource on Family Nights

Susan Vogt gathered many creative ideas for weekly family activities into a terrific book called *Just Family Nights: Sixty Activities to Keep Your Family Together in a World Falling Apart*. Some of the themes covered are stewardship, protecting the environment, appreciating cultural diversity, and dealing with violence in the world, not just sibling squabbles at home, and prayer or spirituality. One night's theme is homelessness; another night, the family explores conflict resolution by trying out activities to defuse anger, such as punching a pillow. The program for each evening includes additional suggested resources.

Family Banner

Deborah Pecoraro is Catholic and started weekly family nights when the family lived in a predominantly Mormon area. "My kids felt prejudice from some of the Mormon kids, and we wanted to make them proud of their own religion," she says. Deborah took her theme from a Catholic prayer titled "God Made Us a Family" and created a special family banner out of felt.

Make it!

How to Make a Family Banner

One of the purposes of Family Night is to create a feeling of team spirit, a sense of shared beliefs, and your banner will help express that.

Materials

At a fabric or craft store, buy two yards (six feet) of felt in the color you want for a background. Banners are long but skinny, so you will want to cut the fabric at home so that it's five or six feet long, by about two feet.

Also buy scraps or small squares of other colors, including white and black.

Instructions

Design: Plan your design on paper first. Give each family member some space, perhaps twelve inches square, in which to create their self-portrait. Save space above, below, or between the portraits for the family name and logo. A logo might include symbols of your heritage, like a shamrock for Irish roots.

Cutting: Have everyone cut out the felt to make their portraits, including details like neckties, hats, and baseball bats. Add pets, favorite toys in felt. Glue them to the background.

Hanging: Cut three or four felt pieces two inches wide and three inches long. Fold them in half, then stitch or staple to the back of the banner, forming loops. Buy a dowel rod from the hardware store to slip through the loops and hang your banner—all the time or just for meetings.

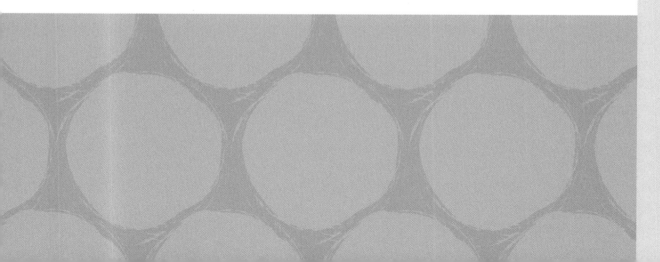

Weekly Family Meetings

Family meetings may include similar elements like prayers and snacks but tend to have "family business" as their central purpose. That includes dealing with issues like scheduling, finances, and behavior. This is a fabulous forum for airing your core values, and a great way to practice communication skills. Stephen Covey, author of *The Seven Habits of Highly Effective Families*, says that regular family meetings help kids move from "me" to "we" in their thinking and that they were the single most effective thing he and his wife did while raising their kids. The sidebar shows some guidelines I've developed.

Ten Guidelines for Great Family Meetings

1. Let Mom and Dad have the last word, but everyone gets a say.
2. Start by sharing the best thing that happened to you all week.
3. Keep the pace brisk and businesslike generally, but meetings should be brief for young kids, maybe fifteen minutes.
4. Go over the week's outings, sports practices, doctor appointments, and so on, with the family calendar on the table.
5. Take turns being the leader when the kids are old enough.
6. State problems without blaming, then brainstorm together. One child might say, "It's a problem that I'm the only one who washes the dishes." He should explain why this is a problem, and the family can jointly discuss solutions.

7. Give a "family star of the week" award to the family member with the most awesome accomplishment.

8. Take five minutes to discuss big-picture questions such as: Where should we go for summer vacation? Is it time to get a dog? This will help make the sessions seem less like nag-fests and create that sense of family as team or tribe.

9. End with a fun activity or dessert treat. This could also be when allowance is paid out.

10. Keep next week's agenda on the refrigerator: Anyone can add to it.

Tip: Barring emergencies, have the meeting at the same time and place every week! Better to have a mini-meeting than get in the habit of skipping.

Say Something Nice

In the Brosbe family, you have to start the family meeting by saying something nice about someone else. Ellen Brosbe says, "It might be mundane stuff like 'Thanks for letting me play your video game,' but it's important for them to thank each other." The four kids have to take turns sharing a bedroom, so "rotating rooms" is almost always on the weekly agenda. Other issues that get discussed are everything from reminders to refill the orange juice pitcher to broad discussions like "Should we keep going to synagogue?" Ellen says her kids began getting surly about meetings when they reached their teens, but she says a lot of family issues got ironed out at these weekly sessions.

Getting to Know You

Writer Jennifer Grant is a mother of four living near Chicago, and her clan has a family meeting at 6:00 PM on Sundays. There are gaps during the summer, but the meetings are pretty regular during the school year. The kids each get a parfait glass filled with 7 Up—and a cherry! The parents usually have a glass of wine, though Jennifer's husband sometimes opts for a martini. The basic purpose of the meeting is simple communication, a chance for everyone to touch base before a new week begins. There is always a simple playful activity, what Jennifer calls a "getting to know you sort of thing." Everyone might finish the prompt: "What I like most about myself is. . . ." Or "What I think people in the family misunderstand about me is. . . ." "I think one reason my kids get along so well is that these family meetings give them trust in one another," says Jennifer.

A Tradition of Debate

The Vogts had weekly Family Nights *plus* weekly meetings. Heidi Vogt, daughter of Susan, says that she and her three siblings got annoyed that family meetings were undemocratic. "We would bring up things we wanted, but they would vote us down even though we were the majority," says Heidi. "But we did get a chance to express our views, and I see now that it gave me a sense of what they really valued. We could never get them to put in cable TV, but they explained it's because they felt they had better uses for that money."

Note to Reader: When I first interviewed the Vogt family, it was more than a decade ago and I remember asking Susan how her kids felt about all the rituals and meetings. She told me to ask Heidi, because she was always the biggest complainer about having to go along with all the family traditions, especially meetings. I interviewed Heidi while she was in college, at Yale, and she told me that even though she was often reluctant, these values-oriented meetings affected her deeply. After college, she joined the Peace Corps. Later, she was a journalist, covering the war in Afghanistan. Her mom went on to write a terrific book called *Raising Kids Who Will Make a Difference*, in which she describes how she and her husband raised their kids. Interspersed in the pages are reactions from Heidi and her siblings to their upbringing, rituals and all.

Dealing with Grumps

The Hassell family always starts their Monday family meetings with a prayer. The kids take turns being in charge of refreshments and supplying a good discussion topic, which includes major family purchases. If one of the children shows up at the meeting in a bad mood, Mary Bliss Hassell says, "We have a family discussion about how to treat someone who is grumpy," and they soon bring the defiant one into the fold.

Family Fun Night

Another way to slant your weekly family ritual is toward sheer fun, carving out one night a week when the television stays off while family members play games, eat treats, and act goofy. You could also call it Game Night.

There's no better guidebook for doing this than Cynthia L. Copeland's book, *Family Fun Night!* First off, Copeland is extremely thorough, so when she does a chapter on board games, she provides a long list of board games that are good for families, including some unfamiliar ones. Then, she closes with tips on inventing your own family game. There are chapters on movie nights, card games, video games, read-aloud family nights, talent show nights, and family memory nights, among others. For low-budget ideas, there is a list of ten family nights costing less than $10.

tech tip

More than 40 percent of American households now have gaming systems. Many are equipped for multiple players, but the favorite of families is the Nintendo Wii. My son loves video games of all kinds and has several hand-held systems, but our Wii has truly been a family-bonding tool. I applaud this device, not only because we often play it together, but because it gets everyone off the couch (unlike my favorite low-tech games: Monopoly, Scrabble, and Apples to Apples)! There are some Wii sports games that come with the basic system, as well as an endless line of additional games. We are particular fans of Wii bowling, but my husband and son also like the golf version. And we have had a lot of fun playing the Wii Guitar Hero.

Discover the Magic of a Talking Stick

One of the hardest tasks for young children is taking turns and learning to listen to others when they urgently want to speak themselves. The talking stick is a traditional Native American sacred object that can be a magical tool in family meetings. Whoever is holding the stick, and *only* that person, has the authority to speak. The stick is a visual reminder to focus on that person, who is supposed to speak truth from the heart. Children love the textures of the stick, and the feeling of literally holding power in their hands. Talking sticks are a good example of the almost mystical powers of focus that good rituals bring: I've seen shy, fidgety children get all solemn and collected when handed the stick. They are so concentrated on doing the "business" of the stick properly, they forget to be nervous and speak what's really on their minds.

A major advocate of this ritual is Stephen Covey, author of the best-seller *The Seven Habits of Highly Effective People.* Covey has lectured and written about the talking stick: There is even a YouTube video of him explaining the principle. He points out that the value of the talking stick is in the listening as much as the talking: People feel understood, because they are allowed to talk long enough to make their point.

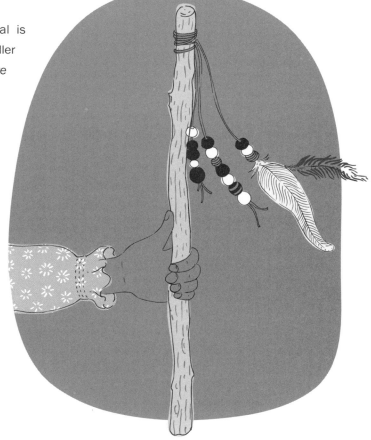

Make it!

How to Make and Use a Talking Stick

Materials

Get a thick stick, about an inch in diameter and ten to twelve inches long (though traditional ones tend to be longer), from your backyard or local park.

Smooth the ends with sandpaper, making sure there are no sharp edges or splinters.

Get bright ribbons from a fabric or craft store, plus feathers from your yard or the store. You can also use shells, beads, buttons, or other adornments.

Instructions

Wrap ribbons up the stick as far as you wish for smoothness and color, then let each family member choose one color of ribbon to represent their "voice," and tie that ribbon tightly to the stick. Spread these ribbons out, so each has its own space. Add as many feathers and other decorations as you want, to the ends or all over. Personalize the stick for your family, perhaps tying on a small stone from your yard, a few hairs from your dog, or whatever suits you.

Traditionally, Native Americans sit in a circle when using a talking stick, and this works well. A circle is found over and over in the natural world, and each person in a circle has the same importance. You may wish to have a ritual way of starting the Talking Stick circle, as simple as holding hands for a moment or bowing to one another before you sit. You can sit on the floor, or at a table.

Decide on who will start, whether it's youngest or oldest, or take turns going first. You may hold the stick any way you choose, but the traditional way is to hold the stick vertically, as though it were planted in the earth. After the first person speaks, he or she looks directly into the eyes of the next person before passing on the stick. Anyone who doesn't wish to speak may pass the stick along silently. One idea is to use the talking stick just at the beginning of your meeting, as you share your thoughts, feelings, and news with one another. Put the stick aside as you move on to issues of family business, games, a snack, and so forth.

Note: If you have younger children, you might be better off with something "safer" than a stick. Some therapists, teachers, and preachers working with young kids actually use a stuffed animal, like a beanie baby, as the object that is passed around from person to person. In some cases, a "talking bowl" is the object used. Not every family will be able to craft a stick, but the concept of using an object that disciplines a group to speak one at a time is a very powerful tool for effective meetings of all kinds, not just family ones.

Monthly Rituals

A month is a naturally powerful, logical unit of time, measured by the cycles of the moon. The good thing about a monthly ritual is that it's regular but also special. There is time for anticipation, and time, if you wish, to create slightly more complex gatherings. At my house, we even change our seats at the kitchen table on the first day of every month, and I love literally getting a new perspective on the familiar backyard scene.

Full Moon Bonfires

Small children are fascinated by the full moon and other celestial phenomena. The James family of Spokane, Washington, started having full moon bonfires when their son was six. The family of four makes a small fire right in the driveway on the night of a full moon and toasts hot dogs and marshmallows on skewers.

Box of Goals

Decorate a small shoebox or cigar box and keep it in the family room. On the first day of each month, have all the members of the family write on a piece of paper three goals they have for that month. It can be a task at school or work they hope to accomplish, or improving on a bad habit, but always something that's in the power of the individual to do: Don't allow it to become a list of "things" your kids hope they receive as gifts. Each month as you fill out a new list, check how you did the previous month.

King or Queen for the Day

Each month, one of Cindy Whaling's kids gets to be royalty for a day. When a new month starts, the child whose turn it is grabs the calendar, closes his or her eyes, and points to a date. Cindy draws a tiny crown on that date, with the kid's name. The royal child gets to pick the dinner and activities that day. As they get older, they wisely learn to point at weekends, when sleepovers are allowed, says Cindy. Her youngest always wants to go to McDonald's for a Happy Meal, which is considered too unhealthy on ordinary days.

Make it!

Calendars for Kids

At an early age, kids want to know what's ahead and to follow along with the family's schedule. It's a great idea and a fun project to make a special calendar for each child to keep in his or her room.

You can do it one month at a time, using colored construction paper. As you make each month's sheet, you can talk about what season that month is in, what holidays are coming, when family members have birthdays and anniversaries, and so forth.

Materials

Construction paper

Ruler

Crayons or markers

Thin ribbon

Instructions

Print the name of the month at the top and use the ruler to draw boxes for each day of the month. Write the numbers in each box, but save room for your child to add stickers or drawings to illustrate important events. Make a small hole at the right and left top edges of the paper, and poke ribbon through the holes, knotting the two ends of ribbon. Hang on a nail or hook somewhere low enough for your child to reach it. Start a ritual of checkmarking or crossing off each day, perhaps just before bed. (Give your kids a washable marker, so your wall won't be ruined.)

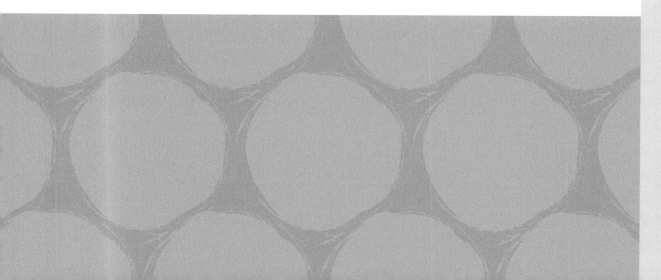

Full Moon Walks

Craig Patchin wanted a special ritual to bring him closer to his children, and he spotted his chance when his oldest child was about to turn ten. His wife had bought a book called *Walk When the Moon Is Full* as a present for their daughter Bethany. Author Frances Hamerstrom, an ornithologist, wrote the book about the nature walks she took with her children during every full moon.

Inspired by this idea, Craig spontaneously wrote in the front of the book, "Happy Birthday. I make a pledge to you that we will go exploring every full moon this year. I love you, Daddy."

The Patchins live in a semirural area, and every month that year Craig and his daughter walked after dark, usually for at least half an hour. Often, they walked to the top of a hill in a nearby meadow where they could see for miles. Bethany loved the ritual so much that her younger sisters and brother could hardly wait for their turn, and they still remember many of the things they saw and heard and talked about.

Says Kelsey, Craig's third daughter, "One cold night when there was snow on the ground, we took a bunch of blankets and curled up in the hammock outside. My dad had to move a branch of the pine tree so we could see the moon, and we talked about memories and stories."

Now that all the Patchin kids have had their year of Full Moon Walks, they can't stand the idea of never doing it again. Plans are that the ritual will be repeated when they each turn eighteen.

> Tip: Vary this ritual to suit yourselves. You can do this every month or just in nice weather. Take turns between the kids, month by month. You can take long or short walks, vary your path, perhaps stay close to home and use binoculars or a telescope to study the sky. Keep a journal about your Full Moon Walks.

Giving-Back Day

I heard about a family that does a monthly community service project. One day each month, the kids in the family fill "activity bags" with coloring books, crayons, and games, and they deliver them

Resource for Monthly Family Service Projects

Sondra Clark began volunteering when she was quite young, and by the age of twelve, she was working on volunteer projects in Kenya and Uganda. Now a young adult, she has really done her homework and produced a very family-friendly book stuffed with ideas for community service projects. *Seventy-Seven Creative Ways Kids Can Serve* is a great book to give to your budding community activist, but these are terrific ideas for projects for a whole family. She starts with very simple ideas like creating a backyard sanctuary for wildlife or collecting tennis balls for the local animal shelter and works up to more demanding projects. As a pre-teen, Sondra became obsessed with Jane Goodall's career working with chimpanzees, and one of the nonprofits she recommends is Goodall's Roots and Shoots project. RootsAndShoots.org, the website for the organization, gives kids and families lots of ways to make a difference. Another Sondra Clark pick is DoingGood Together.org, a website run by a Minnesota family that is full of doable projects for families.

to the local hospital for children who are patients. Other possibilities: Your kids could make monthly visits to a local nursing home and read to elderly residents. They could bake cookies monthly and deliver them to the local fire or police station. Or sign up with a local environmental group to help clean up a nearby park. By going back to the same place, kids can form real relationships with those they help. (You may want to change the recipient of your help annually, as children grow and their interests change.)

Monthly Neighborhood Potluck or Pizza Blast

We're all too busy to stay as close to our friends and neighbors as we'd like. One answer is no-fuss entertaining that is built into our schedules. Designate the first Friday or last Sunday of every month for your Family Pizza Party, but vary your guests. This is the time to meet a new neighbor, get to know the parents of your kids' best friends, invite the woman in your yoga class who looks interesting. Or ask the same four or five families and rotate between each other's houses. Keep the menu simple: pizza, salad, and drinks.

Or start something similar to what *New*

York Times writer Patricia Leigh Brown wrote about in an article: a monthly potluck dinner with her neighbors. The tradition is referred to where she lives as "First Wednesday" dinners, and they went on in her San Francisco neighborhood for decades. No dishes were assigned, everything was casual. At the start of every month, an index card would simply appear in her mailbox with the words: First Wednesday, written in magic marker.

Freedom Day

My son complained that he was overscheduled. "I go to school every day, karate on Saturday, and church on Sunday. When is it *my* day?" he wanted to know. So I designated the last Saturday of every month "Max Freedom Day" when he was young, and he did what he wanted to do on those days (within reason). He would usually skip karate, and I could not schedule hateful appointments like haircuts. The whining over scheduling largely disappeared, and he had something to look forward to all month, every month.

Family Book Groups

There is no more sustaining ritual in my life than my monthly reading group—why not extend this fun to include my own family? A Family Book Group can encourage the love of reading, but it also provides a fun, shared activity. There is a generally greater conversational give-and-take than if family members were to watch a movie together, and unlike such rituals as family meetings, parents get to interact more like equals than authority figures.

Mother-daughter book groups are popular now, especially with pre-teen girls. But father-son book groups are also a great idea. And you could form a book group that paired your entire family with several other families, providing the kids are close enough in age to enjoy the same books.

Six Simple Rules for Family Book Groups

1. **The more authority kids have, the better.** As much as possible, let them pick the books and lead the discussion.

2. **It works well to have members take turns being leader.** The leader should prepare questions in advance to guide the discussion, and present some background about the author or book topic.

3. **You can serve a snack or meal before the discussion begins** and let the group members use this time for chitchat.

4. **Once it's time to discuss the book, stick to the topic for at least half an hour.** Be disciplined.

5. **Even a book group doesn't need to be sedentary and can encompass creative as well as physical activities.** To get the kids moving, dance or do some workout moves to begin. For little kids, ask them to invent a dance or exercise a character in that month's book might do. In addition to talking about the books, include a component of the book group evening when the kids might draw or paint a character, or let them act out a scene.

6. **It's important to have everyone respect others' opinions.** No judging. Members can disagree without having an argument.

More on Family Book Groups

Five Good Questions to Ask About Any Book:

1. Did you like the book? If so, why? If not, why not?
2. Which character was your favorite? Would you have behaved in the same way as that person?
3. Was there anything unusual in the way the author told the story? (flashbacks, multiple narrators, unusual slang, and so on)
4. How does this book compare to other books the group has read and discussed? Are the characters more or less believable? Which had the most exciting plot? Best ending?
5. What did you learn from this book? It could be something about an historical event, perhaps, or a sense of how other people live now and make choices in their lives.

Deciding What to Read

You can get a list of discussion-worthy books from your local library or bookstore. Many bookstores and libraries around the country also host multigenerational book groups on the premises, in case you would prefer having a book group that meets outside your home and includes others.

An excellent site for picking kid-friendly books is KidsReads.com, which reviews both classics and current books and even gives tips on starting a kids' book group. Also helpful is that there are short reading guides for a long list of award-winning children's books that include discussion questions specific to each title.

A good book to help parents choose books and get tips for making reading a big deal in your family life is *Reading Together: Everything You Need to Know to Raise a Child Who Loves to Read*, by Diane Frankenstein.

Awesome Resources on Book Groups for Girls—and Boys

Much has been written about the great joys of mother-daughter book clubs, including the way they encourage teen and tween girls to continue speaking to their mothers. Two excellent books on all-female groups are *The Mother-Daughter Book Club (revised edition)* by Shireen Dodson, and *Book by Book: The Complete Guide to Creating Mother-Daughter Book Clubs* by Cindy Hudson. There is also a very helpful website, www.motherdaughter bookclub.com, run by Cindy Hudson.

However, as the mother of a son who has always been an avid reader, I've been frustrated at the absence of alternatives for boys. Now there is a fantastic website called BookClub4Boyz.com (note the "Boyz" with a "z"), written by Laura, the mother of four sons. This website is just packed with great advice and suggestions about what to read. She even has a topic button on the site for "Biggest Belch Award," listing titles with the type of gross humor beloved by boys. My son sure loved the Captain Underpants books in grade school! One of her tips for a reading group with boys: Start out with twenty minutes of full-out physical activity, so they can settle down afterward and quietly discuss the book.

CHAPTER 3

Family Festivities and Ceremonies

Birthdays

Everything Balloons

One of the best ways to celebrate birthdays is with balloons, which are not only a perfect symbol for the pumped-up excitement of a kid on this day but are also incredibly versatile.

Chairs and Beds

Get a bouquet of helium balloons and tie them to your child's chair at dinner, to designate the "birthday girl" or "birthday boy." Or tie a Mylar® helium balloon to the end of your sleeping child's bed (it must be Mylar® to last overnight; a regular balloon filled with helium will sink by morning).

Balloon Countdown

As toddlers, her kids constantly asked, "How many days till my birthday?" so Debbie Midcalf created a balloon ritual for counting down the days. A week or so before the birthday, she blows up balloons, one for each day, and hangs them on a string across the dining room. All the balloons are the same color, except the last one, which represents the actual birthday. Every day, her child gets to pop one balloon, then count how many are left.

Balloon Forest

A great way to decorate your dining room for a birthday feast is to get twenty-five to fifty regular balloons, in bright colors, inflated with helium. When you get them home, sep-arate the ribbons and let the balloons bounce up to the ceiling. Keep the ribbons long, just reaching to the top of the table, so you have to look at each other through a forest of ribbons. An ordinary room becomes magical.

Balloon Wishes

After blowing out candles, take your child out-side with three helium-filled balloons. Let the child make three wishes, and for each silent wish, let go of one balloon.

How to Make a Balloon Tunnel

Ron Greenberg celebrates the birthdays of his daughters by constructing a "balloon tunnel" on the stairs. When the birthday girl awakes, she must be the first one to squeeze into the tunnel, slide downstairs on her backside, and pick up the wrapped present at the bottom, her first of the day.

Materials and Instructions

Ron starts with about fifty helium balloons. Using ribbons, he ties half of them to one side of the banister and half to the other, and they are crisscrossed in the middle. Because the helium holds them up, there is plenty of room for kids (and adults) to slide underneath them, but not enough room to stand. To close it off and give it more of a tunnel feeling and look, Ron threads crepe-paper streamers through and around the ribbons holding the balloons.

Great Birthday Celebrations

Celebrate Growth and Encourage Maturity

Gertrud Mueller Nelson, author of *To Dance with God: Family Ritual and Community Celebration*, gave her kids two envelopes on their birthdays. One was marked "New Privilege" and the other "New Responsibility." A child turning six might be given the privilege of staying up an extra half hour at night, and the responsibility of feeding the dog his dinner. This ritual "gave them a sense of importance and made them feel grown up," says Gertrud.

Giving Instead of Getting

The Hassells of Winterport, Maine, wanted to cultivate a generous impulse in their kids, so they started the ritual that when a child in the family has a birthday, he or she buys gifts for everyone else. The birthday child still gets a special dinner and cake with candles (plus presents from grandparents and friends). But all the children also look forward to their siblings' birthdays, knowing they'll get presents on each of those occasions. Mary Bliss

Hassell says kids get used to anything if that's all they know: She began this practice when the youngest was a toddler.

Memorable Birthday Photos

When her daughter Dorothy turned one year old, novelist Jean Hanff Korelitz got the idea of photographing Dorothy in a dress that had belonged to her own mother. Every year on Dorothy's birthday, Jean takes more pictures of Dorothy in "the dress," and each year, it comes closer to actually fitting. The photo sessions are full of clowning and silly poses, and the pictures have been compiled into collages that line one staircase. When her son celebrated his first birthday, Jean started the birthday photography tradition for him, shooting Asher in a white dress shirt of his father's.

Stuffed Animal Parade

When my son came home from school on his birthday, his stuffed animals would be lined up along the staircase to the second floor, on both sides. When he got to the top, he would find his first present of the day. (The remainder were opened after dinner.)

Birthday Wreaths

In a ritual she says was inspired by Navajo traditions to celebrate a newborn, Kathleen Metcalf gave each of her children a simple wreath from a craft store when they were infants. The idea is that each year, friends and family give the birthday child a small charm or object to attach to the wreath that symbolizes something special about that year or a positive attribute of their character. A special diary records each little gift as it is added, its significance, and who gave it. The wreaths hang in the children's bedrooms and are now quite crowded with little objects that tell the stories of their lives. In addition, the birthday kid gets one big gift, "usually something useful, like a sleeping bag," says Kathleen.

Boss of the Family

In one family, the birthday boy or girl is "boss for the day" and can order other family members around. They decide on the day's menu and activities, and usually send their parents to bed early!

Make Way for New Toys

Before her daughters' birthdays, Barbara Franco of Florida gets them to help in a major cleanup ritual that includes donating old toys they no longer play with to a local shelter or other charity. They also sort through clothes, and those that don't fit are passed on to the next youngest or donated to the needy.

Birthday Gardens

Amanda Soule, who writes the popular Soule-Mama blog, lives with her husband and five children on forty acres in Maine, and each of the kids has a "birthday garden." To start it off, they all got to pick a type of tree that fit their personality. Then, each birthday, the kids can add plants or flowers or herbs that they like. For those with winter birthdays, on their special day they plan what to plant later on, though they can't put it into the ground until spring. "Adelaide always picks purple flowers: That is all she wants to plant," says Amanda. "My oldest is more practical: He wants something he can eat, like carrots. Ezra is more of a dreamer and likes really different ornamental things, or he will be drawn to something because it has a funny name. His is a kind of Dr. Seuss garden."

Birthday Playlists

Susan Wagoner makes special CDs for her daughters on their birthdays. She thinks of songs during the year, especially the month before. "I have found that most love songs can be used as a mother singing to her child, and I've used things like "She's Got a Way" by Billy Joel and Olivia Newton John's "Let Me Be There." I burn loads of copies and give them out as party favors. I include "good" music like the Beatles, Van Morrison, etc., so they won't just listen to Radio Disney stuff! We listen to these CDs over and over in the car." How perfect: Music to play during the party, and a memento to give the guests.

Great Online Resources on Themed Parties

So, what shall the birthday theme be this year? Winnie the Pooh? Harry Potter? Monster Trucks? Princess Tea Party?

Sometimes parents run out of fresh ideas, but there are a number of excellent online resources for sparking ideas, including for invitations, decorations, games, and treat food.

FamilyFun.com is a website companion to the single most creative magazine for parents. Like the magazine, the website offers ideas for all sorts of crafts, recipes, and year-round celebrations. On the home page toolbar, click on Parties for fun ideas and eats, as well as games and decorations you can download and print out.

Who knew that PBS did kid parties? Go to www.pbs.org/parents/birthdayparties/, where there are lots of ideas for parties themed around such PBS "celebrities" as Curious George, the Cat in the Hat, and the Teletubbies.

BirthdayPartyIdeas.com is packed with suggestions, including a list of more than 300 ideas for party themes, in alphabetical order.

For a change of pace, there is a very classy blog produced by event planners in San Francisco. They show lots of photos of fabulous, fun ideas for parties with clever decorations and food that may inspire you. Just going there makes me want to throw a theme party! Go to CakeEventsBlog.com.

Birthday Cake Parade

Lynn Rosen's house in Philadelphia is laid out so that there is a complete circle from the foyer to the family room to the kitchen, the dining room, and back to the foyer. She figured out when her kids were young that it would be fun to have spontaneous "parades," and she kept a box of instruments nearby. When her son Cooper turned five and she had a room full of noisy children, right before lighting the candles she got the idea to do a birthday parade. "I had all the kids line up behind me, with Cooper first, lit the candles, and marched twice around in a Birthday Cake Parade." The kids loved it, and the parents vowed to copy the idea.

Birthday Treasure Hunts: A Template to Use for All Occasions

One fun way to celebrate a birthday is with a Treasure Hunt, but you might want to bookmark this page because the same basic template can be used just as well for almost any holiday or ceremony honoring a special someone.

It's a frugal idea, actually, because the basic idea is to send your kid on a wild goose chase where one clue leads to another, but the child only gets one prize, at the very end. You can use visual clues for the pre-readers. The older the child, the more complex your clues will be, and the more far-ranging the hiding places. Rhymed clues are easy and fun.

Just to give you an idea, here are a few of the clues I gave my son once. Although this was for Valentine's Day, the principle is always the same:

I won't give you a snub, if you'll peek in the tub. . . .

Your hopes you just might pin, on a look inside the stuffed animal bin. . . .

The spot you want to look, is a place where food is usually cooked! (And that was the final clue—the gift was in the oven.)

Birthday Daddy Dates

Colleen McGuire has three girls, and each year on their birthdays, each girl gets a private date with dad, dressed in her best dress, at a "white tablecloth" restaurant. After that, Dad treats her to a few extra gifts they pick out together.

Birthday Parties for a Cause

Some kids start very early wanting to help others in need. The impulse to donate one's birthday to a good cause shouldn't be imposed on a child, but if this idea excites your kid, there are many ways to organize it and many terrific causes. You can certainly just ask guests to bring a donation rather than a present, then hand over what you raise to a local cause for which your child is passionate. Cole Hodges of Richmond, Virginia, is a boy who asked for money for charity on his birthdays starting at age five, and raised hundreds for causes such as cancer and homelessness.

There are also online sites that take you through the process and suggest national and international charities. The OneDays Wages.org website was founded by the Cho family in Seattle, Washington, because they wanted to do something to help eradicate extreme poverty around the world. The site features a protocol for creating a birthday to raise and collect funds. You pick a charity, set up a special page for your birthday giving campaign, alert your friends and family via social media, and One Days Wages turns all the proceeds over to the charity you designate. Meanwhile, your friends can check your event page to see how close you are getting to your goal. Go to the site, click on Donate, and look for the "Birthday for a cause" logo.

An excellent charity for children who love animals and want to help the poor is Heifer, which provides farm animals to low-income people in the developing world. A flock of chicks is only $20. Go to Heifer.org. If you click on Get Involved, and then Families, you'll find a number of videos that will bring the program to life for your family.

Celebrating the Birthday of a Family Member Who Died

Let's face facts: Your kids will suffer the loss of people they love, including adored grandparents, aunts, and uncles. Here is a very sweet way to honor those loved ones on their birthdays. In December 2005, Cynthia Taibbi-Kates found herself trying to explain to her seven-year-old daughter Mary-Rose why she was so sad one day. The previous summer,

Cindy's father had died and she scattered his ashes at sea: This was going to be the first birthday (and Christmas) without him. Her little girl's matter-of-fact reply was: "I think we should bake a cake for Papa and put candles on it. Then, we should go outside and sing Happy Birthday to him and let the breeze blow out the candles, because now Papa is part of the wind."

They perform this ritual every year on December 22 and get a chance to talk about what a great father and grandfather he was. A little cupcake with a single candle would also work.

The simple power of this brilliant idea reminds me why children of all ages should be asked to help create rituals: They have a more primal grasp on life, and they can often cut to the chase about how to express emotions through action.

Milestone Birthdays

When my son, Max, turned three, it felt like a special milestone to me, and I wanted to find a creative way to celebrate his new powers. I thought about tribal rites of passage, where those initiated into a new stage have to cross over a physical threshold and bravely face the adventure of their future. I decided I could make a threshold with a simple bedsheet. Max would have to go through the sheet to get his birthday gifts, and I could use the blank surface to record his accomplishments. I painted symbols of "big boyness" on the first sheet, including underwear, since he had just been potty trained, and scissors, to symbolize nursery school.

Honestly, I have rarely made him that happy since. He got the biggest kick out of that first sheet, squealing and racing deliriously through the slit to see what was on the other side. I thought he would immediately sit down and open gifts in the family room, but he was having too much fun racing from one room to the next and back again. It was like playing hide-and-seek with a whole room!

I've since made four more threshold sheets, one when he turned five, another at seven, then again at ten and thirteen. At five, the sheet was painted like a pirate's treasure map. At seven, it was a list of breakthrough achievements such as: "Max can read," "Max can write," and "Max can swim." He didn't ask for a sheet at sixteen, so maybe he's outgrown this idea. But each of the others came after he requested them, explaining why he deserved another milestone sheet because of all his new skills and accomplishments.

Ideas vary from family to family about what is a milestone birthday. Is it reaching ten, the first double-digit year? Or twelve? Or the first teen year, magical thirteen?

The most meaningful celebrations come from deep personal knowledge of a particular child, and his or her dreams and aspirations. When my little sister turned sixteen, I happened to know she had "never been kissed" so I assembled half a dozen boys from my high school class (I was a senior, she was a sophomore), who lined up to kiss her during a slumber party. All her girlfriends went spastic with jealousy watching this little parade of kissing boys, and Tracy still says this was the very best ritual I ever invented for her!

How to Make a Milestone Sheet

Materials

One white, full-size bedsheet

A supply of paint, in bright colors, plus black (I used washable paint because that's what I had around; but I never intended to wash any of these.)

Pencil

Scissors

Newspaper

Instructions

Put plenty of newspaper on the floor to protect from stains. Spread the sheet out flat. Cut a slit from the bottom to the middle, ending slightly higher than the child is tall. Sketch your design in pencil first, then paint. Let dry completely before handling. On the big day, use masking tape to hang the sheet across a doorway that leads to the room where the presents are.

Milestone Gifts

In the Chesto family, you get your own alarm clock at age ten, symbolizing that you have the maturity to rouse yourself in the morning and get ready for school without being nagged. Jeff Butler gives his boys *and* girls a Swiss Army knife at ten, proof they can take care of themselves and have good judgment in a crisis. The ritual includes going out to dinner alone with Dad, then picking out the exact right model of knife.

Milestone Trips

For families that love the outdoors, a birthday that signals maturity might be the time for the first white-river rafting trip with Mom and Dad. Or the first night for a sleep-away with friends in the family's vacation cabin (with the parents staying a cell phone call away). Or the first time to try climbing to the summit of the closest challenging mountain. Upon completion of the physical challenge, a good gift might be a keepsake of the accomplishment, like a key chain inscribed with the date.

Half Birthdays

With children, the amount of change and growth that occurs in just six months can be astonishing. Celebrating half birthdays is a way to acknowledge and honor that growth.

Half a Cake

Patrice Kyger says her kids love that she notices how much they change in half a year. For their half birthdays, there are no gifts or parties, but her kids get half a cake (she freezes the rest) and one candle. And they get to pick the menu for dinner.

Half a Song

There are several ways to halve the classic birthday song. You can sing "Happy Half Birthday to You!" or you could try only singing every other word.

Half a Game

Doni Boyd's kids were both born in January, so she always threw them a joint half-birthday party in July, making it as silly as possible. "We would put the picnic table half in our yard, and half in the neighbor's yard," she explains. "I would serve half a cake, and cut ice cream bars in half. Since it was summer, everybody would come half dressed." To increase the fun, people brought only half a present (the board for a game, but not the game pieces, which would be saved for another time) and played half games. "Everybody loved the idea of letting the kids go hide, but no one would go seeking them!" says Doni.

Treats at Breakfast or Lunch

Since many family birthdays involve special dinners, confine the special treats to breakfast. Give the half-birthday child a cupcake or special muffin with one candle. Or send an extra-special dessert in your child's lunchbox that day, with a very small birthday card.

A Stepmom Steps
Up for Half Birthdays

Linda McKittrick understands the stepmother's dilemma: You want to create traditions with your husband's kids, but you run the risk of looking pushy and you can't interfere with beloved existing traditions. But something like a half birthday, which isn't a regular big deal, allows a chance to develop a new ritual and grow a new relationship.

When her stepdaughter was eleven, Linda moved in with J's father. Before long, she was trying to think about ideas for rituals that would make the three of them feel like a family. One of her ideas was to celebrate J's half birthday, but celebrate it each year in a different way. One year they hand-cranked ice cream, another year she took the girl to high tea with a girlfriend, all dressed up. "The important thing is to focus on the changing, ever-evolving *her*," says Linda. "This year she turned twenty-five and a half and we celebrated by going to her favorite Indian restaurant. We brought a Zen card deck and just played with it, not to predict things but for her to zero in on her own intentions. It was quite revealing and she said it was her best half birthday yet."

Star Birthdays

A star birthday, sometimes called a golden birthday, is when someone's birthday date and age are the same, like being seven on June 7. It doesn't always happen in childhood, but it is a once-in-a-lifetime thing, and some families love to honor that rarity.

Stars Everywhere

Some feel the best decoration for this day is stars, and that there can't be too many of them. Patrice Kyger decorates her whole house with shiny star garlands, wrapping them around picture frames, lamps, and furniture. She also buys star-shaped candles and sprinkles stars all over the birthday cake to celebrate a star birthday. You could also make this a day to go to the nearest planetarium for a "star show" or let the birthday kid stay up late and look at the stars outside your home.

Star Treatment

Give the birthday child the total movie-star treatment. For a girl, this could include a beauty makeover at the local beauty parlor or a special gift of age-appropriate beauty products. For a boy, get a costume for a spaceman or safari guide, and photograph him in heroic poses. Make a movie of the whole day, featuring your star. You could write a script in advance about the history of the birthday star's life and success, "up from humble beginnings," or you could have the star help write it. Make sure you include an on-camera interview with the star, about his or her tips on life. Ask for autographs often! (And get everyone in the family with a camera to play paparazzi.)

Star Gifts

Some families give the child with a star birthday the number of presents equivalent to their age. But if a ten-year-old is getting ten gifts, only one will be something big and the rest will be tokens and trinkets. Wrap each one, even the smallest, in the biggest boxes you have, and tape a big number on the side or top of each package. Save the best for last, so you build up to it as a climax.

Adoption Rituals

Growing up in a family where two of us were biological kids and two were adopted, I'm very sensitive to the less-than feelings that adopted children sometimes have. All four of us were loved and wanted, but in recent years, I've become more aware that it was harder for my adopted brother and sister to feel equal in the family equation, and that makes me very sad.

I think my parents, who adopted in the 1950s, were fairly typical in thinking that it would be wrong to hide the fact of their adoptions, but it would be odd to make a fuss about it: Best to just go forward as a family, seemed to sum up their plan. Now that I've spent years studying ritual, however, I can see the importance of creating rituals that acknowledge and celebrate the differentness of that relationship.

These days, many parents of adopted children celebrate the anniversary of the day they adopted a child as well as his or her birthday. If their child was born in another country or region, they take pains to create rituals that incorporate the food and songs and culture of that place. If they can locate other adoptive parents with children from that same culture, they'll create occasions for the adopted children to get to know peers, others of their generation from that place. And someday, they may plan a "heritage trip" with the child to her or his native land. This all seems right to me.

Raising one's own child is fraught enough with challenges, and there can be additional ones related to adoption. But thoughtful parents can create a whole body of rituals and ceremonies as needed to keep these wanted children feeling loved and fully known. You can't always know what episodes and moments will arise that call out for ritual's magic touch, but you can become sensitive to the need for ritual and ceremony in your own clan. There is so much emotion inherent in adoption, and ritual is about recognizing, celebrating, and channeling that powerful energy in a good direction.

Open Adoption Ceremony

There has been a trend in recent decades toward more transparency in adoption, and in open adoption cases, the biological mother continues to be a presence in the life of her child. Mostly, this is a win-win situation for everyone. And it is just one example of the extra layers of complexity in twenty-first-century family life: further proof that we all need expertise in ritual creating now.

Families in this situation must invent new rituals of connection, figuring out how the biological mother and the adoptive family interact and marking all the usual big occasions. But even in the case of very open adoptions, it isn't at all usual to have a ceremony marking the adoption in a public place. Women who are forced to give up a child are understandably not keen to publicly act out this difficult milestone, and in many cases, the logistics wouldn't work. Often, the adopting family picks up a child in another state or country and brings them home.

I'm not suggesting everyone should do this, or would want to, but I wanted to include the example of Gail Simpson's open adoption ceremony. It's one of the most courageous and powerful ceremonies I know about, and it was written and enacted with dignity by all the parties involved. There are many ritual occasions during which there is more than one central emotion operating, and Gail managed to honor both the sweet and the bitter in this one.

This was actually the second open adoption for Gail Simpson and her husband, but in this case, the young college student whose baby they were adopting had lived with the family during the final months of her pregnancy. There was a real bond there and mutual trust, and the young woman agreed she was up for the gesture of literally placing her infant daughter in the arms of her new family in front of a church congregation. Gail created the ceremony that took place at her church, working hard to make it supportive of everyone involved: When it came time for the young mother to speak her piece, a member of the congregation who had given up a baby years earlier stood next to her to speak with her.

To give a voice to the tiny baby being adopted, anyone in the congregation who was adopted was asked to say these words, which are addressed to both the adopting and biological parents:

I bring you together in this mysterious intersection of nature and nurture which is adoption. I am the music to which you will dance of love and loss for a lifetime. Dance well. My melody is the sweet yearning for life. Teach me the language of love from which to compose my lyrics.

You can read the entire ceremony in Appendix 2 at the back of the book. Both Simpson girls are young women now, and though their relationships with their birth mothers have waxed and waned over the years, the mothers continue to stay in touch.

Homecoming Day

The Hoddinott family celebrates the adoption days of two children born in Korea but is sensitive to the feelings of a biological daughter. "To us, it's a way to keep the door open, to allow them to ask questions and hear their stories over and over," says Julie Hoddinott. "It's obvious they're adopted because they don't look like us, and it's important to acknowledge their histories." The family has a special dessert on Homecoming Day, but it's important to Julie that the cake be shared by all. On each boy's Homecoming Day, she shows the video taken the day he arrived from Korea, and the family looks at baby pictures from that time.

tech tip

Like some others who adopt these days, Marla Michele Must has blogged extensively about her adoption journey, but her experience included especially extensive preplanning and wise use of available technology. Obviously, this sort of thing isn't always possible, but Marla was able to introduce herself to the child many months ahead by using Skype, the free Internet videoconferencing tool. The little girl was with a foster family in China that had a computer and was willing to participate. Also, Marla was able to visit the foster family shortly before picking up Sasha Jade: She brought a tape recorder and got some comforting words translated into Chinese. So the foster parents were able to record a tape that said things to the child such as, "It is okay to be happy with your new mommy and brother and sister. We want to hear how you are doing." Marla says playing this tape over and over for Sasha Jade in the early days was very helpful, adding, "I didn't want her to think anybody had disappeared." Hearing those familiar voices would make those caretakers feel present. Besides, although Marla and her kids had been studying Mandarin for some time, they weren't any more fluent in Chinese than Sasha Jade was in English in those early days.

Forever Family Day

There are many different names given to the day when a family takes an adopted child home. Some families call it "Gotcha Day"; others use "Airplane Day" because they brought their child home on a plane. Marla Michele Must and her two biological kids decided that June 21, 2010, will always be called "Forever Family Day," and they will celebrate each year. That's the day they all got to pick up a toddler named "Tian Tian" in China, who is now called Sasha Jade and lives in Michigan.

Marla and her family did many thoughtful things to make the transition easier for the girl. She even mailed a blanket to the girl months before they came to get her, so it would be a comfort object when she moved to the United States. And the three of them put together ten photo books in the course of six months, so their new sister could get to know them.

Family Day

A couple in Minnesota adopted two Romanian orphans in 1991 and decided to celebrate the adoptions on an annual day they called Family Day. At a festive dinner, they retell the story of the adoptions but also take time to talk about a biological daughter who committed suicide in her teens. There are five candles on the cake, including one for this girl.

When I share this story, I sometimes hear from people who are disturbed by this and express a concern the kids might think they were adopted as "replacement children" for the suicide. But I believe in the positive intention of this family, which is to communicate that no matter what, once a person joins this family, he or she is part of it forever, and everybody's story matters. I think that's ultimately deeply comforting, conveying permanence.

Many Roots, Much Love

Adoptive parents try to raise their families to appreciate all aspects of their children's roots, both the genetic ones and the cultural and personal traditions of the family they join. There is so much cross-pollination now, and scientists have shown that genetically, the people of Earth are a very mixed-up but nonhomogenized brew. I'm always heartened by stories I hear about adopted kids celebrating their multiple cultures with energy and creativity. My friend's Korean-born daughter was trying to pick just the right wedding dress to show off the tattoo on her back: It's a Celtic knot, in tribute to her "Irish roots."

Talking to a Star

When Lucy Steinitz noticed that her daughter, adopted as an infant from Guatemala, got sad on her birthdays, wondering about the mother that let her go, Lucy invented a special birthday ritual. She told Elsita she didn't know much about the woman but suggested, "If you look out your bedroom window and talk to a star, and tell her what she needs to know about you, I just know she'll be listening." The ritual always made Elsita feel better, and as a teenager, Lucy took her for a "cultural heritage" trip to Guatemala.

Mia's Life Book

Jennifer Grant and her husband already had three children when they decided to adopt a fourth. They adopted Mia from Guatemala when she was about eighteen months old. She is the youngest now at nine, but her sister and two brothers are all only about two years apart.

Like most adoptions, there were emotional bumps along the way, many of which Jennifer explores in her fine memoir of adoption, *Love You More*, but the family found several rituals that helped greatly. A major one was the "Life Book" that Jennifer made even before she brought Mia home, and it's something many adopting families do.

"It acknowledges that an adopted child's life began when they were born, not when they come to your home," says Jennifer. "I tell a little about Guatemalan history, what the culture and geography are like, what I know about her birth mother, and where she spent her first year and a half." The book includes photos of Mia's foster mother, that woman's own children, and also pictures of Mia meeting her new family.

This book was an anchor, a love/security object, for Mia for quite some time. "I think Mia has read her Life Book about 100 times," says Jennifer. "When she was little, it was her favorite book to read. I had the whole thing copied on cardstock, so she could carry it with her everywhere."

Every year, they reread the book on Mia's "Homecoming Anniversary" when celebrating her arrival. It's a special day for the whole family, and the older kids write notes to Mia telling her what she means to them, and what they remember of her earliest days there.

Resources for Adoptive Families

There are many specialized resources for adoption, but here are some basic guides. Any parents contemplating adoption are advised to search for and work with reliable agencies, which will be able to suggest all manner of resources. The best agencies tend to have websites packed with articles and links and also offer occasional workshops and other programs for parents.

Magazines

Adoptive Families is an award-winning national magazine that is published bi-monthly. You can read some of the content on the website AdoptiveFamilies.com, and the site links to many good online resources. *Adoption Today* is also excellent, an all-digital publication that focuses particularly on international and trans-racial adoptions. That website is Adopt Info.net.

Books

There are hundreds of books, including many heartwarming individual adoption memoirs. Some of the good general-interest titles are:

- *The Connected Child: Bring Hope and Healing to Your Adoptive Family* (especially for parents who adopt from other cultures or have special-issues kids), by Karyn B. Purvis, David R. Cross, and Wendy Lyons Sunshine.
- *The Whole Life Adoption Book: Realistic Advice for Building a Healthy Adoptive Family* (new edition, 2008), by Jayne E. Schooler and Thomas Atwood.
- *Adoption Parenting: Creating a Toolbox, Building Connections*, edited by Jean MacLeod and Sheena Macrae, which includes essays from more than 100 experts in the field.

Summer Vacation Rituals

A balance needs to be found between the overprogrammed school year life of many kids and a summer of loafing. Family rituals for this time of year often center on summer food, trips to the local pool, and backyard games, when kids are not off at camp. Here are some fun ideas to try:

Books and Cones

One reason my son reads so much in the summer is that the local library gives the kids a "summer passport" to list all the books they read (or have read to them). Any child who clocks twelve hours of reading in a summer gets a free sundae at the local ice cream store in the fall. Why not make books a sweet treat now: Go to the library every two weeks, and stop for an ice cream cone after every visit.

Tour Your Town

One summer weekend each year, pretend your family just arrived as tourists and see the best your town has to offer. Visit historical sites, eat in the cool new restaurant, take a long bike ride through neighborhoods you've never visited. Take photos in front of landmarks, buy T-shirts, and send postcards.

New and Barbecued

Once a week, have a simple backyard barbecue, but invite a family in the neighborhood or from your children's school that hasn't been to your home before. Make a pact with your kids that you'll serve some of their favorite foods like hot dogs and chips, but try one new grilled item each time, like grilled peppers, corn on the cob, or chicken and mushroom kabobs.

After-Lunch Siesta

During summers, whether they were at home or away, the Vogt kids had a period of thirty minutes to an hour after lunch when they went to their rooms to read or daydream. It was a serene time, no distractions, in the heat of the day, and it calmed and rested everyone.

Make a Movie

After school ends, have a "story conference" and come up with a wacky plot in which every family member plays at least one character. Design costumes. Over the course of the summer, shoot one scene at a time, in different locations. For credits, film one of your kids typing the title and list of actors on a computer screen. At summer's end, invite friends and family to the "premiere." Next summer: Shoot a sequel, or the prequel to a movie still to come.

Master a New Skill Together

Long summers and vacations are the absolute best times to learn a new skill that takes practice. Why not pick one, or several, that everyone in the family takes a hand at?

It could be old standards like playing a harmonica. Or learning simple juggling. Or basic magic tricks, starting with those that require only a regular deck of cards. There are tutorials on all of these and more available online, and additional resources at your local library. Many of these are quite portable too, so you can keep practicing if you travel for part of your vacation. And some satisfying skills like whistling require time and patience, but no props at all.

The fun of taking on something like this as a family is that you can build up to a talent show or other event at summer's end, and find out which family member learned the most.

Getting There: Rituals for Cars and Planes

Vacation spots are mostly heavenly, but getting there can be challenging. Many families have created rituals that make the journey actually feel like part of the vacation.

Fuss Towns

Polly Mead drastically reduced the number of car fights between her four kids by creating the ritual of "fuss towns." Before a long drive, she would locate a town roughly halfway to the day's destination. The kids were not allowed to fuss and yell until they got to the outskirts of the designated fuss town, when those behaviors became mandatory. The kids would erupt and explode with a vengeance, but once they reached the other end of town, they calmed back down. Mostly.

Vacation Treasure Balls

Public Radio personality Marty Goldensohn told me his mother used to make these balls for car trips. She started with a small hard ball, wrapping it with half-inch ribbon around and around, folding in little toys, tokens, pieces of candy. During a long trip, each kid got one and could only unwrap to the next treasure at designated intervals.

If you try this with your kids, I assume you'd use different-colored ribbon for each of them so there would be no fights.

Rhyme Games

Car games are essential, and many of the best don't even require props. Have one of the parents start a nonsense sentence, which every person in the car has to rhyme with another sentence. Nancy Shaw used to play a game like this with her children in the car, and later turned it into a series of best-selling picture books with such names as *Sheep in a Jeep* and *Sheep on a Ship*.

Storyteller for Hire

Many parents keep their kids occupied watching TV shows and movies on portable screens during long rides, but I'd argue for a story the whole family can share. We always take chapter books on car trips, but the designated reader gets pooped before long. A great ritual is to get an unabridged book on CD from the local library. The story becomes a memorable part of your summer. Ask the librarian for age-appropriate books, but our favorites are the Harry Potter books; *The Trumpet of the Swan* read by author E. B. White; and *The Indian in the Cupboard* read by author Lynne Reid Banks. The story becomes part of your shared family culture. And the driver doesn't get so bored.

Great Online Resource for Car Games and Activities

Laurel Smith is the former high school teacher and mother of three behind the website MomsMinivan.com. She boasts that her site contains 101 road trip games for kids, and I believe it. Here you will find rules to lots of classic games, along with fresh ideas for license plate games and on-the-road scavenger hunts and car bingo, for which you can download and print cards.

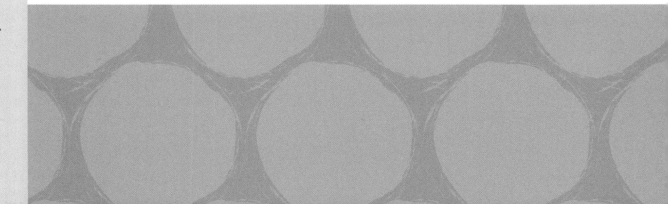

Being There: Rituals for Peak Vacations

Porcupine Award

The Routh family of Iowa spotted a live porcupine while hiking in the Rocky Mountains and declared it the strangest-looking creature they had ever seen outside a zoo. Thus was born the Porcupine Award, given to the family member who spots the weirdest animal on any trip, or even a long family hike. Mary Routh says it's great because even the baby of the family sometimes wins. There isn't an actual certificate given by the Rouths, but your family could create one. Or buy a cheap trophy and pass it from room to room back home, as different people "win."

Every Picture Tells a Story

Think ahead about a loose plot that could be tied to your destination, and take a series of fun photos to tell that story. It could be as simple as creating a scrapbook travelogue starring your toddler daughter's frayed teddy bear. Photograph him at the pool (not too close to the water), asleep in her bed, viewing the local sights. One family I know has a goofy Christmas gift exchange in which the same wacky object is passed from household to household: Whoever gets the thing in a given year invariably takes it on vacation and photographs it somewhere scenic.

An alternative: No matter where you travel in the world with your family, try to take the same photo. Have everyone make the same gesture, or photograph everyone making the same silly face or wearing hats or Groucho glasses. Save one photo from everyone you travel with to make a big collage for your family room.

Super Sand Castles

The Bonner family visits the same beach every year, and the whole family collaboratively makes a very large, complicated sand castle in their annual ritual. There are turrets

galore, and lots of shells and stones placed carefully along the edges to embellish it. Then they take lots of photos of their work. They try to outdo themselves each year, and sometimes, this is the image on their Christmas card. There can be many parting rituals for leaving a special vacation spot, such as enjoying a special feast, flying kites, blowing balloons, and taking group photos.

Arriving in Style

Some families vacation at the same cabin, resort, or campground every year, and they love to settle in with a ritual that makes them feel at home and ready to relax. They might head to a nearby stream, take off their shoes, and go wading, or might stop by the same fried-clam stand for their favorite vacation chow. When we visit my husband's cousin on a lake in New Hampshire every August, we always watch the sun set while sitting on the dock and sipping a special lemon drink. But you can also start an arrival ritual that works wherever you go. If you arrive after dark, for example, you can give the kids glowing florescent sticks and let them run wildly in circles around your cottage or campsite.

Garden Rituals

Gardening and kids definitely go together, and there is much ritual inherent in growing things. Planting something by themselves and then having it grow is a very powerful experience for children, giving them a sense of real accomplishment. This isn't just a drawing or structure of blocks, but life that they created.

Plant Early and Often

Marcela Villagran's kids start by planting seeds in little pots in February, giving them a tiny bit of water daily. The kids also help take the kitchen garbage out to the compost pile. At nearly five, Marcela's daughter said to her: "So whatever we put in the kitchen bowl, the worms eat and then we have this nice soft dirt? And the plants like it, and that's why they grow so pretty?" Yep, she gets it.

Personalized Scarecrow

Erica Rawson's family had a gardening routine that included making a scarecrow every year. "We create someone new, give him/her a name, make up a story about them, and refer to the scarecrow often during the summer. The kids love this!"

Resources for Little Green Thumbs

Good bets for small children are sunflowers and nasturtiums, which have big seeds. For vegetables, best bets are lettuce, tomatoes, and pumpkins.

A fantastic website is KidsGardening.org, produced by the National Gardening Association. A great book for young gardeners is *Roots, Shoots, Buckets, and Boots* by Sharon Lovejoy: It includes twelve clever themed gardens for kids, such as a Pizza Patch and a Moon Garden (full of night-blooming flowers).

For another fun idea, see Amanda Soule's "Birthday Gardens" in the Birthday section, earlier in this book.

Family Reunions

According to Edith Wagner, editor of *Reunions* magazine, more than 200,000 families in this country celebrate family reunions annually, averaging fifty people each. A regular reunion, even a small one, helps kids grow up with a sense of family history and a feeling of belonging. With extended families so far-flung today, such gifts are even more valuable. Here are some fun reunion ideas shared by families:

Big Event

The Love family reunion, begun in 1976 as a weekend get-together, now attracts 300 family members and lasts four days. The semiannual reunions always include a golf tournament and talent night, but a special feature is the family mentoring program. Every child between seven and fifteen is paired with a family mentor. Even between reunions, the children check in with their mentors about their career aspirations, listing five steps they'll take to achieve them.

One Generation Is Enough

Every year, Amy Cordell has a weekend reunion with her five sisters (and one brother), and they call it the Sisters Convention. They meet at a hotel or one of the sibling's homes and the main activity is talk. "Because the gap between youngest and oldest is twelve years, this has finally made it possible for us to really know each other," says Amy. They have been known to make reunion T-shirts, but usually each one brings a favorite book or product (hair mousse, once) to share with the others.

Two Generations Are Great, Too

When I was a little girl, I know my parents used to take us to some pretty large Cox family reunions. Alas, all I remember from these is faded black-and-white photos showing us children in summer outfits, sitting on the laps of relatives who are now unknown to me. Because the tradition didn't stay alive long enough for me to remember it—and given my patchwork family with four very different kids going completely different directions—it didn't look like we'd ever do the reunion thing.

I don't see much of my adopted brother since my parents are both gone, but something funny happened recently, thanks to Facebook. My brother's sons are now in their teens, and one of his twins reached out to me and my sister via Facebook, wanting to get to know us. Next thing you know, we were planning a sibling reunion on the North Carolina coast, in the town where our parents last lived. We did a low-key three-day weekend, all staying at the same motel and mostly eating meals out. We went to the dock where my mother's ashes were scattered and the golf course where we scattered my father's ashes, and scattered rose petals in their memory. Best of all was the night where we gathered in my sister's room and the siblings spun stories of some of the wilder parts of our childhood and our parents' lives: It was great to see the teenagers silent and rapt, taking in their family history. I also brought copies of some letters written during the Civil War by an ancestor of ours. And we're planning to do this now every other year. Yes! (Thanks, Stephen!)

Cousins Camp

One form of reunion is when Grandma invites all the grandchildren to visit her at the same time, for a weekend or longer. Because she misses many of her grandkids' birthdays throughout the year, every summer Patty Mac Hewitt celebrates "Everybody's Birthday" at her summer house on a lake in New Hampshire. There is plenty of cake and ice cream for all the kids, and everybody gets a present, usually a toy good for either gender that can be left at Grandma's till next year.

Family Farm

Seidemanns come from twenty-four states on the third Sunday of July for a one-day reunion of this clan at the patriarch's Wisconsin farm. The descendants of German immigrants always have a kuchen (coffee cake) contest, and the entries are auctioned off to help pay for the reunion. Annual features include food, games, and a talent show, and the barn is full of family furniture and artifacts from eight generations.

Ask and Ye Shall Receive

The McNair-Brazil-Scott family traces its origins back to the 1800s, when two brothers named McNair left Mississippi for free land in Arkansas. They've been having reunions for many years, and they know how to leverage their large reunion for freebies. Many convention hotels will throw in a free room to a group renting a large block of rooms, but one year, the reunion chairman, who worked in Milwaukee, got the Coca-Cola company to pay for the reunion banquet and give free Cokes to the 250 family members who attended that year. The reunion organizers are also savvy in their fund-raising, and every year, they give scholarship money to all the McNair-Brazil-Scott kids who are graduating from high school. Because they got the reunion organization declared a nonprofit, they can deduct the scholarships. Check out the family website, www.mbsfamily.org.

Family Alphabet Chant

Create a family cheer or song in which each letter of the family's name stands for something. Try to weave family history into it, letting the letters stand for a special hometown, professions of prominent family members, or family lore such as war heroism. Repeat it at every reunion.

Family Olympics

The Bode family picks a special theme for each reunion. The Olympics was one of the most popular, kicking off with a parade in which each family represented a different country. The games were things like "chugging contests" with Dixie cups full of root beer, and the day ended with an international buffet (Swedish meatballs, German potato salad, and so on) and a medals ceremony.

Family Circles

Linda Grenis belongs to a family that has an annual picnic, and an annual business meeting. Her extended family meets in a structured gathering called a family circle, an old-fashioned tradition especially popular with Jewish families but essentially nonreligious. Her family circle is called "The Weber Family Circle Bagel and Lox Hunting Club" as a joke, she says, because "Jewish people typically don't hunt." In some family circles, you have to be twenty-one: In this one, you join when you graduate from college. After eating typical Jewish fare, the forty to fifty people sit in a circle and read minutes from the previous meeting, then go around doing what they call "good and welfare," updating relatives on their lives. There are lots of repeated jokes. (You can get the flavor by checking out the website, webercousins.com, which states in the About Us page: "Begun in the Eisenhower era by a small group of (mostly chain-smoking) Webers, who thirsted for companionship and hungered for smoked fish, the Club has a long & illegibly written history. . . . ") Linda says there are five generations of cousins attending, and that after a recent "membership drive," the family circle is expanding again.

Great Reunion Resource

Reunions magazine is a bimonthly publication that is packed with ideas for organizing and running successful reunions of all kinds. A subscription for a year is only $10 and comes with a reunion-planning workbook. But an enormous amount of excellent information is also provided free on the magazine's website, ReunionsMag.com. There are lengthy lists of ideas for overall themes, ice-breaker activities, fund-raising possibilities, and tips on choosing a place. Even without subscribing to *Reunions* (and you can get a trial issue free), users of the website can bid here on discount hotel rooms, via ReunionsMag .hotelplanner.com.

Reunion Quilt

The Gines family takes turn hosting their reunion, and each year the host family passes out fabric already cut into six-inch squares. Each family unit attending decorates their fabric (with fabric paint if they don't sew), and the seamstresses in the clan stage a sort of quilting bee during the get-together. The finished quilt is given to the family that hosted that year.

Family Cookbook

Many families that hold reunions regularly sell items like coffee mugs and T-shirts. If it's a big reunion, this can be a good moneymaker, and even if it's a smaller group, at least everyone gets a neat souvenir and there is some money for postage and other reunion expenses. A number of families sell reunion cookbooks, thick with favorite family recipes. With reunions that attract 300 or more guests, this, too, can help raise funds. But it doesn't have to be ambitious: Ask every family coming to your next reunion to bring five or ten favorite recipes, then publish the resulting "cookbook" on your home computer in time for Christmas.

Memorial Service

Many families like to include a memorial service to honor both departed individuals and the family's collective history. The Bullock family reunion, inspired in part by Alex Haley's book *Roots*, features an especially dramatic candle-lighting ritual during its Saturday night banquet. The lights are turned low, gospel music plays in the background, and candles are lit: a thick white one for the patriarch, George Bullock Sr., and smaller white ones for his departed children.

tech tip

Your Reunion Needs a Website Because . . .

In the olden days, reunions were run by telephone and snail mail, and it was a bloody nightmare trying to keep track of everything. Now, many well-established larger reunions do everything online, from sending invitations to tracking RSVPs, selling tickets, and posting both historic and current family photos. A website is a great vehicle for doing all that.

If you've been invited to a nice wedding or major party lately, chances are you've used one of those online invitation services that lets you RSVP easily and keeps you updated on event details, like who else is coming and whether you need to bring something. Weddings are big and complicated and so are some reunions, but unlike weddings, the reunion keeps happening again every year or two, so a website allows people to maintain the structure they build for the event. Typically, the services that provide templates for and host reunion sites cost around $10 to $15 a month, but many families swear by them and use the websites to keep family members updated all year long.

Here are two examples: GuyFamilyReunion.com is the reunion site for "descendants of Civil War veterans Baldy Guy and George Guy." Apgar Family.org is a site for a New Jersey family that even includes a virtual family museum.

Offbeat and Made-Up Holidays and Rituals

It's a wonderful moment when a child realizes that nobody else on the planet celebrates the same wacky holiday that his or her family invented, or engages in the same silly ritual.

Crazy Food Day

The Taylor family of Stratford, Connecticut, started this tradition one year during Christmas vacation: On Crazy Food Day, all the meals are mixed up. They might eat lunch or dinner for breakfast, and breakfast for lunch. This day usually gets chosen when school is closed because of snow or when there's a vacation day with no events planned. Everybody stays in his or her pajamas all day.

Kids' Day

Some kids have lobbied their parents for a children's equivalent of Mother's Day and Father's Day. The Hains girls of Maryland get to pick a special family activity, and each gets a small gift. Patrice Kyger takes it a step further: Son's Day is the second Sunday in July, and Daughter's Day comes on the second Sunday in August. A special outing like a picnic or miniature golf is planned, and the siblings talk about what's good about having a sister or brother, depending on the day.

Family Happiness Party

In Merchantville, New Jersey, Susan Lynch and her daughters know just what to do on days when everyone in the family is down in the dumps. They declare a Family Happiness Party and get ready to cheer themselves up with such treats as make-your-own sundaes.

Yes Day

Darcie Gore wrote in *Family Fun* magazine that she got tired of saying "no" to her three girls constantly and decided to declare the next Saturday "Yes Day." She started a "Yes

Jar," so her daughters could deposit written requests for things they couldn't do immediately, such as "wear my Cinderella dress all day." On a Yes Day, the activity requests are read, and all the kids pick one special thing they want to do that day. The first Yes Day began with a breakfast of chocolate milk and donuts, and included such activities as freeze tag, a pillow fight, and the application of toenail polish.

You can decorate almost any container you have, but one simple idea is to take a Quaker Oats cardboard box and decorate the outside with colored paper. Perhaps the kids can cut out pictures from magazines of foods and activities and toys they love and glue them on. Cut a slit in the plastic top, so they can write their Yes Day requests during the month and save them in the container.

Invite the Stuffed Animals

There were always a lot of stuffed animals in our house, and a good number of rituals were created around them. The stuffed platypus my husband gave me for Valentine's Day years ago, Boris, has his own team sports gear, especially a Cleveland Browns shirt (made from an old sock with a team patch stitched on) that he wears during games (he keeps it on all week if the team wins). Another fun ritual was the stuffed animal football games my husband and son would stage on the floor in the playroom.

But the best ritual of all was the "New Toy Interview," in which the esteemed platypus Boris, who was sort of the dean of toy town here, would give every new stuffed animal our son got a little orientation. My husband would help Boris make his presentation, and there was always stuff about how Max might not always pay them this amount of attention, and warnings that some of the stuffed animals were leaning toward the dark side and should be avoided. But in general, it seemed like a very sweet rundown and reminder of our family values, a tutorial about what it means to be one of us.

Groundhog Day

This holiday isn't invented, but who do you know who actually celebrates it? Nancy Dodge, the mother of five in Princeton, New Jersey, says her family really needs a holiday around February 2, "when the winter is looking endless and bleak." Basically, the Dodge family eats a lot of junk food on Groundhog Day and watches back-to-back movies, mostly on a baseball theme, though they've been known to watch the movie named for the holiday.

Alice in Wonderland Day

Declare a fantasy day, and let everyone pick themes, food, and activities. Go to a special place where you'll feel really huge or really tiny, like Alice after she eats the magic food. Have a Mad Hatter's Tea Party. Read or talk about your favorite fantasy books, such as Harry Potter. Mix magic potions. Learn magic tricks.

Mess Day

The idea is to take all the ordinary household rules, and for one entire day, turn them upside down. Let everybody wear their grubbiest clothes and never comb their hair. Table manners aren't allowed, and all meals should be eaten on a picnic blanket on the floor, preferably while watching television. Toys are never put away, so playing never has to stop.

Overcoat Day

In New York City, Mary Beaton and Jels McCaulay celebrate this holiday with their two daughters. On the first really cold day of the year, they call friends and family and proclaim Overcoat Day. Depending on whether it is a weekend or weekday, up to thirty people show up in mittens, scarves, and warm coats and crowd onto the family's outdoor deck. The adults drink champagne, while the kids clink sippy cups of juice together. "Wintery" books like *The Snowy Day* by Ezra Jack Keats are read aloud, and the kids make snowman decorations out of cotton balls and construction paper.

Speranza'a

This is the invented winter holiday of the Speranza family and it lasts six days and starts the Monday after Valentine's Day. Each member of the family gets a dedicated day of his or her own (including the pet bunny, Charcoal). On that day, the chosen one gets to pick the food for dinner—even if the choice is bacon and popcorn—and eat by candlelight. After dinner and blowing out the candles, everyone dances in the living room. Loosely inspired by Kwanzaa and Hanukkah, the holiday has its own principles, explains Carol Sulcoski (whose married name is Speranza). "So far, we've got the principles of Irony, Gluttony, and Magnetism, but I think they need tweaking." Next, the family is considering making a special candleholder, to be called a "spenorah." Doesn't it sound fun? "All silliness aside, it is sweet and surprising to see how much this family tradition means to my kids," Carol wrote in her blog Go Knit in Your Hat. "They talk about it for weeks beforehand, and it is heartwarming to feel like we are making some special memories for our kids."

Between-the-Seasons Dinners

Cindy Taibbi-Kates has a novel way of celebrating the transition to a new season. When they celebrate the event in September and prepare for fall, she explains, "We eat watermelon slices right alongside butternut squash soup and we drink lemonade and hot chocolate! We dress in shorts and a long-sleeved sweater—or maybe a T-shirt and snow pants. We play Beach Boy tunes and Christmas music." The decor echoes the theme: One year, the family hollowed out a pumpkin to use as a centerpiece, placing within it a bouquet of daisies in a glass vase. Says Cynthia: "It's always so much fun to see how silly we can make it!"

Best Guides for Finding Something New and Fun to Celebrate

Every single day is a major holiday or anniversary somewhere in the world. If you are looking to invent a holiday at your house or celebrate something new, you can't beat these online resources that document all the days.

The old go-to resource is Chase's Calendar of Events, published by McGraw-Hill, which is the standard text many libraries own and includes a wealth of detail, including astronomical information like moon phases, lists of famous people born on a particular day, every holiday proclaimed by Congress, and lots of national and international special occasions. Along with totally goofy things like January being Oatmeal Month (or so proclaims Quaker Oats), you will find valuable news such as what actual day Easter or the summer solstice will fall on in a given year. This is updated each year and distributed electronically: You can access much but not all this information free online (www.mhprofessional .com/templates/chases/), but you can very likely access Chase's Calendar at your local library's website. It's hard to overstate what a great tool Chase's can be, because in addition to creating new celebrations, you can use it as a tool to teach and discuss history with your clan. I mean, look at just two holidays in Chase's for the date August 14, which just happens to be the day I'm writing these words: China celebrates the "Festival of Hungry Ghosts," and the Navajo Nation marks Navajo Code Talkers Day (look that up; it's fascinating World War II history, and a movie was made about it).

Here are two other invaluable resources, websites maintained by private individuals, but also packed with ideas of things to celebrate: HolidaysForEveryday.com and Earth Calendar.org.

Belly Laugh Day

Did you know that passionate, persistent individuals (as well as nonprofits and corporations) can invent a holiday and then actually get it listed on various "official" calendars? Elaine Helle did this when she created Belly Laugh Day in 2006, which happens every year on January 24. She thought winter was a good time to get people to laugh and relax. The idea is to "throw your arms in the air and laugh out loud" on that day, at 1:24 PM (local time). See www.bellylaughday.com.

Jack Horner Pies

This seems to be a widely practiced, old idea but the person who told me about her family doing it is Lee Vogelgesang. Her family does this at every family gathering, whether Christmas, Easter, or family vacation. "A Jack Horner pie is made of little special prizes or trinkets that are given specifically to the person whose name is on the other end of a string or ribbon, to which the gift is secured," Lee explains. "The gifts are placed in a big bowl or bucket and covered with tissue paper, so no one can see the prizes. The ribbon is poked through the tissue paper, with the name of the recipient on the end." When the time comes, everyone recites the rhyme: "Little Jack Horner, sat in a corner" and when they get to "What a good boy (or girl) am I," everyone tugs at once.

Bookapalooza

When my son outgrew celebrating the birthday of Pooh's creator, A. A. Milne, he suggested we have an annual full day that is all about celebrating books, as winter vacation winds down. We wake up and read in bed, then dress up as favorite characters (Hermione Granger for me, but I do have a Mary Poppins costume left from Halloween), and watch one of our favorite movies based on a book. Other ideas: Play book-title charades, visit the library, make pilgrimages to a statue of a famous fictional character (the Alice in Wonderland statue in Central Park is awesome) or an author's birthplace.

SFFF Outings

Carol McCarthy Heald is the mother of four grown kids, and she says for years she would plan some sort of special night or outing labeled with the initials "SFFF." The letters stand for "Spoon Fed Family Fun." "Back when it was only $15 for the Santa Fe Opera, I'd buy tickets for all of us. But this also included nature outings, backpacking, canoe trips, and more," says Carol. She says they had a blast and many memorable adventures, but sometimes she had to force the kids to try new things. "We told them: You don't have to like it, but you do have to do it."

Fairy Godmother Induction Ceremony

My friend Anne Kalik had a good friend whose eleven-year-old daughter kept saying that she wasn't fond of her godmother and wished Anne could take over the job. Anne explained that being chosen a godmother was a lifetime position, but that she would be happy to become the girl's "fairy godmother." Wow. During a camping trip, Anne created a little ritual to mark this new relationship, painting the girl's face with a moon and stars before beginning. She drew a circle on the beach by a river. While the girl and Anne and some other family members stood inside, Anne lit the end of a smudge stick and waved it around to add atmosphere and make the space sacred to them. (For an explanation of smudge sticks, see the sidebar in Chapter 1.) The smudge stick was lit and passed around the circle, says Anne, and each of them "said something from our hearts."

This one-time ritual was simple, but profound. Says Anne, "I've loved this child since she was born, but the ritual made me feel I had formally made a promise to be responsible. It added something special: I pay more attention."

In today's world, when everyone creates new connections and decides who belongs in their extended family, is there a bond you need to mark and celebrate?

Sarah Stengle's Half-Baked Party

I've always been a fan of the free spirits who go way outside the box to create rituals that celebrate the authentic and messy lives they actually live. The greeting card companies have gotten better at including some more unusual occasions in the mix, but I get a thrill from a holiday or special occasion celebrated by so few people that there will never be a commercial card for it. We live in a DIY (do-it-yourself) world, and that's happening more these days, I think. Here's a good example: May it free you to nurture the kids you've got rather than someone else's idea of who your children should be.

Not every kid marches to the beat of the same drummer, and that includes Sarah's daughter Sophie, who went off after sophomore year to take some college classes in art. After that, she couldn't bear high school and wanted to bust out, get her GED, and move on to college as soon as possible. Having left home herself at sixteen to tour Europe, Sarah, a book designer, understood the girl's impatience. So, halfway through her junior year, the girl dropped out of high school, with her mom's blessing. Later, she secured the GED and was accepted into college (Academy of Arts in San Francisco, where she had previously done the summer program). But even before that, when she dropped out of school, the family decided to throw a playful party, alluding to the fact that Sarah was leaving high school half-way through.

"We have a long tradition of playing with our food, having cupcake baking parties, and doing our Peeps of Destruction ritual at Easter (see Easter traditions in Chapter 4)," says Sarah, who has two teen girls. "For the half-baked party, we made dough for chocolate chip cookies but only cooked half of it. The half that we left uncooked didn't include any eggs [experts say cookie dough with raw eggs should be avoided, in case the eggs have salmonella or other bacteria], so people could eat both cookies and unbaked dough."

Sarah admits that some parents she spoke to thought she was nuts to celebrate such an occasion. The party crowd included extended family and Sophie's friends. "We didn't want the fact that she was stopping high school to seem apologetic. This wasn't a failure but a decision," says Sarah. 'We wanted to celebrate this personal transition, but with humor."

House Blessings

The place where we live is immensely important to our well-being, and the idea of blessing one's dwelling is an ancient one. Before sharing some really creative ways families have blessed their homes, including when moving from one house to another, does anyone remember that sweet blessing from the movie *It's a Wonderful Life*? Mary Bailey (played by Donna Reed) says this when a family moves into a new home in the development the Baileys have helped make possible. She stands on the threshold with these objects in her hand, and passes them along to the new homeowners:

"Bread, that this house may never know hunger. Salt, that life may always have flavor. And wine, that joy and prosperity may reign forever."

Thanking the House

When Karly Randolph Pitman's family left a house where they had lived for a long time, she said they felt compelled to ritually thank the house. "We found a place in the bowels of the house near the furnace, where we all signed our names. At one point, I remember literally hugging the walls of my bedroom and thanking my house in the room where I gave birth to my son."

Good-Bye to the Old House, Hello to the New

Mary Ann Paulukonis had to leave a house in South Dakota in 1992 that the family had built and lived in with their children for twelve years. The now-grown kids came home for the last weekend there and Mary Ann designed a brief ceremony. "We went on a house tour, telling stories in every room and then blessing the room with thanks to God for all that happened there," recalls Mary Ann. "Then we went out to the driveway, remembered shoveling, guests arriving and all of that, and lit some forgotten sparklers our son found in a closet. There were tears and laughter mixed through-out. We concluded by eating ice cream and everybody said they felt better, more ready to move on."

Seven months later, after moving to a new house, the kids came to visit. "We did a new house blessing in the same spirit, " says Mary Ann, "and concluded by going to a local dairy farm for fresh ice cream, symbolizing a union of the old with the new."

Ritual Dedication of a Remodeled Kitchen

This comes from Elisabeth Fuchs of France, who e-mailed it to me after reading my monthly *Ritual Newsletter*. She said the renovation had taken weeks and disrupted the family of six a great deal.

"After the last kitchen cabinets were put in, we invited family members, including my parents and grandmother, to the inauguration of our new kitchen. Everybody gathered in front of the closed kitchen door. Ahead of time, I taped a red ribbon horizontally across the door frame. My husband, our four kids, and I each had a pair of scissors, and we all cut at the same time."

The family then entered the kitchen, in a sort of parade line, each bringing back a tool or appliance that was special to them. "Our three-year-old daughter had her breakfast mug, our eight-year-old daughter the cookie box, and so on. Everybody came in and admired the kitchen, we got some lovely gifts (unexpected), and sat down for a buffet-style meal." All present were invited to sign their names on the calico tablecloth with markers: Elisabeth later embroidered over the signatures so they would stand out and last as a keepsake of the day.

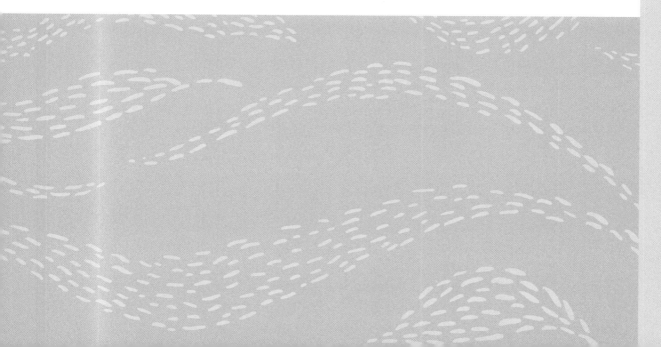

Milestones and Coming of Age

The major recurring theme of human life is change, and rites of passage help us to celebrate and fully experience each major change as it happens. By staging meaningful rites of passage for our children, starting at a young age, we teach them how to flexibly and creatively welcome change all their lives.

It has been said that modern societies have largely lost the ability to create deeply meaningful coming-of-age ceremonies. But I see many families and religious communities struggling to make workable contemporary rites of passage and often succeeding. And I think families can produce enormously powerful rites of their own.

Rites of Passage

Change is both scary and exciting. Our kids want to be "big," but they're frightened of that unknown place. Modest rituals can help them make the leap, and feel celebrated. Some children have a rough time with these transitions, but don't push or make them feel they've failed; celebrate that they're trying—and consult your pediatrician for advice.

Bye-Bye Pacifiers

To get her daughter to give up her "sissies," Andrea Majewski told the girl that if she left the pacifiers in a special box for the Easter bunny, she'd get extra treats. The box was set out on Easter eve, and next morning, sitting next to the Easter basket was the same box. The pacifiers were gone, but the box was full of special candy and a note from the Easter bunny about how grown up the girl was. The girl was thrilled, and her little brother was eager to follow this magical ritual a few years later.

Big Boy Day/ Big Girl Day

Experts say the best way to improve our kids' behavior is to "catch" them being good, and praise them immediately. If you're trying to help them grow out of a behavior like thumb sucking or needing a pacifier, talk about how once they get through an entire day without doing that, they'll be celebrated as "Big Boy (or Girl) of the Day" after supper. The celebration could include a treat food, a special crown, or a privilege like extra story time.

If there's a "big kid" activity they've been wanting to try such as a sport or helping you cook, pin that experience to a full week without the baby habit.

Bottles to Cups

Have the child help pick out a special "big girl" or "big boy" plastic cup, perhaps one illustrated with a favorite character. Tell him or her that new babies are being born in the world who really need their bottles. If there are no baby siblings, have them pretend to use a bottle to feed a doll or stuffed animal "baby." Pack up all the old bottles in a box and leave them inside the front door at bedtime: Help them invent a little good-bye song for the bottles. The next morning, serve the child's favorite drink in the new cup, with a fancy straw.

Tooth-Fairy Visits

According to the children's book *Throw Your Tooth on the Roof,* there have been prescribed rituals for disposal of baby teeth for ages, in countries all over the world. Some of the oldest rituals, like throwing the tooth over the roof, into the woods, or simply as far away as possible, had to do with superstitions about evil beings who might take a tooth and bewitch the child who lost it.

Two Fun Tooth-Fairy Resources

The website/blog called ToothFairy.org includes many fanciful posts about the tooth fairy and good information about the importance of brushing. There is an online shop here that sells tooth fairy themed books and other items.

Another site, OfficeOfTheToothFairy.com sells kits with very official looking "Certificates of Record" to write down all the important details–which tooth was lost, under what circumstances, and so on, with a tiny envelope attached to each certificate stamped with the words "Official Tooth-Fairy Deposit." (Obviously, you could use this as an idea to make your own official paperwork.)

The ritual of the tooth fairy is well established in this country, and many of us who grew up with the tooth fairy like to pass this tradition along to our kids. My son was given a sweet but simple tooth-fairy pillow as a toddler, which included a small pocket on the front into which he could insert the lost tooth before stowing the pillow next to him on the bed. When he awoke, there was a quarter or a dollar (depending on the tooth) in the pocket, and the tooth was gone.

There are lots of charming variations: Some families have the kids put their tooth in a jam jar or glass filled with water. When they awake, the tooth is gone, but the water has turned a pretty color and is full of sparkles, with some coins resting at the bottom. (This seems to be based on a Swedish ritual, according to *Throw Your Tooth on the Roof*.)

Confirmation Ritual

For many Christian families, this is a very special occasion, and there are myriad ways to celebrate. The nature of the ceremony will be much influenced by the family's church and that isn't what this book is for. But just to get families thinking about how to carry the celebration home, here is one family's idea.

Wanda Stahl bought a gift box at Target,

eight inches by eight inches, with an elastic ribbon and a butterfly on the top for her daughter's confirmation. She called it a "Blessing Box" and cut up pastel-colored card stock with decorative edged scissors into a pile of pretty blank cards, putting them next to the box on the coffee table in the living room. When everyone got back to the house after church, "I asked folks to write a blessing, prayer, scripture, good wish, etc., for Caitlin on a piece of the paper and put it in her box," says Wanda. "Later, I encouraged my daughter to use it for future remembrances or symbols of her faith journey, such as poems, Bible and inspirational quotes, and stones."

Braces

This has become an ever more common experience and often happens in those key middle school years when kids can be so self-conscious. In one sense, it's a transformative ritual and comes with a sense that sometimes a person has to go through unpleasant and uncomfortable trials to emerge as a better, older, more mature person.

Certainly, feel free to include those topics in your "Before" and "After" twin rituals, or just keep it playful. Many a mother has planned a "soft foods dinner" for after the braces are first applied, or subsequently tightened.

Laurel Van Ham used to schedule braces appointments right before lunch at her daughter's school, so that after she got them tightened, they could spend time relaxing at a pretty park. Meg Miller's braces ritual was to create a "time capsule" full of treats for after the braces would be removed—filled with sticky candy like taffy, gum, and Starbursts. And on days when the braces were tightened, she scheduled a ritual treat of soft ice cream.

Pierced Ears

How tribal does this feel? Here's a ritual in which one's body is pierced, allowing the wearing of a new type of ornament.

I will never forget that when I turned sixteen, my mother went with me to the doctor and we *both* got our ears pierced. (I had one of those cautious moms: We would *not* be doing this at the mall earring shop!)

Many families raising girls have to confront this decision eventually: At what age can their daughter get her ears pierced? I have one friend who made it contingent on her daughter's studying Latin, but usually it's more a personal decision about maturity.

Karly Randolph Pitman, decided that in their family, their two girls would have to be ten years old before they could get their ears pierced. And here is the beautiful part, at least to me: They couldn't have the privilege until after writing an essay about why they should be allowed to take this step. "My girls wrote about why it was important to them, and how they would take care of their ears," says Karly. "The oldest wrote about how having pierced ears would help her be creative. This all began because my husband said he needed persuading: He told them, 'Write an essay, and persuade me.'"

Then the girls started asking for cell phones. You know the next part: They have to write essays and persuade their father that this is a good idea.

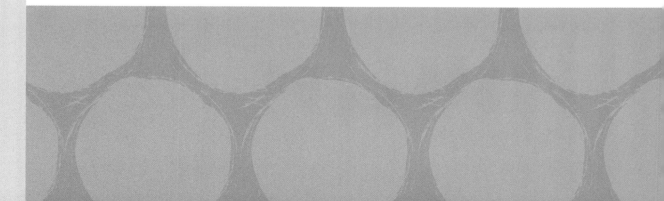

Coming-of-Age Rituals

First Period

The older our children get, the more vital it becomes that they help shape their role in any rituals they perform. That is especially true with coming-of-age rituals. After all, these rituals emerge from and celebrate a primal impulse to separate from one's parents. We defeat the purpose and power of such rites of passage if we deny our children a voice in how they ritually dramatize their coming independence.

Especially delicate is the question of creating ceremonies to celebrate a girl's first period. There are organizations around the country that stage group womanhood rituals involving girls and their parents. And this is fine, if the girl is comfortable with the idea. I've heard of some, for example, where fathers are present and make a crown to put on their daughter's head and express their love. But most of the teen girls I know are extremely shy about this private matter. However you honor this milestone, be sure to include some frank talk about the responsibilities that go along with this new stage in life and try to set the stage for continued openness.

Let me add that I received a little push-back after including this in the first edition. Some readers posted in online reviews that the very idea of creating a ceremony around a girl's first period seemed creepy. That's fine: Obviously, there are families and girls who would never want to do something like this. But for others who feel differently, perhaps this will inspire a thoughtful, meaningful ritual all your own that will make your daughter feel proud and mature. For those who are interested in a global perspective, Wikipedia provides a list of how families in many cultures mark this milestone: In Japan, the family eats red-colored rice and beans. In this country, the Mescalero Apaches still put on an eight-day ceremony with exhaustive dancing to celebrate girls who started menstruating in the previous year.

Private Time

DeeAnn Pochedly let her daughter play hooky the day she got her first period and took the girl out to lunch for a private celebration. As a gift, she gave her daughter pretty, colored underpants "to wear on those special days." DeeAnn says the event brought them closer: It was the first time in ages her daughter called her "Mommy."

Bejeweled

Marilyn Clark and her husband have accompanied each of their girls to a jewelry store to pick out a ring as soon as they started their period. Wearing the ring reminds the girls that their womanhood is worthy of celebration, but no one else needs to know the significance of the ring. I know another family in which the girls get rubies, the red being symbolic of blood.

Circle of Elders

In one Kentucky family, an all-women dinner is held when a girl is about to start menstruating. The older women share stories of their periods and offer advice. The girl is given gifts, and expected to phone all those women relatives when her period actually arrives.

A New Name

The Gardiner family of Stanchfield, Minnesota, takes this milestone very seriously and has created a detailed coming-of-age program. This might be awkward if there were any boys in the family, but with all girls, it's been lovingly embraced. Barbara Gardiner and her husband, Kevin, spend time with each girl before the period starts, reading and discussing a book called *The "What's Happening to My Body?" Book for Girls,* by Lynda Madaras, co-written with her

Tip: The overwhelming favorite book at the moment, which covers not just menstruation but healthy eating, body image, and a great deal more, is *The Care and Keeping of You* (American Girl Publishing), by Valorie Schaefer. A recommended book that focuses more tightly on this big life change is *The Period Book: Everything You Don't Want to Ask (But Need to Know).* It was co-written by Karen Gravelle and her fifteen-year-old niece, Jennifer.

daughter, Area. As a family, they talk about how the change to womanhood is also a time of mental and emotional challenge and encourage the girls to try new sports and other activities. Also, each girl is allowed to choose a new middle name, based on a sense of her emerging adult personality. On the day the blood comes, there is a special family dinner, Dad brings home flowers, and the girls get a special gift from Dad.

Flower Ceremony

There is a lovely first-period ritual for a mother and daughter in the book *I Am Woman by Rite: A Book of Woman's Rituals* by poet Nancy Brady Cunningham. On the same day the period starts, she suggests the girl and mother go to a quiet room after supper and light two red candles. Then the girl takes some red roses from a vase and cuts off the stems, symbolizing letting go of childhood. She lets the rose blossoms float in a glass bowl filled with water, "honoring her ability to bring forth life from her womb." Other elements suggested by Cunningham include giving the girl gifts of a new brush, comb, and mirror, and having the mother brush her hair. To suggest that womanhood will bring both sweet and bitter experiences, the mother feeds the girl a series of things from a spoon: bitter tea, salty water, and last, honey.

Coming-of-Age Rituals for Boys and Girls

In Japan, there is a national holiday every year to celebrate adulthood for those turning twenty. America has nothing like it, though some religious and ethnic groups have deeply meaningful coming-of-age rites. These include the bar mitzvah and bat mitzvah for Jewish children, the vision quest still practiced by many Native Americans, and the Quinceañera, a lavish celebration for fifteen-year-old girls in the Latino community.

Louise Carus Madhi, a Jungian analyst and editor of a compilation of essays called *Betwixt and Between: Patterns of Masculine and Feminine Initiation,* wrote: "The need for some kind of initiation is so important that if it does not happen consciously, it will happen unconsciously, often in a dangerous form."

Look no further than initiation rituals for street gangs—or college fraternities. Or consider the drinking games popular with those who want to celebrate turning twenty-one, the legal drinking age in most states. One drinking game that is all the rage is called "21 for 21," in which young people go into a bar at midnight and try to scarf down twenty-one shots in a row, while friends cheer them on. Some do not survive this "rite of passage."

Psychologist Julie Tallard Johnson calls that a "street initiation" and says it isn't the real deal. She explains that it doesn't qualify as a real rite of passage because it doesn't include a ritual to integrate the newly formed young adult back into his or her community and family. It isn't enough just to endure a harrowing trial. This topic is a difficult one for parents to confront, but here are some examples of what intrepid parents are doing to help their kids mature in a meaningful, but safely mentored way.

Manhood Trip

The summer after they turned thirteen, the sons of John Fergus-Jean of Columbus, Ohio, were taken on a three-week camping trip out west alone with their dad. The destination each time was Yellowstone Park, but the route wasn't pre-planned. Along the way, father and son read about Native American manhood rituals and talked about how boys don't have a single milestone to signify maturity, as girls do. Each boy found a "secret spot" within Yellowstone and engaged in a physical challenge, jumping from the cliffs above Fire Hole River. They both smoked their first cigar with their father and talked about the ritual history of tobacco and the importance of handling its power in an adult way. John says the trips deepened his relationships with both sons.

Cutting Dad's Hair

Richard Boardman, a guidance counselor from Wisconsin, wanted a hands-on ritual that would signify the passing on of power to his children. When they complete eighth grade, they give him "the haircut of their choice." He literally puts his head in their hands. Naturally, the kids love it, threatening wild hairstyles for months in advance, such as a pink Mohawk. The rules are that their father has to wear the resulting cut for a week without revisions, though he can wear a hat in public. (And if they are with him, they can ask him to remove the hat.) He has attracted quite the stares in church after the kids' cuts, the story goes.

To me, this is the sort of offbeat personal ritual that is truly unforgettable to kids. I also applaud Richard's ceremony because it follows my precepts about the emotional truth at the heart of a ritual. As a guidance counselor, he totally gets it—teen years are about kids testing boundaries and taking on their own power and reconfiguring their relationship to the next generation. He created a ritual that includes that testing, but in a playful way, one that conveys clearly he's open to the coming power shift.

African American Coming of Age

Charles Nabrit and Paula Penn-Nabrit of Columbus, Ohio, created an unusually rigorous and academic rite of passage for their sons. At thirteen, each of their three sons had to study scripture and African American history, reading sixteen assigned books and writing reports about them over six to nine months. Both a church ceremony and a party capped each boy's efforts, and the ceremony included a speech given by the boy to family and friends about "the future of black men in America." The Nabrit boys grumbled loudly while enduring this tradition, moaning that they had to rewrite their essays and that they didn't get a lot of new power once they completed the initiation (I bet lots of bat mitzvah boys would say the same thing). But they were confident and poised young men by the end, and every one later attended an Ivy League college.

Vision Quest: Adapting the Native American Tradition

When done creatively and with conviction, this ancient Native American tradition can translate powerfully into modern life. The basic elements of vision quest are similar to those of many tribal coming-of-age rituals around the world.

The ritual includes a period of preparation and learning with the help of a mentor/elder, followed by a difficult physical trial designed to push the initiate past his normal limits. Often, Native American questers go alone into the wilderness to fast for days, seeking a vision of their future (and a new name). They return, share stories about their experience, and are welcomed and celebrated as an adult by their tribe.

In our culture, it's important that the teens be treated differently in some way after the ritual by their parents, perhaps given new privileges in the household.

One Mother's Version of Vision Quest:

Before her oldest son turned thirteen, Diane Sanson of Malibu, California, decided she wanted to create a coming-of-age ritual for him and a group of his peers. The ritual took nine months to complete for five boys and their fathers. Once a month, the boys and men met in a "council," discussing everything from what it means to be a man in our society to the series of challenges the boys would undertake. The challenges included camping and kayaking. Each boy had to perform some sort of community service, and each kept a journal about the process and his dreams and goals. Several times, the boys were taken to a cliff above the ocean at dawn and given forty-five minutes of quiet time to work on their journals. There was also a "sweat lodge" ceremony, performed by a hired Native American guide, in which the boys sat in a canvas "lodge" full of steamy heat. A big party was the final event, at which each boy spoke about what he had learned, and what sort of man he wanted to become.

Tip: Vision Quest leaders aren't exactly board certified, and if they don't know what they're doing, they can do harm. Check credentials of any you plan to hire very carefully.

Vision Quest Resources

If your pre-teen or teen is interested in exploring this possibility, you won't find a better guidebook than *The Thundering Years: Rituals and Sacred Wisdom for Teens* by Julie Tallard Johnson, a Wisconsin psychotherapist. Among the many authorities who recommend this book, it has been praised by the Dalai Lama. It is packed with advice on meditation, writing a journal, and spiritual ways of exploring nature, but the section on rite-of-passage ceremonies is particularly strong.

Julie suggests that teens start planning their coming-of-age ritual months in advance, and that they choose a "wisdomkeeper," or mentor, "who represents the qualities of an adult that you aspire to." Like many experts, she says it can be difficult for parents to mentor their own child when the goal of the exercise is separating from the parent. She says the most important aspect of the trial or challenge is that it be "bigger than anything you've done before . . . Something that pushes you beyond your comfort level. By succeeding at this challenge, teens realize they are powerful and able to create their lives. They feel what it's like to push the limits without harming themselves or anyone else. This proves they are ready to be adults."

Here are some of the possible trials she suggests for an authentic rite of passage:

- sleeping under the stars alone
- running a race, a marathon, or a designated distance alone
- giving a performance of some kind
- doing your first hunt
- writing an article for the local paper
- climbing a mountain, rafting, or kayaking (all which you've prepared for)
- creating some artistic piece (painting, sculpture, poetry, a play)

School of Lost Borders:
Serious Rites of Passage for Teens

If you have the kind of kid who really wants to test himself or herself, the School of Lost Borders has been running serious wilderness vision quests for more than thirty years. Co-founders Steven Foster and Meredith Little lead a well-trained team that also does wilderness spiritual quests for groups of adults.

Young people between sixteen and twenty-two spend ten days on a vision quest that includes three days and nights in the California desert without food or shelter. A great deal of preparation is done before the kids trek off, and there are reintegration ceremonies after the ordeal.

Find out more at SchoolofLostBorders.org, where you can see videos of teens talking about what the quest was like for them.

Steven Foster has written multiple books, including *The Book of the Vision Quest: Personal Transformation in the Wilderness.*

Plate-Breaking Ritual for Turning Eighteen

You may have been to a Greek or other ethnic wedding where part of the ritual was the breaking of a plate or plates. In many cultures this is done to symbolize the break in the dependent relationship of child to parents: Mom and Pop are no longer going to be the meal ticket.

The Englebert family of Joplin, Missouri, does something like this when their kids turn eighteen. "Our family chooses to celebrate that transition (from childhood to adulthood) with a plate-breaking ceremony to symbolically represent our child leaving their childhood behind and venturing into the unknown adult world, where they will be responsible for themselves," father Steve Englebert says. "When we do the ceremony, we always say: 'From this point forward, everything we do for you is because we love you, not because we have to.'"

A special ceremonial plate is prepared with sayings painted on it such as "Childhood . . . when you know where your next meal is coming from" and "No Free Food." After a fine meal, jokingly called "The Last Meal," the family troops outside. Part of the tradition is that the coming-of-age child comically refuses to let go of the plate, and there is a crazy tug of war with a parent, until the plate gets smashed on the ground (with a bedsheet underneath so shards don't fly). The celebration continues with cake, ice cream, and gifts for the eighteen-year-old. One ritual gift is a note-card binder given to each child called "Book of Wisdom": Any family member over eighteen is allowed to share his or her wisdom in the book. Each kid saves a chunk of broken plate as a memento.

Steve says he and his wife, Virginia, have always tried to create lots of fun rituals to build bonds in their blended family: The six children include two each from a previous marriage, and two they had together. Five of the Englebert kids have experienced the plate-breaking tradition now—just one more to go.

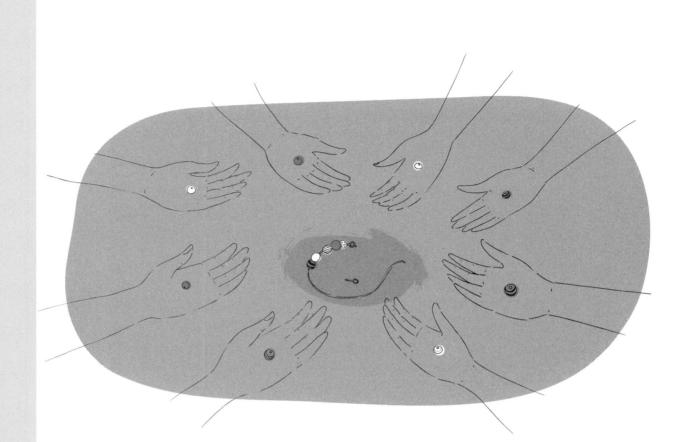

Bead Ritual

Linda in Tucson, Arizona, wanted to do something special when her daughter turned eighteen. She didn't want to call it a ritual, because her daughter and friends might think that un-cool, so she just called it a party. Beforehand, she cleared all the usual furniture from her family room, scrubbed the floor, put a low round table in the middle, and spread pillows all around it. "Then I filled the room with so many candles that it glowed. We did not use one artificial light. I had asked each of her friends and family members to bring one bead and say something they loved about her or wished for when they gave it to her. Then we strung a bracelet right there at the table (which meant going to a bead store and getting wire and clasps and having a small pair of pliers handy). She told me a few days later it was the best part of her eighteenth birthday, way better than the facial someone treated her to, or being allowed to stay out all night."

Bead Basics

Beads have been used in rituals for thousands of years, including religious rituals, so they evoke a sense of history and layers of meaning. This same principle of having many people come with a special bead is extremely versatile for family milestone celebrations. I know a woman who was about to undergo chemotherapy for breast cancer, and she had a ceremony in which each of her friends brought a bead and said a prayer over it. She wanted to take this string of brightly colored beads with her, to be cheered by their colors and have something concrete to hold during her treatments. And I know women who followed a similar template for their baby shower.

There's a great website, FireMountainGems.com, that has been selling beads in its store and online for many years. The website is packed with how-to videos and advice for getting started and doing simple beading. You can buy beads and all the attendant supplies, such as wire and the metal fixtures to create a bracelet or necklace. Or, you can check out your local bead store.

A special source for beautiful beads is Beads of Courage, a nonprofit begun by a pediatric oncology nurse to celebrate and encourage kids with cancer. There is a codified system practiced in eighty hospitals in which kids who sign up for the program get specific beads for particular treatments: white for chemo, brown for losing your hair, a glow-in-the-dark bead for radiation. To raise money, the charity sells exquisite artist-made beads on its website: BeadsOfCourage.org.

How to Make a Ribbons-of-Love Curtain

When someone we love reaches a significant milestone, we are sometimes at a loss how to celebrate. Just getting a fancier gift than usual seems insufficient. This is a ritual gift that also provides a ritual activity and is best done when you want the celebrated person to feel embraced by a whole community of family and friends. It would be a great activity to cap a coming-of-age ritual.

Materials

Extra-wide ribbon in bright colors (from a craft or sewing store), cut in four-foot lengths

Glue

Pens or markers

A wooden dowel rod, one-half to one inch in diameter and from three to six feet long, depending on how many people will participate

Instructions

When you are finished, the dowel rod will be covered by a row of bright ribbons, hanging down like a beaded curtain. Unlike a maypole, where all the ribbons are attached to the top of a vertical pole, these ribbons will dangle down all along a horizontal pole. The ribbons will have writing on them: Every family member and friend will take one ribbon and be given instructions on what to write, such as "something you wish for (the celebrated person) in the future" or "a quality you love about (the person)." For many milestone celebrations in our lives, there are friends and family who simply cannot come, so you'll want to send ribbons by mail ahead of time, for those who can't make it but want to express their love. (And you can always add some ribbons after the event, if they don't arrive till after the party.)

You may choose to attach the ribbons ahead of time and present the finished ribbon curtain to the honoree, or you could opt to make the finishing of the curtain part of your celebration. Perhaps each celebrant could come forward with his or her ribbon, reading out the sentiments written there. In any case, you will wrap the ribbon around the rod and attach it using craft or fabric glue: Make sure the ribbon reaches over the top and covers part of the back of the wooden rod.

When completed, this ribbon curtain will be a gorgeous keepsake that can be hung in the child's room on two hooks or nails.

More Coming-of-Age Rituals for Girls

Sparklers in the Sand

The day my niece Jenny turned thirteen, her mother and I were sharing a condo on the beach in North Carolina, so I created a ceremony there. We asked Jenny to write down things and feelings from her childhood she was ready to leave behind, and she took these private papers and threw them in the ocean. After dark, I drew a circle in the sand, marking it with shells, candles, and sparklers, and we stood in the middle, facing each other. I brought a bottle of red (for blood) wine, and poured us each a little. As the sparklers burned, I toasted Jenny and spoke about the awesome woman I knew she would become. We sat on the beach for a long time afterward, talking. Later, I gave Jenny thirteen symbolic gifts, including a tiny globe, in the hope she will travel a lot, a red rose for her beauty, and so on.

Scarf Ceremony

This would work well for a group of girlfriends and family, as part of a celebration. Instruct each invitee to bring a beautiful scarf for the girl, something light in weight like chiffon or silk. Tie all the scarves together, making one long, colorful "rope." As the girl stands still, have her hold one end of the scarf rope, while the girls and women wrap it around and around her, covering her. Tell her that as she moves forward through life, into independence, she will always be embraced by this community of loving women. Then, help her unwrap the scarves, and run forward, trailing them like a banner.

Circle of Love

I love the smooth solidity of river rocks. If you don't live near a river, you can buy them by the pound from a plant nursery or landscaper. Buy enough for each person attending your ceremony, and let everybody paint one word on a rock with permanent paint. The word could be something you hope for that girl. Have the participants place the stones in a circle around the honored girl, one rock at a time. Standing in a bigger circle, the girls and women can give toasts or words of love. Later, the girl can display the rocks in a bowl or plant them in a garden.

Gift of Inspiration for Teenagers Who Only Want Money

When my nieces and nephews hit the teen years, I no longer had the magic touch when it came to picking out gifts. I didn't know their taste in music or clothes and they wanted to have the pleasure of shopping for the *exact right thing*.

Thus began a period where I usually sent them a check or a prepaid credit card when a gift was called for. But on milestone birthdays like eighteen and twenty-one, I still wanted to give them something memorable, something that would last longer than the cute boots or the latest video game.

I created "Money-Plus," a tradition of writing down things on narrow slips of pretty paper, then folding those papers into little scrolls with money rolled inside. For significant birthdays, I would use $5 bills (getting new crisp ones from the bank), and there would be one money-plus-message scroll for each year. The comments written on the papers were all of a kind: Either they were all things I wished for that child, or aspects of his or her character and personality that I wanted to applaud. In other words, "things I love about you" or "things I hope for you." Each scroll was tied with a ribbon, and then I would put all of the scrolls inside a small, pretty box, maybe a wooden one from the Ten Thousand Villages store. I have no clue whether this went according to my wishes, but my hope was that my dear niece and nephew would save all the messages in the pretty box and reread them in the future.

Rituals for New Drivers

Car accidents are the leading cause of death for teenagers, but studies show that "parental involvement" can reduce the risks. Special rituals can help you celebrate the milestone of a first driver's license while preparing your kids for a huge new responsibility. In our culture of speed and mobility, earning a driver's license is a major rite of passage and deserves to be recognized as such.

Prayer for a New Driver

In the Vogt family, a new driver is celebrated with a brief ceremony in which the teen is given not only a personal car key but a house key as well. The ceremony is part of a special dinner, with treat foods. Most of the family's rituals include a religious element, and this one is no exception. Susan Vogt's simple prayer goes: "God bless our child as he gains independence at this new stage in life, and bless this car, and keep our son safe in his travels."

Fitting Gifts

Whether you celebrate with a little family party or dinner out, there are a number of things that would make meaningful gifts for a new driver, such as a special key ring. In addition, you might give a fancy set of tools and safety gear, things like flares.

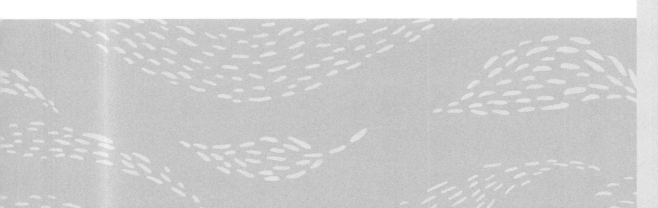

A New-Driver Contract

However you celebrate, one vital aspect of the ceremony is the solemn signing of a pact between the parents and the new driver. The elements should be discussed and understood in advance, but you may want to read it aloud and have the new driver verbally agree to each statement, like taking a vow. The glove compartment might be a good place to keep the contract, as a reminder.

Usually, such contracts include an agreement to observe all motor vehicle laws. Sometimes they spell out the consequences of breaking such laws. In the Chesto family, each kid was allowed one speeding ticket and one fender-bender, but anything beyond that resulted in reduced driving privileges.

Other ideas for the contract: regulation of how many passengers are allowed, how far the teenager is allowed to drive, and rules for driving after dark.

Here is a contract written by one of Kathy Chesto's daughters, when she was a teenager. It could easily be modified:

- I believe that driving a car is a serious responsibility, to myself, to passengers in the car, to those in other vehicles, to pedestrians, and to the environment.

- I believe that traffic laws have been made for our protection, and I will obey them.

- I believe that others have as much right to the road as I do, and I will attempt to always be courteous.

- I believe that a car is a means of transportation, not a symbol of power, and I will use it wisely and share in the responsibility of being a driver in this family.

- I believe that a car is an expense that should be shared justly by all who use it.

- I believe that the less parents know, the more they worry, and I will try my best to call when I am late and keep them informed.

Graduations

All graduations are rites of passage. And though I remember laughing at lavish graduation ceremonies for five-year-olds, I did give a pizza party when my son finished nursery school. For each child, I made a "medal," which consisted of a gold construction-paper star, to which I glued a blue ribbon. "Crossroads Graduate" was written in the star's center, and each child had one of these draped around his or her neck.

A high school graduation is another thing entirely. Indeed, it's one of the only ceremonial occasions (outside of weddings) for which we still dress up. Wearing caps and gowns as they walk alone past a roomful of classmates and family, teenagers find themselves physically enacting the crossing of a major threshold toward independence and adulthood. For many, it's a powerful emotional experience.

But I think families can do a lot to enhance that experience, helping their graduates to celebrate their past and eagerly anticipate the future, to acknowledge in some ceremonial way that though a separation is coming, the love and devotion of the family will follow them wherever life's journey takes them.

High School Graduation Letters

Three months before her daughter graduated from high school, Betty Ruddy sent a note to the girl's relatives and close family friends asking them to write a letter in honor of her graduation. Some wrote the girl advice for the future, and others shared favorite memories of her childhood. One aunt sent a poem; another made up a mock "report card" charting the girl's triumphs and character traits. Betty gathered all these papers into a beautiful box and presented it to the girl as one of her graduation gifts. "She was in tears before she unfolded the third letter," says Betty.

Dutch Tradition: Garland for the Graduate

Janneke Van der Ree grew up in Holland and loves the Dutch tradition called "slingers," which are garlands, long strings of ribbon on which hang colorful triangular flags. These garlands are often used for birthdays and other milestones like baby showers, and the simple, store-bought ones are often made of plastic or paper. Janneke, who is an excellent seamstress and quilter, decided to make a special slinger for her daughter's high school graduation. She made the triangle-shaped, three sided flags out of fabric, attached to a long string of bias tape. For her girl, Janneke printed some special photographs on paper and attached them to the fabric, and she made some individual flags out of old dresses, linens, and other mementos, even Girl Scout badges. Her daughter loved the brightly colored, highly personal garland, which is a portable memento she can keep hanging in her room at home or take off to college.

Great Graduation Gifts to Start in Kindergarten

Novelist Jean Hanff Korelitz writes a letter every year to her children on their birthdays and keeps them sealed and hidden away. Another mother I know asked each of her children's teachers to write a letter about her child at year's end, and she saves all those letters from kindergarten on. High school graduation is a logical time to gather together such material that documents a complete childhood, along with a collage of school photos from every year, and present them to your amazed child.

Let me add a confession here: I heard about the year-end letter idea when my son was in first grade, but in the chaos of a busy life (and an unwillingness to stalk teachers who didn't follow through), I only managed to secure letters from three or four of his grade-school teachers. Never mind: Each letter is wonderfully specific and heartfelt, and I can't wait to give them to Max when he graduates from high school in 2013. As we quilters like to say to one another, "Done is better than perfect."

Framed Needlepoint: The Tassel Is Worth the Hassle

Kunni Biener made a needlework sampler for each of her children before graduation. It included the name of the child, the school, and the date, all in school colors, and the inscription: "The Tassel Is Worth the Hassle." She put a tiny mortarboard on the sampler with a small button on top of it, which was a place for the grad to hang said tassel.

College Acceptance Celebration

Martha Hess, a mother of six in Utah, had a special ritual to celebrate her children's college acceptance. She got sweatshirts from that college for the whole family, prepared a big family dinner, then took a group photo of the whole clan in their matching sweatshirts. When the time came to depart for college in the fall, a framed copy of that photo was packed in that kid's luggage.

Bonfire of Childhood

As part of a party involving a group of close friends, you might build a fire (in a safe place) and have all the graduates write on slips of paper those aspects of their childhoods they are ready to let go.

Knowledge Threshold

Think of a special threshold you can create that is symbolic of where your teenager is headed next. If your son is headed off to mechanic's school, you might get big sheets of cardboard and paint car logos or a car engine on the front. Tape the cardboard over the entrance to a door and give the graduate a knife, telling him he has to "cross the threshold " to his future. If your child is heading to college, create a threshold using sheets or cardboard that is a listing of great works of literature or other subjects that child is likely to seek out.

Gifts of Values

One of the greatest gifts we give our children over the years is the values we teach and share. Find a way to symbolically present your graduating teen with a reminder of the gifts of character they

Pitch-Perfect Gift for
Milestone Rituals: VoiceQuilt

Note to readers: I'm not a shill for any company, but I wanted to include this idea and this product because of multiple rewarding experiences with it.

Whether you're celebrating a high school or college graduation, a milestone birthday, baby shower, or major anniversary, a terrific gift that can also become part of the event is something called a VoiceQuilt. The way these work is that a bunch of family and friends are directed to call a toll-free number and leave a voice mail message for the person being celebrated. All the messages are assembled into a sort of audio playlist (like those on an iPod) by whomever is leading the tribute, and that person can add a beginning and ending message. For example: "Hello, sweetheart, this is your mother, and I've put together a special tribute on this big occasion and called on some of your nearest and dearest to give you advice on life as you leave for college. . . ."

The finished VoiceQuilt can just be burned onto a CD, but typically, people order a handsome wooden gift box for the recipient. The box looks a bit like a music box, and when the lid is lifted, the messages began to play. There's space inside the box for small tokens or gifts, and there's a paper naming all the speakers. These also work wonderfully for retirements: When the minister of my church retired, they got over seventy people to record messages, and the children's choir sang several of the minister's favorite hymns as their message.

When my husband had a major birthday, I gave him a VoiceQuilt, and he said it was probably the best gift he ever received. He was so moved to hear everything from his two-year-old granddaughter singing him silly songs to his elderly aunt sending her love to his cousin Larry saying that in their childhood arguments about "who was the best cowboy," my husband was actually right. Not all his extended family members could come to the actual party, but we played all the messages and sat together laughing (and crying) alongside the birthday boy: It was memorable.

You'll find the details at VoiceQuilt.com.

carry inside, such as giving them a slim, blank book in which you write one value on each page. When Kathleen Chesto's children went off to college, she gave each one a basket of essentials for dorm life, things like shampoo and a dustpan. As she gave them the gifts, she voiced a parental wish with each one: "I give you this soap. Never be afraid to get your hands dirty in the service of others."

Special Twenty-First Birthday Ritual for a Loved One Far from Home

Much as parents want to be there to celebrate their kids when they hit that major milestone of adulthood, turning twenty-one, often their child is off at college or perhaps working a job far from home.

Alma Fisher of Lake Bluff, Illinois, came up with a brilliant plan to celebrate her son Scott's twenty-first birthday when he was away at college, but it involved a lot of forethought. About a year before the big day, Alma was already busy searching for perfect cards because she was going to buy one for every single year of Scott's life. She wanted each card to reflect something that had happened to him in a particular year. One example: On Scott's fifth birthday, a friend of his slammed the door of the tree house on Scott's fingers, and at the time, he felt his parents underplayed the injury because they didn't want the *other* kid to feel bad. So the card for that year showed a little boy with a suitcase walking out the front door of his house.

Also important was the way the cards were delivered: They started arriving at Scott's fraternity twenty-one days before his birthday. Enclosed with the first card was a photo of Scott as an infant and a letter from his mother recounting the story of his birth. There was also $1 in the envelope. Next day, Scott got another card and another letter, a photograph from his second year of life and $2. So it went, day after day. By the day of his birthday, Scott Fisher had collected $231 in cash, the story of his life in words and pictures, and a demonstration of motherly love he will never forget.

Later, Scott told his mother, "I can't begin to tell you how much this meant." He saved everything she sent, and he's planning to follow the same ritual someday for his own children.

CHAPTER 4

Holidays

Every ritual and tradition we practice is a distillation of our identities, and a vivid expression of the lessons we want to teach our children. The little rituals we do every day accumulate a quiet power and make a deep impression over the years, but they are like the pop songs of life, whereas holidays give parents a chance to create something more on the scale of an opera: monumental, bold, and unforgettable. Kids everywhere look forward to the major holidays with great anticipation, and holidays are always an opportunity to move family to center stage, whether your traditions are loud or quiet, intimate or crowded, secular or religious.

The same principles laid out for daily, weekly, and monthly rituals apply here as well: be thoughtful and intentional in your approach, balancing out the edicts of your religion, ethnicity, and family history with loads of personal touches. Start by thinking not just about what foods you'll prepare or how you will decorate your house, but what messages you want your children to soak up from the proceedings. What are the overarching two or three themes that underlie all your holiday celebrations? And what are the major themes within each one?

Never forget that traditions are people made, and by nature they are always works in progress. Don't be afraid to make changes as your kids grow up, or to drop and add not just specific traditions, but entire holidays, as you go forward.

Party on!

You Have My Permission to Change How You Celebrate

Warning: Holidays can be harmful to your health and sanity!

It's not surprising that plays and movies often show family psychodramas bursting out into the open on major holidays like Thanksgiving and Christmas. It's not only that we're often thrust together with more members of our extended families and conflicts can arise, but we also have such high expectations. We've seen all the sentimental movies, magazines, and commercials about family holidays, and most of us have wonderful childhood memories of intense anticipation and excitement. Often, parents have worked very hard ahead of time to create memorable gatherings, and if something goes wrong, we feel crushed. Or exhausted. Or both.

So, before getting into fun ideas for celebrating lots of different special holidays, here are a couple of ways to prevent holiday burnout.

If you are celebrating something for the first time, don't overdo it. Be realistic in the number of activities you plan, the number of people you invite, and the number of new recipes you decide to prepare.

If you're celebrating an occasion you've marked previously, when it is getting close, do a quick evaluation of how it went the last time or last couple of times. Ask other members of the family, too, for their suggestions. If it felt overwhelming, figure out which foods, activities, and decorations were the most fun and rewarding, and skip a couple of the others. Sometimes more is less.

Just because something has been a tradition in your family for years doesn't mean it has to be in the future. There are many different reasons for making drastic, as well as minor, changes. Perhaps your children have outgrown the annual Easter egg hunt or are too old to leave cookies and milk for Santa. Maybe the matriarch or patriarch of the family has died, or moved, and you need to change both where and how you celebrate. Or maybe someone who has been doing the heavy lifting tradition-wise is injured or suffering from a chronic illness.

When author and family educator Kathleen Chesto was diagnosed with multiple sclerosis in 1986, she had to make considerable changes to her holiday plans. Her kids were old enough to be able to help with the cooking, so she put this question to them: Would you like to prepare our traditional feast yourselves, or should we pick a new menu that's doable for me? They chose the latter, so the family switched from turkey to roast beef for Thanksgiving. Kathleen says it was a positive exercise because the whole family realized that being together was the centerpiece of their holidays and was more important than what they ate. They revisited the issue later, and when the kids got a little older, they switched back to more elaborate menus: They were ready to do the cooking themselves.

One more example: I know a family that had stopped celebrating Christmas together. The parents had divorced when the children were young but in later years still insisted on having fancy, formal dinners together for holidays. Everyone was miserable, suffered from indigestion, and began to dread the holidays. When the kids grew up, they all went their separate ways. But when they began to have children of their own, one sibling raised the idea of getting together for Christmas. The response was: only if we can completely reinvent the ritual for our generation. The new tradition is the opposite of their childhood dinners, a completely informal seafood feast. They throw tablecloths on the floor, eat with their hands, drink a lot of wine, and laugh a lot.

For Families of Divorce

As painful as divorce generally is, holidays rub salt in the wounds. They are fresh reminders of what's been lost, and there are often awkward negotiations about who gets the children during what hours, on which days. If everyone is willing to be reasonable (a major "if"), then some kind of cooperative rotating system is created. I'm not equipped to suggest formulas, and people's lives and preferences vary widely, but I think the real watchword is flexibility. This is the time to make delicious lemonade and invent yourself a whole new holiday, if need be. I know of a stepmom who wondered how she could celebrate

Christmas with her stepdaughter on the weekend before the holiday without confusing her two young sons. She came up with a creative idea that was sensitive to everyone: When the stepdaughter comes for the weekend, the family celebrates "Practice Christmas." Santa fills the stockings for all three kids, brings multiple gifts for the stepdaughter and a token gift for each of the two boys. They all loved the new holiday immediately and have celebrated that way for more than a decade.

As a mother and a stepmother, I've grown accustomed to celebrating the major holidays in more than one venue, and I've learned to roll with it. Sometimes Thanksgiving is at my house, and other times we head to my husband's ex-wife's house. Because she's a much better cook than I am, this is more pleasure than hardship, and I know my sausage stuffing and pumpkin pie are welcome additions. Now that my stepdaughter is grown, she alternates Christmas holidays between her husband's family in New Mexico and her parents. But even if she isn't celebrating Christmas at our house, her mom will be here, enjoying Christmas morning with us and bringing along her mouthwatering puff pastry angels. Naturally, one of the six stockings that I made and hang on the fireplace mantel every year has her name on it.

I learned long ago that nobody likes a "traditions dictator," even if it's somebody who gets paid to write about celebrations. So I'm careful not to push my ritual agenda on others in my blended family. But I do take time to consider which ones are the most central to my own appreciation of a given holiday. With Thanksgiving, I insist that the three of us find a time to make our usual Thankfulness Tree (described later in this chapter), but if we aren't eating turkey at home, we may create the tree the night before or even the day after Thanksgiving. (I remember one time when my son was little and we were having Thanksgiving elsewhere, and at a one point he grabbed my hand and said, "Let's go sit on the porch and talk about the things we're grateful for!")

Celebrating Holidays

New Year's Celebrations

New Year's Family Blast

A great way to celebrate the coming of the New Year is to pay tribute to the year ending, while also welcoming the new year. Have a family-focused party and choose things from the following menu of ritual activities, depending on how much time you have and what suits you. Add your favorite food, drinks, music, and decorations.

Depending on your preference and the ages of your kids, you can do this either on New Year's Eve or New Year's Day. If your kids want to ring in the new year but can't stay up till midnight, turn the clocks ahead.

Review the Past Year

Sitting at the kitchen table or the family room sofa, look together at all the family photos you took in the past year and watch any family videos you made. Then, everybody gets a chance to vote on the best and worst day of the past year. Also, everybody fills out this list:

My most embarrassing moment this year was when I . . .

I should have had my photo on the cover of *People* magazine because I . . .

You guys can be annoying, but you really came through for me when . . .

Give annual family awards for "best athlete," "worst school picture." Use your imagination for more awards.

Make Resolutions

Cut small strips of paper half an inch wide and about six inches long. Take whole walnuts from a bag of mixed nuts in the shell and, using nutcrackers, carefully open the nuts and remove the nutmeats inside. Each person makes three resolutions and writes each one on a paper strip, which is then carefully folded and put into the nut. Glue each nut closed. Using markers, each person writes his or her name on a nut.

This idea comes from the Hilton family of Henderson, Nevada, and they glue ribbons into their walnuts and use them to decorate their Christmas tree. They reuse the same nuts every year, and once they started the practice, they began a tradition of reading last year's resolutions aloud before writing new ones. That way they can review how well they've done. Nanette Hilton, the mother of four daughters, says she thinks it's great for her girls to see that "life is fluid. They see Mommy and Daddy working on goals, too . . . and sometimes failing."

Best and Worst List

We fill out the same survey every year. On New Year's Day, it's great fun not only to compare notes on the year just ended but to see what we all loved and hated in past years.

These are the questions we always ask:

- Best thing that happened to you?
- Worst thing that happened to you?
- Best thing you accomplished?
- Best thing you did for another person?
- Best movie you saw? Worst movie?
- Best book you read?
- Best TV program of the past year?
- What current events of the past year will make history?
- What will you remember most about this year?
- Name three things you hope for most in the new year.

First Footing: A Scottish Tradition

The Sanford family of Warren, Vermont, likes to honor its Scottish roots with a New Year's tradition called "First Footing," tied to ancient superstitions about the first person to cross one's threshold in a new year. It was said to be good luck if the person was a dark, handsome man, and typically, that person would walk into a house just after midnight carrying symbolic gifts of food, whiskey, salt, and coal.

Jim Sanford, a Vermont architect with three sons, decided early on that he wanted to have one special tradition that was exclusive for each of his kids. First Footing was done with Owen, his dark-haired middle son, from the age of seven. (When Owen grew up and left home, his younger brother, Cooper, took over.)

They break with tradition by doing this on New Year's morning, but the items they bring are true to their roots: bread (or a traditional sweet cake made by the boys' mother),

Scotch whiskey, logs (instead of coal, but also for warmth), and salt. Jim added cashews as well, to "promote a sense of humor" in the new year (nuts, get it?). And Jim and his son both wear kilts.

Except for reading aloud from a card explaining the ritual, the Sanfords don't talk much, which is especially interesting when they come to a neighbor's house for the first time. They come to the door without calling ahead, knock, bring the items to the kitchen, and Jim reads the card. Typically, he'll pour two shots of whiskey, toast the head of the house, and then the son and father leave.

"I love that this is unique to us," says Jim Sanford. "Lots of folks send Christmas cards, but who goes around drinking Scotch with their friends at 8:30 AM on New Year's Day?" (Just so you know, this nonconformist also likes to wear a tie every year on the first day of deer-hunting season—to show respect for the deer.)

Toast the New Year

Use plastic wine or champagne glasses but serve sparkling water or cider to the kids. All family members get to make a toast, saying one thing they hope happens in the new year to himself or herself, the family, or the wider world. End with a shared family toast "To the (Name) Family!"

Celebrate with a Burst

It's an ancient tradition to open the doors (and sometimes windows) to let the New Year and good luck into your home. It's also a tradition to make lots of noise, so get wooden spoons and bang on pots, pound drums, and ring any bells you have. Make a tissue paper banner to tape across the opening to the family room, and at midnight (on your family's clock), burst through the paper, holding hands.

Balloon Treasure Frenzy

In Texas, the Minich family loves to make noise by bursting balloons, but the balloons are also full of "treasure," a good omen for a prosperous year ahead. Beforehand, the parents purchase about 500 balloons and fill them with a piece of candy or a coin, with a few containing dollar bills. They're inflated with an inexpensive, handheld balloon pump, then stuffed into a room that has mostly been emptied of furniture. At midnight, the family's kids and sometimes their friends get the signal to dive in, when their mother tosses in some extra quarters and nickels among the balloons.

Family Unity Day

Perhaps while working on your resolutions, you might also spend some fun time thinking about your family as a tribe or team and brainstorm along those lines:

- **Invent a family song, chant, cheer, rap, or motto.**
- **Design, make, and hang a family shield, using symbols from your ethnic heritage, religious traditions, and shared passions.**
- **Have everyone finish this sentence: "Members of the (insert last name) family are known for (fill in the blank)." Make the list as long as you can, then vote on the top three or four choices, which can be serious or silly, or some of both. Actually, if you do this exercise first, you'll be better prepared for the chant and the shield.**

Dinner Day

This has been a declared state holiday in Pennsylvania since 2002. On the second Saturday in January, every family is supposed to invite a neighbor family of slight acquaintance for supper. The man behind the idea is Jeffrey Smith, a Doylestown-based software designer, who came up with the idea after the 9/11 tragedy. The homepage of the DinnerDay.com site says: "Invite your neighbor to dinner as a celebration of the values that make America a terrific place to live. Ask a neighbor you've never met or one you've only waved at, but never taken the time to get to know. Take a moment to break some bread together in one of your homes or out on the town. Either way, be sure to build a bridge to your neighbors and take down any fences that have kept you apart."

Try this idea yourself, even if you live in a different state or another date works better for you. As Jeffrey Smith told *Cooking Light* magazine in 2008, "You can change the fabric of your neighborhood, give something special to yourself, your community and the world, just by stopping neighbors in the street and inviting them to dinner."

January 18: Celebrate the Birthday of A. A. Milne, *Winnie the Pooh* Author

Getting a sense that there is a person who creates the books and characters we love is a great way to make reading special and personal. Kids love knowing that A. A. Milne wrote the books about his real-life son, Christopher Robin, and his stuffed animals. In addition, mid-January is a good time for a party, deep in the winter doldrums. When my son was young, this was probably his favorite thing to celebrate other than Christmas and his birthday,

Setup

Spread a picnic blanket or bedsheet on the floor of the family room or playroom. If there are any stuffed animals in the household from the Hundred Acre Wood (Pooh, Piglet, Tigger, Eeyore, or others), place them on the blanket, along with paper plates or plastic ones from a child's tea set.

Foods

Because Pooh loves honey, serve honey graham crackers or honey cookies. We have Pooh cookie cutters and a book of Pooh recipes, so we always ate honey cookies in the shapes of Piglet and Tigger and the rest. If blowing out candles is important, use a cupcake. Drinks could be juice or herbal tea with honey.

Activities

Sing "Happy Birthday" to A. A. Milne, then blow out any candles and eat treat foods. Read some of Milne's work, either the classic books *Winnie the Pooh* and *The House at Pooh Corner,* or his poems "When We Were Very Young" and "Now We Are Six." There are also some terrific, practical Pooh books from Disney, such as *Oh Bother, Someone's Messy*. If someone wrote a book about the stuffed animals in your house, what adventures would they have? Imagine the titles.

Some Other Favorite Authors and Their Birthdays

March 2: Dr. Seuss

How about green eggs and ham for breakfast or dinner?

June 10: Maurice Sendak

Have a Wild Things party!

July 31: J. K. Rowling

This is also the birthday of her best-known character, Harry Potter. Have a magic-themed birthday, and go find a Pumpkin Juice recipe at Mugglenet.com. (If you can't find fresh pumpkin in July, use a can of pumpkin puree.)

Snow Day Rituals

There are two kinds here: rituals to *make it snow,* and rituals for celebrating at home when school is closed.

Making It Snow

Somehow, this is a trend/superstition that has spread like wildfire, and there are a bunch of variations that kids use all over the country to make it snow overnight. Among them are: wearing your PJs inside out and backward, flushing ice cubes down the toilet one at a time, sleeping with a spoon under your pillow (some say the spoon must go in the freezer first; one family I know uses a potato instead of a spoon). It is widely agreed that there must also be some sort of Snow Day Dance. For tips on that, there are YouTube videos, plus several children's books about Snow Day Dances.

Snowed-In Rituals

When Max was little, I started baking gingerbread with a light lemon frosting on every snow day, using the wonderful recipe in *The Silver Palate Cookbook.* What's great about gingerbread is that it is quick and easy to make, plus all that cinnamon and molasses smells so fabulous after you come in the house from sledding and snowman building. If there are a slew of snow days during the winter, we skip the gingerbread baking and enjoy our leftovers.

A Snow Day potluck: One year, after an especially heavy snow that made driving impossible but didn't shut off the power, our neighbors decided to have a potluck dinner and cook up a big ham they had on hand. People brought what food and drink they had, and we sat around the fireplace and got to know many of our neighbors for the first time. It was magical!

Valentine's Day

Valentine's Garden of Sweets

Lori Prew's kids love her Valentine's Garden. She grabs a small planter, fills it with actual potting soil, then her children "plant" Valentine seeds (those candies called Red Hots). Every day, they water the seeds. On Valentine's Day, they wake up to a miracle: the seeds have grown to full sized lollipops, which they "harvest."

Treats Undercover

Pam Skripak says that on Valentine's Day, family members give each other cards and small gifts. All these items are placed underneath their plates, which are turned upside down. They sit down to eat a special meal, and all of them lift their plates simultaneously to reveal the surprises they hid for each other.

A Valentine for Nature

On this day when you declare your love and affection, make a heart in your backyard or in a local park or on a favorite trail. Shape it out of materials at hand, like pinecones or twigs or rocks. Or bring along biodegradable food like cranberries, so you will also be leaving a treat for local wildlife. Snap a photograph of your heart art before you leave: Turn it into a homemade card for someone you love, or post it on Facebook.

Valentine Tree

Trees are a great centerpiece of ritual action because they grow and change like families do, symbolize life and hope, and can be easily but beautifully decorated for any season or occasion. Every year, the Dodge family buys a small tree in a pot, such as a three-foot-tall pine, and decorates it with a string of tiny white lights. Everyone helps cut out red craft paper to make teddy bears and hearts, pokes a hole in their tops, and uses thin ribbon to tie them onto the tree. The decorations stay on until spring, when the family plants the tree in the yard. If you do this every year, you could designate a special Valentine Grove on your property.

Red Food Night

At the Straw household in Plano, Texas, all the food for Valentine's dinner is red. Sue Straw serves beets or red cabbage, mashed potatoes mixed with red food coloring, and either ham (pink) or pasta with red sauce. Red fruit might include grapes, raspberries, or strawberries. Even the milk is red. Dessert can be brown, as long as it's chocolate and shaped like a heart.

Have-a-Heart Awards

Each member of the family gives an award to each other member for a special act of love or kindness. Buy round, fuzzy, ping-pong-ball-size pom-poms at your local craft store, to which you can glue little eyes and mouths and feet. Cut hearts from a piece of construction paper four inches square, and glue the feet to the paper heart. Write on the heart the name of the person getting the award and what they did. Perhaps one child helped a younger sibling learn to tie his shoes. Perhaps Dad earned his award coaching Little League last summer.

The Book of Love

Who wrote the Book of Love? You did. Buy an inexpensive blank book, one with a heart on the cover, or glue one there. Call it The Book of (your last name) Love, and each year, have every member of the family write one loving thing about every other member. Take dictation for young kids. Every year on Valentine's Day, read what has been written the previous years.

Heartbooks

One of the best traditions I ever invented is the heart-shaped book I made for my son every year on Valentine's Day. I created a simple heart-shaped template, about six or seven inches long and wide, and cut out ten of them from white computer printer paper. Then, I cut another heart from something stiffer, like card stock, to use for the book's cover. I decorated the cover with stickers or cartoon characters cut from old calendars or magazine photos, and on top of that, I wrote the words: Ten Things I Love About Max, from Mom. (After the first year, I wrote "Ten More Things I Love About Max.")

I used a hole puncher to punch holes at the top curves of the hearts, so I could hold all the pages together with a piece of narrow satin ribbon, which was knotted a few times in the back to stay put. This made a nice handle, so I could hang the heartbook on the doorknob to my son's bedroom while he slept.

To me, what makes a gift like this the most meaningful is to be thoughtful and specific in the text. I wrote things like: "I love that your favorite animals are spiky or extinct," and "I love that you're open to new things (sometimes)." The last page is always something like: "I could never fit everything I love about you in one book," or "Actually, I love *everything* about you!"

From the time he became a teenager, I was forbidden to make a heartbook for my son, but no matter. I have discovered they make great birthday gifts as well: I once made one for a friend's milestone birthday that was "Sixty Things I Love About Joan." For that, I used fancier papers, and since I wasn't going to be hanging it on a door-knob, I used the ribbon differently: I cut two pieces instead of one, and rather than making a handle, I threaded each ribbon through all the holes and tied it into a bow for the top.

Make it!

Valentine Craft: What's Sweet About You Poster

This is like giving your kid a giant Valentine card, but much more personal. Make one for each child. If you're having a special dinner, you could bring the posters out then. Or prop them up against the kitchen chairs, so your kids find them when they come downstairs to breakfast or come home from school.

Materials

Large sheets of poster board in white, pink, or red (one sheet for each poster)

Red and pink construction paper

Scissors

Glue

Small Valentine candies, such as chocolate hearts wrapped in foil

Markers

Instructions

Cut nine to twelve hearts from the construction paper. The hearts should be about four inches high and three inches wide. On each heart, write one trait you love about that child's nature. Make it specific, focusing on positive aspects of his or her personality. Also, praise behavior you'd like to reinforce, such as putting away toys or progress in potty training.

Across the top of the poster, write "What's Sweet About (Child's Name)." Glue the hearts to the board, but just put glue on the bottom edges and up the sides of the hearts. Leave the top open, so they work like pockets. Put a piece of Valentine candy in each pocket.

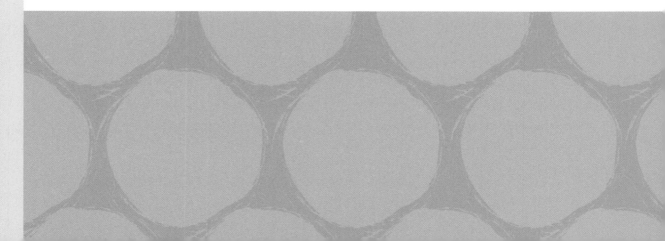

First Day of Spring

The official beginning of spring, March 20 or 21, is marked by the vernal equinox, when the sun crosses the equator from south to north. Some fresh ways to mark this joyful transition:

Plant Flowers

Kids love to dig in the dirt, and if the weather is bad, you simply plant in pots indoors. Best bet for small hands: nasturtium seeds, which are about the size of peas. Bulbs are also an excellent choice. My birthday is in March, and the year I turned fifty, I planted fifty daffodil bulbs by the birdbath in my backyard: I wanted to be able to see them from the kitchen table when they bloomed.

First Picnic of the Year

The Suks of Evanston, Illinois, have a picnic on the first day of spring, no matter the weather. Letitia Suk prepares picnic food such as deviled eggs and iced tea and packs it in the family car along with a Frisbee, a baseball, and a bat. Their destination is the nearest park. Even if they have to eat in the car, trek through snow, and wear gloves, they throw out the first ball of the season.

Paint the Rocks

The landscape of winter is drab and bare, but colors will burst forth in the spring. One way to symbolize and celebrate that transformation is to color your surroundings. If it's not raining, grab some washable poster paints in primary colors and some big paintbrushes. Pour small amounts of paint into paper cups for portability, and go paint any rocks you've got on your property. Paint pictures of flowers, write words, splash and drip like Jackson Pollock. My son absolutely loved doing this: I remember him painting words, listing his favorite toys at the time, like Legos. If you haven't got rocks, paint the driveway or use colored chalk. You might want to add favorite warm-weather activities, like kite flying or bubble blowing, and mix up the season's first pitcher of lemonade.

Make it!

How to Make a Bird's Nest Basket

Birds flying north after the winter are looking for material to build their nests. You can help them and attract birds to your yard, by supplying nest-making material in an inviting way.

Materials

Plastic berry baskets from the supermarket (use the ones your blueberries came in, or ask the produce department for some extras)

Short pieces of string or ribbon

Feathers in muted colors (birds won't take anything in a bright color that might attract predators' attention)

Twigs and leaves

Instructions

Simply arrange the nest materials in the basket, then tie string or ribbon to the four corners and use string to hang the basket from a tree branch, preferably one you can see from inside the house. Then watch birds as they swoop over to the basket and grab a scrap of ribbon to use in their nest building elsewhere.

Celebrate Big Bird's Birthday

Every year on the first day of spring, Big Bird celebrates his birthday, and he always turns six. If your kids love *Sesame Street*, you can adapt the idea of Susan Lynch of Merchantville, New Jersey, and mark this occasion at home. Her kids always make a cake with sprinkles on top to represent birdseed. They invite friends and hand out party favors like pinwheels or flowers. There are plenty of great *Sesame Street* and Muppet CDs, if you're looking for perfect sing-along songs, though "Happy Birthday" is a must.

Vernal Equinox Fun Facts

Show your kids the equator on a globe and help them research what is actually happening to Earth on this day, when theoretically the day is divided equally into twelve hours of light and twelve hours of darkness. Then, explore the myth that only on the vernal equinox can a person balance a raw egg on its end: Actually, you should be able to do this any day of the year, but it takes patience!

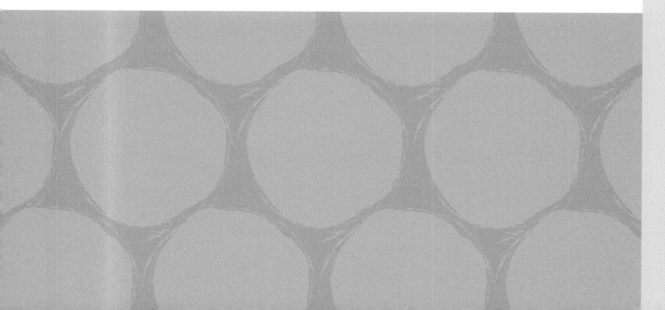

Passover

The oldest holiday in Judaism, Passover celebrates the liberation of the Jewish people from slavery in Egypt some 4,000 years ago. The observance lasts eight days, but the highlight is the seder, or ritualized family dinner, that begins the holiday. Of all the Jewish holidays, this one is of special interest to Christians because the Last Supper is believed to have been a Passover seder.

Like other major religions, Judaism remains strong partly because of its effectiveness in using holiday rituals to teach the tenets and history of the faith to children. And one of the great strengths of the Passover seder is the flexibility of this tradition: Families feel free to riff on the basic structure and make it their own. And because it's about storytelling and not just prayer, it can be made especially appealing to children. A seder is guided by a Haggadah, a book that contains prayers, readings, songs, and stories about the holiday, but there are also many different versions to pick from. Here are some of the ways families go about making seders memorable and fun:

Emphasizing Freedom

Passover is a great time to talk about the joy as well as the responsibilities of freedom, then and now. Laurie Salen, a social worker in San Francisco, has all the people who come to her seder bring a symbol of their own liberation to put on the table. One brought termination papers from a hated job. A workaholic friend brought her dancing shoes, because she had finally fulfilled a fantasy of working less overtime and taking dance classes. A guest with AIDS brought some of the drugs that keep him free to enjoy life. At other seders, people discuss countries in the world today where the citizens have limited freedom.

Kid-Friendly Passover

Julie Stockler's seders with her two daughters are especially playful. She has been known to use troll dolls to act out the story of the holiday (the troll with a star in his hand was God), and she always has a "movie night' the week before so her girls can watch *The*

Ten Commandments because "the plagues are so vivid." In trying to dress like ancient Hebrews, the family has wrapped themselves in bedsheets for the seder, and once ate while lying down. While slaves, the Hebrews were not allowed to recline while eating, a position reserved for free people, so some seders are eaten while reclining.

Fleeing Egypt

At the appropriate moment during the seder, the Brosbe family of Santa Rosa, California, has one of the dinner guests ring the doorbell and run away, leaving a note on the front steps that says *"Get Out of Egypt Now."* The family and their guests strap on backpacks and rush out the back door to march around the backyard singing a traditional Passover song.

Acting Out the Plagues

Many families get creative in depicting the ten plagues sent down by God when the pharaoh broke his repeated promises to free the Israelites. Some families take a blank roll of paper and tape it around the dining room like a mural, putting crayons on the table so the kids can draw each plague as it's described. Some discuss how modern-day plagues affect the world, such as AIDS.

An Intellectual Seder

When the Weber family of Los Angeles sends invitations to thirty or more people three weeks before the holiday, many of the guests are sent a question to discuss during the seder. Sometimes an individual is asked to answer, and sometimes a whole family. Often the guests do research to prepare their responses, and some families choose to put on a rehearsed skit. The end result is a stimulating discussion that lasts for hours, and just being asked is considered an honor. Some questions are repeated most years, but there is usually at least one new one. Some questions asked in the past are:

1. **There is no mention of Moses in the Haggadah, despite his importance to the story: Prepare an argument to include Moses.**
2. **What are ten plagues that threaten us today?**
3. **There are four questions traditionally asked at a seder: Develop four others to share with the group.**

The Weber seder is also a good example of how rituals must grow and change: Jerry Weber, a devout Jew fluent in Hebrew, started the family Passover tradition, but he was tragically murdered in 1989 in an ATM robbery in Los Angeles. His widow, Sally

Weber, wasn't at all sure she could carry on the tradition for their two daughters, because she didn't grow up in a religious household and didn't know Hebrew. After some studying and prodding by her daughters, she resumed holding the Seders at her home, with help. She found friends proficient in Hebrew willing to read those parts of the ceremony, and others who could carry a tune (unlike herself) to lead the songs. Much to her daughters' delight, Sally hosts, develops the questions, and leads the evening.

Finding the Right Haggadah for Your Passover Seder

There are truly a staggering number of Haggadahs available, including medieval ones, cartoon ones, feminist ones, Orthodox ones, even one for Buddhists. Here are some of the more popular ones for different audiences, and you'll find free ones online.

A Passover Haggadah, by Elie Wiesel, combines a full-length seder text with historical and personal commentary by the Holocaust survivor and author.

Uncle Eli's Special-for-Kids Most Fun Ever Under the Table Haggadah, by Eliezer Lorne Segal, a colorful book that covers the basics, defines terms, and includes a text for the evening that is full of rhymes and cartoonlike photos.

A good website for those celebrating Passover with children is Torahtots.com/holidays/pesach.

Our Haggadah: Uniting Traditions for Interfaith Families, by Cokie and Steve Roberts, was created by the journalists based on their forty years of figuring out how to celebrate this holiday as a couple and a family: Cokie is Catholic and Steve says he was raised mostly as a "cultural Jew."

Interfaith couples will also find a lot of thoughtful ideas on Passover and other Jewish holidays in the blog of Susan Katz Miller, OnBeingBoth.wordpress.com. (She was raised Reform Jewish but married a Protestant.)

Easter

Easter is the most important festival of the Christian church, and it celebrates the resurrection of Jesus after his crucifixion. The forty-day period leading up to Easter, called Lent, is generally a time of fasting, praying, and serious contemplation about suffering and the message God wanted to send with the death of Jesus. During Lent, devout Christians deprive themselves of things they especially enjoy, often foods like sweets or meat. Like the date for Passover, the date when Easter is celebrated changes every year: To find out when it will fall in the current year, check a calendar, whether online or on your wall.

Some people celebrate Easter strictly as a religious holiday, but even non-Christians often enjoy such fun and festive activities as outdoor egg hunts and Easter baskets. Here are some ideas that cover a range of ritual approaches.

Sunrise Bonfire

Light is a symbol of Jesus, and "seeing the light" figures in many hymns. At dawn, or as early as you can wake the family, walk outside and make or bring a light of some kind. You may choose to make a small "bonfire" in your yard (or even your outdoor grill), or if it's still dark, have everyone bring a flashlight. Read from the book of Luke about the resurrection, and break your fast with sweet rolls, perhaps some hot cross buns. These buns, often decorated on top with a cross made of white frosting, are traditionally eaten on Good Friday, the Friday before Easter.

Washing Hands

Because Jesus washed the feet of his disciples, bring a bowl of water, soap, and a towel to the table one night at dinner and have family members wash one another's hands, with care and tenderness. Talk about what it means to be a disciple, and the importance of being humble, even as a leader.

Fasting Ritual

Fasting isn't a good idea for small children, but having occasional meals when the family eats less than usual is one way to ritually experience fasting. The next night, talk about whether everybody was a bit hungry when they went to bed, and what that felt like. One family tried an experiment of computing how much money a family their size would get for food for a week if they were on welfare, spending only that much money at the supermarket and eating only that food for the week.

Handmade Crosses

Using simple twigs from your backyard and twine, have each member of the family fashion a simple cross. Each person can keep a cross on their bedside table, then hold it while praying and thinking about the suffering of Jesus on the cross.

Peep Destruction

Sarah Stengle of Princeton, the mother who created a "Half-Baked Party" (see Chapter 3) when her daughter left high school early, also has a creative way to celebrate Easter. A divorced mother of two girls, Sarah says when the girls were very young, they started taking the marshmallow Peeps out of their Easter baskets and creating little tableaus, which got more elaborate each year. "One year, it was a scene with plastic horses and the Peeps were warriors, and we gave them little plastic swords (cocktail toothpicks)."

Eventually, the tradition evolved so that a photojournalist friend of Sarah's would record the Peep scenes, and the girls' cousins would come help with the building. And often, part of the fun became sticking the creations in the microwave, then nibbling on the melted mass. They began calling the ritual "Peep Destruction."

"This year we did a river scene with boats and a prison made from sugar cubes and marshmallows," says Sarah. "We have often melted these creations in the microwave and eaten them with chopsticks. It is sooooo stupid, but we really have so much fun!"

Candle Ritual

Julie Young had just moved and needed a simple ritual. For the week leading up to Easter, she gathered pretty candles and set them up in the living room. Right before bedtime, she would turn out the lights, light the candles, and read about "the events of Jesus's last week on earth" from a book called *The Book of God for Children*. Each child was allowed to blow out one candle before going up to bed.

Garden Celebration

Rain Mako in Arkansas celebrates Easter with her family as the earth's rebirth. They put a brightly colored flag at each of the compass points in the family garden, and the flag colors represent the four elements of earth (brown), air (blue), fire (red), and water (white). As they drive in the four stakes, they talk about how these elements are required by all living things. The family members dress up in party clothes, beat drums, and sing songs about spring.

Creative Egg Hunts

To avoid fighting over eggs, designate a color for each child and make sure to hide the same number of each color. Some people add extra eggs that are specially marked with an " X" or a sticker: Anyone finding those eggs gets a special treat or prize. Betsy Muir's family in California has big family Easter celebrations with a double hunt: After all the plastic eggs are found the first time, they're re-hidden in the house, often stashed somewhere on one of the grownups, for instance, in a pocket, shoe, or handbag. When Letitia Suk's children got too old for egg hunts, or so they said, she wasn't ready to end the ritual, so instead of putting candy inside the plastic eggs she hid outdoors, she included gift certificates (in modest amounts like $5 or $10) to her children's favorite retailers. Suddenly, they were eager for the hunt once more!

One family makes finding the Easter baskets more fun by hiding them in the house but attaching long ribbons to them: The kids wake up to find one end tied to the foot of their bed, then have to follow it to the basket.

Egg-Cracking Rituals: Cascarones

Many cultures, among them Greek, French, Lithuanian, and Mexican, have an Easter tradition of cracking eggs together. Andrea Majewski, whose background is Polish and Lithuanian, calls this "bucking eggs," and her family does it with dyed, hard-boiled eggs. They have contests on Easter and smash their own against another person's egg.

Vicki Adkins is Mexican American and grew up with *cascarones,* which are hollowed out eggshells, stuffed with confetti. The open end is sealed with brightly colored tissue paper, secured with a dab of glue. Her family hides these, then after the egg hunt, they smash them on each other's heads! That may sound painful or mean, but it's more like a confetti shower than getting punched with food. Sometimes *cascarones* are also made on such

Mexican holidays as Day of the Dead and Cinco de Mayo. When I first started writing about *cascarones,* they weren't widely known in this country, but now there is a Wikipedia entry on them, and you can search for how-to videos on YouTube. I've even seen some *cascarones* packed in egg cartons for sale on Amazon.com, but it's more fun to make your own.

Bunny Tracks

Susan Wagoner and her husband in Charlottesville, Virginia, have a tradition of going out to homes in their neighborhood with kids ("or the young at heart"), to sift flour or powdered sugar over a stencil they made that looks like large bunny footprints. They leave a trail snaking up to the front door. They then throw a few Tootsie Rolls on the mat and a carrot with a leafy top still attached. "Kids loving seeing the Easter Bunny's evidence left behind," says Susan.

Kindness Wreath

Hang a plain wreath on your front door. About ten days before Easter, give each family member about ten brightly colored ribbons about eight inches long. You decide whether to give each person one color, or just let them grab what they like. Until Easter, every time a person performs an act of kindness for someone else (not just a family relation, but also friends, schoolmates, a stranger who needs help at the store, for example), he or she gets to tie on another ribbon. This will focus everyone's attention on doing good deeds and will result in a prettier and fuller wreath as the days pass. (Adapted from "Family Traditions for Easter," by Susie Cortright, from ezinearticles.com.)

April: Celebrate National Poetry Month

For little kids, poetry is indispensable and fun. They seem to be born with rhythm: Kids love a beat, and they're always banging words together. I think it's great to raise kids who don't think of poetry as intimidating or fussy. And in this age of hip-hop, why should they?

National Poetry Month was launched in 1996 by the Academy of American Poets, and the organization runs a fantastic website to help you celebrate. Go to Poets.org for lots of fun activities, and check out some good poetry anthologies from your local library.

Five Ways to Celebrate at Your House

1. Read a poem aloud every day during April at dinner or bedtime. They can be short, funny poems mostly, and you can save a few longer ones for the weekends. You can find them online, or just read from a few favorite poetry books.
2. Organize a Family Poetry Slam and have every member of the family "perform" several favorite poems, written by themselves or any writer they choose.
3. Considering how popular rap music is, why not write a family rap together? Don't forget the dance moves and hand motions. Don't have a real drum set? Tap on pots and tables to make a background beat.
4. Pick out some really short nonsense poems you like and write them in colored chalk on your driveway and in the street.
5. Put a poem in your child's lunch box or backpack every day.

So you know how much fun you'll have celebrating Poetry Month, here's one to start you out:

"My Robot"

by Douglas Florian, from his collection *Bing Bang Boing*

I have a robot
Do the dishes,
Phone my friends,
Bone the fishes.
Rub my back,

Scrub the floors;
Mop the kitchen,
Open doors.
Do my homework,
Make my bed;
Catch my colds,
Scratch my head.
Walk the dog,
Feed the cats;

Hit my sister,
Knit me hats.
Do my laundry,
Clean my room;
(Boy, he's handy
With a broom.)
Comb my hair,
Darn my socks;
Find my lost toys,

Wind my clocks.
Mix me milk shakes,
Fix my bike;
Buy me all
The things I like.
Grill me hot dogs,
Guard my home—
Who do you think
Wrote this poem?

Three Terrific Poet's Websites

ShelSilverstein.com is incredibly interactive. His famous line drawings come alive, and the site is full of silly sounds. There is a special section for kids that includes games and puzzles, so they can do things like finish a poem he started.

JackPrelutsky.com features his own poems, but also has tips for parents on how to read to children. He has written many great poetry books for kids, and has edited some anthologies. One of the fun poems he includes on the site is called "My Mother Says I'm Sickening" and it's about bad table manners.

Douglas Florian is another awesome poet, and his blog offers samples of his poems, plus others he loves. He's done many books that are filled with humor, clever wordplay, and his wonderful illustrations. Go to FlorianCafe.blogspot.com.

Here's a neat idea: If you send text messages regularly, try to send at least one a day during April that rhymes!

And if you are itching to download a poetry app, go to Poets.org and order the Poem Flow app, which for a small sum will deliver a poem a day to your smartphone or other device. Or go to the iTunes store and download the free app from the Poetry Foundation called, simply, Poetry.

Arbor Day

National Arbor Day has been celebrated since 1872 and is observed in most states on the last Friday in April. Planting trees is a fabulous activity for families and a great opportunity to create hands-on environmental awareness. Trees produce oxygen, moderate the temperature, diminish smog, and provide a home for wildlife. Any kid can help dig a hole, stick in a sapling, spread the roots, fill with dirt and tamp it down, and pour water on it.

You can always go to the nearest nursery and buy young trees, but if you're organized enough to plan ahead, an alternative is the National Arbor Day Foundation. For a $10 donation, the nonprofit group will mail you ten young trees, a variety of types that will thrive in your part of the country. They will look like dead twigs when they arrive, only about a foot long, but they'll come with planting instructions and your kids can watch them grow, year by year. The toll-free number for the Arbor Day Foundation is 888–448–7337, and their website is www.arborday.org.

A Scrapbook for Trees

Tarrant Figlio has been celebrating Arbor Day with her kids for years, and they have developed some special rituals. "On Arbor Day, we always plant a tree together as a family. I tell the kids how special trees are and we talk about how birds nest and how paper is made from trees. They are sort of like mini-science lessons." Tarrant's children also keep a special scrapbook for their Arbor Day trees, and every year they measure each tree, count branches, and take a photograph. Because the picture includes the kids, they can look back and see how they grew, alongside their trees.

tech tip

One great way to celebrate Arbor Day is to appreciate trees in your area by simply going for a long walk or hike in a nearby park. You will have your cell phone along, most likely, so why not download one of the excellent free apps that help to identify all the tree species you find on your walk?

The app called TreeBook covers the 100 most common trees found in North America.

Another app is LeafSnap, which includes more species and gorgeous photos and was developed by researchers at two universities and the Smithsonian Institution. You can find out more at the website, LeafSnap.com.

May Day

The first day of May is a fascinating holiday because its history is so diverse. Centuries ago in Europe, it was raucously celebrated as a spring festival and fertility rite, with feasting, crowning of May Queens, and dancing around a maypole. Devout religious types frowned on all the wild drinking and partying, including the Puritans who came to this country. What celebration is done in the United States today tends to be somewhat muted, though flowers still figure as an important element, and some schools and community groups erect maypoles. In Hawaii, May Day is "Lei Day," and the local people drape one another with those colorful flower necklaces. Still another aspect is May Day's association with worker's rights: At the end of the nineteenth century, union organizers were fighting hard for the right to an eight-hour workday and had big May Day rallies in support of this.

Here are some ideas for families who want to mold this background into traditions of their own.

Flower Garlands

Flower crowns and garlands are lovely, but the flowers quickly die. Instead of using live flowers, get some small dried or silk flowers at a craft store, and using florist's wire and ribbon, make a crown to fit the head of each young girl in the family. Tie additional bright ribbons to the back, so they stream down past the girl's waist. Improvise your own May Day party and feast, with music and dancing. If you haven't yet, start working in your garden on this day.

Flowers Forever

Kate Smith helps her kids gather flowers on May Day and then preserve them. They make a simple flower press, placing the blooms between two layers of cardboard, then squishing them together with heavy books such as phone books. Leave the flowers to dry and flatten, then glue them to picture frames, turn plain paper into pretty stationery, or glue the flowers into a diary or other special book.

Because the flowers take some time to dry (two to four weeks pressed in a book), you could pick your flowers several weeks before May Day but turn your dried flowers into craft projects on the day itself. For lots of advice on how to dry and press flowers, including in the microwave, go to http://preservedgardens.com/how-to-press.htm.

Maypole Festival

Nancy Goddard shares a property in Sebastopol, California, with several other families in what they call a "co-housing international community" named La Tierra. They have their own homes but share a garden and many tools, and love to throw a major celebration every year for May Day. They erect a forty-foot pine pole and up to 300 people wind up dancing around it.

"This ceremony is about the renewal of life," says Nancy. "It's a celebration of the season of fertility and growth, and the weaving together of our lives and our community. And it's great fun."

Here is how they do their maypole dance: They staple about sixty ribbons onto the top of the pole. It takes a long time to wind down the ribbon on a pole this tall, so it's a progressive type of thing, whoever wants to start doing the dance jumps in. People are positioned so that every other person around the pole faces the opposite direction. They dance over and under each other while holding the ribbon. When one person gets tired, somebody else picks up their ribbon and keeps going. Everybody sings. Then, when the ribbons are all woven down to the end, and the people are all clumped together close to the pole, everybody hoots and hollers and we tie the ends down so it doesn't pull apart.

Not to worry: A maypole doesn't require 300 people and a forty-foot pole. Your local lumberyard will be happy to cut a ten-foot-long wooden pole in a standard diameter of one and five-eighths inches. There are various ways to lodge it firmly in the ground, including planting a metal cylinder (from the hardware store) in your yard and then slipping the pole into the cylinder. Half a dozen or so eager children is sufficient to weave the ribbons and cover the pole. Play any lively music you like, or you can always play the "Spring" section from Vivaldi's Four Seasons or Beethoven's Sixth Symphony (the Pastoral).

How to Make a May Day Basket

Materials

Paper plates, either floral or colored, or white ones if your kids would prefer to decorate and color them

Crayons, markers, or stickers

Instructions

Bend each plate into the shape of a cone, and staple the place where the sides meet. Glue or staple a pretty ribbon to the inside of the top of the cone, so you can hang the "basket" on someone's doorknob.

Fill the basket with daisies or other spring flowers, and if the recipient of the May Day basket won't be home, wrap the stems in a wet paper towel covered with plastic wrap to keep the plate dry.

Deliver the baskets to the homes of special friends and relatives.

In Casper, Wyoming, Mary Sutton's children often fill their May Day baskets with candy or homemade cookies instead of flowers. There are many elderly people living in their neighborhood, and they love to leave the baskets at their homes, anonymously. Her kids sneak up to the house, place the basket on the doorknob, ring the bell, and then run. Kunni Biener and her daughters had another method: They made May baskets using Dixie cups with ribbon handles. They would put a marigold plant in each one, then hang them on neighbors' doors: One year, they put a May marigold cup on the door of all seventy-seven houses in their development. Now in their twenties, the girls still talk about this tradition and make the May cups for their college roommates.

Family Job Tree

To honor the history of labor in your family, create a family tree going back several generations that shows not only family members' names but also what work they did during their lives. Talk about the history of work and labor, the movement away from agrarian life in this country, and imagine jobs and work in future times, including the adulthood of your kids.

tech tip

Websites for Lei Day and Maypole Dancing

Study the culture of Hawaii with your kids by learning more about the tradition of Lei Day on May 1, and try your hand at making your own leis from paper flowers or other artificial ones you pick up at a craft store. A good website for background is LeiDay.net.

Have you always itched to make your own community maypole? It's not as hard as you might think. You won't find a better resource for celebrating with a maypole dance, including how to coach the children and the optimum number of dancers (six to twelve), than the website of the Atwood-Smith family. They call themselves "Smatters," and their award-winning site includes everything from wedding photos to family recipes. See www.smat .us/maypole

Mother's Day

Here's a little quiz to start us out. Who invented Mother's Day?

If you answered "the greeting card companies," then bzzzzzzt, you lose.

Generations ago in England, there was an annual custom known as "mothering Sunday," in which it was customary to visit one's mum, take her a cake, and do the midday cooking so she could attend church. Although Americans assume our Mother's Day tradition was created to sell stuff, the originator of the celebration was actually a very churchy lady named Anna M. Jarvis. A genteel spinster who spent her life caring for a blind sister, Jarvis started lobbying in 1905 for a special day to honor mothers, including her own, recently deceased. Her idea for celebrating was very church-focused, and she was said to be alarmed at how commercial the holiday became during her lifetime.

As for me, I'm totally cool with family members buying me stuff on Mother's Day, and I will never forgot how thrilled I was the first time I got a card: It came from my stepdaughter while I was still pregnant with my son. As the years go by, I know I can count on a lot of hugs and special treatment on this day, even now that Max is a teenager. I usually take the day as a gardening holiday, heading off to my favorite nursery to load up with spring flowers.

Breakfast Out of Bed

Judy Elkin finally confessed that she hated getting breakfast in bed on Mother's Day: all those crumbs in the sheets, plus she would rather eat with her kids than alone. So her family came up with a creative twist: They don't bring her food, but rather a menu. She decides whether she wants pancakes or eggs, and while the kids and her husband cook, she lounges in bed drinking coffee and reading. When it's time to eat, she joins them downstairs and receives flowers and home-made cards.

Role Reversal

For a full day, have your kids mother you. They can pick out your clothes, cook your breakfast, kiss your boo-boos, read you a story, and tuck you in bed at the end of the day. You'll probably also get some lollipops and new toys.

Mother Wisdom

If you're like most mothers, there are probably a handful of sayings and certain types of practical advice (also called nagging) for which you are known. Your husband or an older child can get each of the kids to write on sheets of letter-size paper something they've learned from you that's proved valuable, or something they promise to pay more attention to in the future. The sheets can be stapled together in a sort of book.

Queen for a Day

Remember the old television show *Queen for a Day*? Get the kids and your husband

prepared in advance to bow down to your commands, and get a robe and tiara ready. Have them give you flowers when they dress you in your robe and crown, then have an "audience" with them while they tell you just why they think you are a royally spectacular mother. It's also important that they prepare a feast, and that you don't do any dishes.

tech tip

Good Mother's Day Website

At MothersDayWorld.com you will find a wealth of information about how it is celebrated around the world, as well as crafts, quotes, recipes, and gift ideas. My personal favorite among the quotes is from Abraham Lincoln: "All that I am or ever hope to be I owe to my angel mother."

Father's Day

In these enlightened times, dads do more of the heavy lifting of parenthood than ever before, and they deserve to be honored and celebrated. Would you believe that presidents as far back as Woodrow Wilson tried to get Father's Day recognized as a national holiday? Wilson first proposed the holiday in 1916, but it didn't happen until Richard Nixon signed it officially into law in 1972. Now it is celebrated globally, including in the Arab world, also in June.

Father's Day is a great day to do "guy things" like grilling, but the best approach is to spend time with your dad doing the things he truly loves. Take a hike, go to a baseball game, pack a picnic to the park with all his favorite foods. And get mushy: Dads need hugs, too.

Guy Day Adventures

The McCandless family decided to create a Father's Day ritual that celebrates all the menfolk in the family at once, including the sons. "About ten years ago, we got tired of just buying another shirt for Father's Day, so we started planning a special 'Guy Day' for all the dads in the family. Every year it's a new adventure and it includes my father, my father-in-law, my husband, and our son. The first year it was a local air show, another year they toured a naval shipyard, and another time they visited a train museum."

The womenfolk, "who would be bored by these things," says Sue, pay for the whole excursion but don't attend, appearing only at the picnic dinner that ends the day.

Daddy's Toolbox: A Survival Kit for Fathers

Adapted from a workshop for kids at Blue Tulip, a wonderful New Jersey gift shop that no longer exists.

Take any sort of box, shoebox size or smaller, and let the kids decorate it with torn paper, markers, glued-on decorations. The items listed are just a starting suggestion: Let the children add little tokens, toys, drawings, anything they want their dad to keep close. If they can't write yet, the parents can help, or let the kids explain in their own words what these items stand for.

- Marbles—to replace the ones you will lose
- Penny—to give you cents (sense) to know how valued you are
- Heart (paper is fine)—to remind you that I love you
- Rope—in case you are at the end of yours
- Rubber band—to remind you to be flexible
- Paper clip—to help you hold things together

Other ideas: candy, Band-Aids, Lego blocks, mini-sports tokens (football and so on), friendship bracelet, buttons, stickers.

Make it!

A T-Shirt to Melt His Heart

Materials

White cotton T-shirt

Fabric paints in one or more bright colors

Paintbrush

Instructions

Pour some paint into a shallow foil baking pan, then have your kids place either the palms of their hands or their feet in the paint. Have them make a print of their hands or feet on the front of the T-shirt and write next to the prints either "I'm in good hands with Dad" or "I want to walk in Dad's footsteps." If you have more than one child, you can change the wording to "We're in good hands," and the like. Have them wash all the paint off their skin immediately. Tiny baby feet and hands are adorable mementos, but you can make this an annual tradition, a clever way to chart the kids' growth.

July 4

Write Your Family Constitution

The Declaration of Independence was a passionate and detailed argument advocating liberty from British rule, complete with a long list of grievances about how the colonists were treated. But the Constitution, which came later, was all about how the new country would govern itself. This is a good time for you to sit down and create your own document about the rules in your house, and the values from which they spring.

You can get as formal as you want to, but if you are looking for a good model, Scott Gale made a fairly complete and realistic one for his family. He wrote about it in his 2009 book, *Your Family Constitution: A Modern Approach to Family Values and Household Structure.*

You can access a lot of his ideas free at the website YourFamilyConstitution.com, including an e-book that includes multiple templates for creating your own constitution. Typically, the templates cover such topics as manners and attitudes, chores, homework, and rules about screen time, but what's clever is that Gale has designed themed constitutions that will really appeal to kids, including a Pirate's Code (consequences for not following required duties are listed as "Deadman's Curses") and one with a football theme (consequences of bad behavior are listed under "Penalties.")

Everyone in the Gale family signed the constitution, and the kids were consulted in its creation. Like the nation's constitution, this is a living, changing document. At the family's weekly meeting, there may be a discussion if some aspect of the constitution isn't working and small tweaks may be made. Otherwise, they give it a thorough examination once a year to see if it needs a more serious amendment.

You get the idea. For all of you parents struggling to create rules about fraught issues like how much time your kids can spend plugged into their various screens, this may be a godsend. To flesh out your rules and then get everyone to sign off on them (consent of the governed) is a great way to reduce friction, while also teaching about how nations and groups are governed.

A "Happy Birthday, America" Party

Food

Typical barbecue fare such as burgers, hot dogs, or chicken, but be sure to include a cake with white frosting, topped with strawberries and blueberries. Instead of regular candles, use sparklers if you have them.

Music

Get a CD with Sousa marches and patriotic favorites, or lead a sing-along of *Yankee Doodle Dandy*, *America the Beautiful*, and other suitable songs. Provide printouts of the lyrics by going to the website ScoutSongs.com. Be sure to sing "Happy Birthday, America" before lighting the sparklers or candles and cutting the cake.

Party Hats

You could use construction paper to fashion hats, such as Uncle Sam's stovepipe hat, in red, white, and blue. Just make a cylinder of paper about eight inches high, glue the edges so it fits the child's head, and cut a matching brim (cut it extra wide so there's paper you can tuck and glue to the bottom of the hat. No need to worry about a top). Or you could use green paper and make some simple Statue of Liberty hats, just a crown shape with spikes sticking up. Your local party store will also stock hats.

Activities

Read aloud from the Declaration of Independence. Although the long list of complaints about King George III gets boring, the initial section is very inspiring. "We hold these truths to be self-evident,

that all men are created equal," and so on. Borrowing from the Jewish tradition of thinking about the importance and joy of freedom, have all the people at the table talk about why they value freedom, and what life is like today in countries whose citizens are not free.

Sign a Declaration of Interdependence

Although independence was the way to go for the American colonists, and our children want to be as independent of us as possible, there is no question that the fates of all the people living on Earth are tied together. We realize this truth more and more as we go along.

As it turns out, historian, philosopher, and public intellectual Will Durant created such a declaration after World War II, making the point that future world wars might be avoided if people would generally acknowledge this truth, and live it. Because so many of the horrors from that war were related to religious and ethnic persecution, Durant's declaration argued particularly hard for tolerance.

A more recent declaration has been developed by a nonprofit group called WE, which is attempting to get people all over the world to work together on such issues as environmental stewardship. Prominent social activists and religious leaders, including Desmond Tutu, Deepak Chopra, Jane Goodall, and others have signed this Declaration of Interdependence. Sign it and learn more with your family at: we.net/declaration.

This is the basic language of the document:

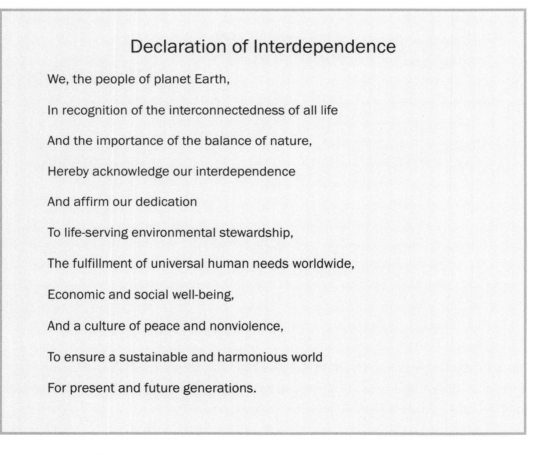

Declaration of Interdependence

We, the people of planet Earth,

In recognition of the interconnectedness of all life

And the importance of the balance of nature,

Hereby acknowledge our interdependence

And affirm our dedication

To life-serving environmental stewardship,

The fulfillment of universal human needs worldwide,

Economic and social well-being,

And a culture of peace and nonviolence,

To ensure a sustainable and harmonious world

For present and future generations.

Certainly, you can also write your own Declaration of Interdependence, including your personal commitments to your family and community.

tech tip

Fireworks Apps and a Few Good History Websites

If you live in a part of the country where firework sales are illegal, as I do, or you just want to be able to take a fireworks show everywhere you go, check out one of the many firework apps now available for various cell phones and other devices. Two good ones for Apple-made devices are iLoveFireworks (99 cents) and FireworksArcade. The latter puts a fireworks show in the palm of your hand and includes a number of firework games. It is free, but if you want the embedded ads to disappear, you have to pay 99 cents.

There is also a free app for downloading the Declaration, located in the Reference section of iTunes. Look for Declaration for iPhone and iPod Touch, and the developer is Clint Bagwell Consulting. (They also have a free Constitution app.)

To bring history to your celebration, go to this amazing website: ushistory .org, created and hosted by the Independence Hall Association of Philadelphia. This deep resource includes many options, including a virtual tour of historic Philadelphia, and a series of changing virtual exhibits and explainers. You can even buy bronze replicas of the Liberty Bell, or buy a flag. Especially nifty is the chance to click through to the sister site on the Declaration of Independence: Your family can read the document and also click on the name of each person who signed it to read that man's story.

Although the History Channel on cable television is sometimes attacked for inaccurate portrayals of historical events and silly reality programs, their website has some good resources, including many short videos. Go to History .com and click on Topics, where you will find, among other things, a good four-minute video about the Declaration.

Halloween

What is now called Halloween has its roots in ancient Celtic celebrations of New Year's: October 31 was the last day of summer in the ancient Irish calendar. People believed that on October 31, the barrier between the worlds of living and dead got thin, and the spirits of the dead could walk among the living. To frighten away those spirits, the villagers would dress in ghoulish costumes and party loudly. Another ancient Celtic tradition was to ritually cast out all the evil from the year just ending, to prepare for a good new year. It was the latter tradition that inspired Lucinda Herring to create the unusual ritual described in the box on page 247.

At my house, we aren't fanatics about Halloween, but my son has always loved the tradition of inventing (or buying if we run out of time) a creative costume and going trick-or-treating. Because our house is set far back from the road and we don't live in a good area for this activity, we have developed a tradition of taking him over to the apartment complex where my husband's ex-wife lives. Every year, we pick up a pizza on the way to her house, and after we eat it together, she and her dog (who often wears a costume) go from door to door with our son, while I stay at her house and hand out candy to the kids who come to her door in the meantime.

Harvest Festival

Families that wish to steer clear of gory, scary Halloween celebrations can follow the example of the Gines family of Michigan. They celebrate the month of October as a continuous Harvest Festival. One weekend, they take a hayride at a local orchard and pick their own apples and pumpkins. One week, they make a scarecrow as a family. And one weekend they make "sun catchers": they collect fall leaves, grasses, and flowers and lay them down on waxed paper, then shred crayons on top of them, cover it all with a second layer of paper, and then iron the waxed paper till the crayons melt. They cut the paper into circles and other shapes, poke a hole in the top, and hang their sun catchers around the kitchen, to catch the fall light.

Pumpkin Burial

It's wonderful fun and a great family project at my house to carve one or more pumpkins every year. Even the annual outing to the local farm that grows pumpkins is festive, as we eat donuts and drink cider and make sure we pick exactly the right specimens from the vast pumpkin patch.

Once they are carved, we usually put one by the front door and a second one on the screened-in back porch with a candle inside, so we can see it from the kitchen table. We turn out the lights inside and light the pumpkin's candle, for a great spooky effect.

But a carved pumpkin, especially one kept outdoors in the weather, starts to cave in and get gross after just a few days, and then you've got to dispose of this squishy orange and black thing.

The family that maintains a website called Pumpkin Carving 101 (no family name appears on the site) provides terrific resources on pumpkin-carving patterns, but I especially like their personal ritual for disposing of their crumpled pumpkins after the holiday. "It seems so heartless, cruel and undignified to simply toss them in a bag to be hauled off with the trash," they write. So they created a small patch in the backyard, where they bury their old pumpkins every year with a small bit of ceremony. "We think the Great Pumpkin would be very impressed," they write. And I agree.

Here is their simple eulogy:

We are gathered here to pay homage to our dearly departed Jack O'Lanterns.
Throughout their short lives our Halloween Pumpkins
Have brought both us and our Trick or Treaters much joy.
We now consign them to the earth where they first came.
May They Rest in Peace.

How to Toast Pumpkin Seeds

Separate seeds from strings and toss with a spoonful of vegetable oil. Spread seeds across a cookie sheet and sprinkle with salt. Bake at 250° for 90 minutes to dry, then raise heat to 350° to toast. Done when lightly brown.

Ghoulish Fun

Kyna Tabor of Salem, Illinois, takes her kids to a nearby graveyard every Halloween Eve day to make grave rubbings. This particular graveyard dates to the Civil War, and many of the graves are old, with interesting markings. She uses butcher's paper, which you can get from your local supermarket, and either charcoal or sidewalk chalk. If your kids are older, you can sit around in the dark, with only the light of candles (in or out of carved pumpkins), and take turns telling ghost stories.

Make it!

Gloom Dolls: A Healing Activity for Halloween

This idea comes from Lucinda Herring, a writer and educator who lives with her daughter, Eliza, on an island off the coast of Washington state.

Materials

Paper

Pencils or crayons

White cloth cut into squares measuring twelve by twelve inches (you can use an old sheet)

Newspapers or wood, and matches, to make a fire

Instructions

Have each person write his or her "glooms" on pieces of paper. These are things and feelings that family members don't like about their lives, from not making the soccer team to a serious illness or other crisis in the family. Unless the children need someone to write for them or want to share their glooms, these should be private. After the glooms are written down, crumble the paper into a ball. This will be the doll's head. Stick it in the middle of the fabric square, then use a piece of string to tie the fabric around the balled up paper, thus forming a head and letting the rest of the square form a ghostlike body. In a fireplace inside or a grill outside, start a small fire. Talk first about letting go of all the bad feelings that "haunt" us, and then let everyone throw their gloom dolls into the fire and watch them burn.

tech tip

Super Halloween Websites

There is a mega-website that lists the links to a lot of Halloween-related sites. HalloweenWebsites.com will lead you to recipes, costume ideas, ghost stories, and tips on safe trick-or-treating.

For the app-happy parent, there are loads of downloadable apps, with everything from costume ideas and pumpkin-cutting patterns to a Halloween-themed version of the hot game Angry Birds.

Thanksgiving

The core emotional truth of Thanksgiving is the expression of gratitude, and the best model for kids is a joyful tradition of giving thanks.

Corn Kernels

Put three kernels of corn next to each place setting for Thanksgiving dinner, and at some point, have each person count out three things for which he or she is grateful.

Thanksgiving Scroll

Each year before the feast, the Butman family of Walkersville, Maryland, unrolls a paper scroll across the kitchen table. (Arts and crafts stores sell paper rolls, which are about one foot wide.) To start, Bryan Butman or one of his three kids picks out a Bible verse having to do with giving thanks, and they write it across the top. The paper is taped to the table and divided into five sections, one for each family member. All of them draw or color something they were thankful for that year, whether a pet, good grades, or close friends. The Butmans keep adding on to the same scroll until it's full, but you could also cut off each year's section and carefully tape it to the dining room wall while eating your feast.

Thankful Box

Put a cardboard box with a slit cut into the top on the kitchen counter the week before Thanksgiving, with a pile of blank paper and a pencil next to it. Have your whole family write down things they're thankful for. Read them aloud during the feast, and guess who wrote what.

Thank-You Notes

Kim Meisenheimer realized that many of the people for whom her kids were thankful didn't come to their Thanksgiving dinner. So she started having her sons write (and mail) two or three special thank-you notes a year to special people, anyone from the soccer coach to Grandma. On Thanksgiving Day itself, each family member could be required to write a thank-you note to each other person attending the feast. Slip them under the plates before the meal.

Gratitude Walk

Stacey Sharp practiced a simple but profound Thanksgiving ritual as a child that anyone can practice, with or without children. "Every year when I was a kid, my mom and I would take a walk in the morning and go over each month of the past year and find something to be thankful for in each month. We were migrant workers for some of those years so you can imagine there wasn't always a lot to find, but we always did. It might just be the memory of an apple pie with donated apples. My mother is gone now and my own circumstances have improved, but I still take that walk every Thanksgiving morning."

A to Z Thanksgiving Countdown

Amy Candland wrote in *Family Fun* magazine (February 2006) about how her extended family goes around the table detailing their gratitude, using the alphabet as their guide. The first person says something he or she is grateful for that starts with A, and so forth. One year, Amy's mother secretly arranged things to be sure Amy was the one to get the letter U: She used her turn to announce she was grateful for the ultrasound that showed she was pregnant (her first child), and she waved the ultrasound photo triumphantly!

A Chair for the Absent

After the September 11, 2001, terrorist attacks, I suggested in a newsletter that people include one empty chair at their table that Thanksgiving to honor the memory of the thousands who died. Monica Hall wrote me later, "We always have a craft corner for people to make their own place cards for Thanksgiving. This year, we made an extra place card, so that all of our twenty guests could write the name of someone they wish was sitting there. Kids who were divorced wrote the name of missing parents, some adults wrote the name of an estranged family member. Then, during the meal, two dads prayed for all the people whose names were on that card." I think this is a powerful tradition, and a simple one, that can apply to every Thanksgiving.

How to Make a Thankfulness Tree

Materials

Construction paper in red, yellow, and orange

Pencil

Scissors

String or ribbon

Bare tree branches about two to three feet long

Vase for branches

Instructions

Trace the maple leaf shape on this page, or draw a template of your own. Once you have the template, use a pencil and outline the leaf shape on the colored paper. Cut out as many leaf shapes as you wish. If your children are very young, you may want to do this part ahead. Spread the leaves across the table, and let everybody in the family write things on the leaves for which they are thankful that year. Poke a small hole in the stem part of the leaves, thread with string and hang on the branches. Afterward, save all the leaves, either gluing them into the family scrapbook, or stuffing them in a plastic Baggie marked with the year. (When he gets older, my son will love that he was thankful for "my brane" at age six.)

This is one of those activities that I sometimes need to nag my menfolk about, but once we are actually sitting at the table and filling out our leaves, it has invariably been a wonderful and illuminating shared experience. I never think ahead of time about what I'm going to write, and it's always a revelation, as are the things for which my husband and son are grateful. Looking back over the past leaves provides a real window into what mattered to us most as the years passed.

Alternative Idea: Make your thankfulness tree as a poster, drawing a picture of a tree, then having the kids trace around their hands on colored paper and make those handprints the leaves. Glue "leaves" to tree on poster.

Thanksgiving Reader

Various attempts have been made over the years to create a book or script like the Haggadah used for the Jewish holiday of Passover, so that families can take turns reading during the Thanksgiving feast. The idea of making the meal more than just an exercise in planned overeating is a laudable one, and people can craft their own version, adding prayers and readings from historical accounts of the first Thanksgiving.

If you are looking for a good script that has already been compiled, I recommend "America's Table: A Thanksgiving Reader," which was created by the American Jewish Committee after 9/11. You can use as much or as little as you choose, and it includes some strong writing celebrating America's traditions of freedom and compassion. Go to AJC.org and search for "America's Table." (Note: the site lists different versions, by year, but it doesn't matter which you choose. The central text is the same in each one. All that changes is the sidebars that feature profiles of various Americans telling their own stories.).

Here is a sample, taken from the last page of the seventeen-page booklet:

We are the stewards of America:

- **We are thankful for the freedom to worship.**
- **We are thankful for the freedom to speak our minds.**
- **We are thankful for the freedom to change our minds.**
- **We are thankful for the freedom to celebrate this day.**
- **In America, each of us is entitled to a place at the table.**

Connecting When You're Apart

On the day before Thanksgiving, Gines family members all over the country make pie at exactly the same time, using Grandma Betty's piecrust recipe. Betty, who has six children, calls each household in turn and speaks to each grandchild. This is a wonderful idea for today's far-flung families. If you wish, you can do this and take photos or videos and collect them on a shared family blog.

tech tip

Instant Holiday T-Shirts for Your Family

For people who can make crafts, the website of online crafts supplier Dharma Trading provides great materials as well as tutorials and patterns for family craft projects. This idea, which would also work for other major family holidays, takes a little pre-planning, but it's entirely doable. If you'd rather not be rushing around completing the T-shirts that day, another option would be to take a group photograph of your celebration and send the T-shirts out later as mementos.

The basic idea is to take a group photograph, then run off to the computer while everyone else is hanging out and chatting. Download your chosen digital image to your computer. You will use your computer printer to print the photo on chemically treated inkjet transfer paper, then use an iron to transfer that photo image onto plain white cotton T-shirts. Before the turkey (or maybe the pie) is out of the oven, voilà! You will be handing every family member a matching themed T-shirt to wear. Dharma sells everything from the white cotton shirts to the inkjet transfer paper.

You'll find the tutorial at: www.dharmatrading.com/html/eng/2548071-AA .shtml?lnav=home.html. Or go to DharmaTrading.com and search for Family Holiday Photo Transfer Tutorial.

Fun Thanksgiving Dinner Ideas

Autograph the Tablecloth

In Mindy Robinson's family, thirty or forty people regularly attended the feast, and every person would sign the tablecloth with a pen during dinner. Afterward, her mother would embroider over the signature lines, in a different color thread each year. (The year is embroidered around the edge of the tablecloth, in the color used that year.) The cloth became a visual history of the holiday, reminding the family who was missing this year and how much the little ones had grown, as signatures changed.

Turkey Parade

There can be a lot of pressure when preparing a major feast. One family finds that once all the dishes are finally ready, all of them need to let off some steam and stretch their legs before sitting down to eat. Each person attending is given a pot or pan and a spoon, and the cook carries the finished turkey on a large platter. The group literally parades down the street (briefly, before the bird cools completely), banging on pots and screaming "Happy Thanksgiving!" to the neighborhood. This has to be one of my very favorite "problem-solving" rituals of all time!

Pilgrims and Indians

Allison Dafferner's family had a tradition of making Pilgrim and Indian hats. It gave the kids something to do while her mother cooked, and it sure was festive. The hats were made from colored construction paper and glued or stapled together. Tradition had it that the kids could pick first whether they wanted to be Pilgrims or Indians, and the adults, who also participated, balanced out the numbers.

Kid-Friendly Feast

Monica Hall of Baltimore, Maryland, got tired of cranky kids, forced to sit too long. She puts the little ones at a separate table, buys extra turkey legs, and gives them cranberry Jell-O® instead of cranberry sauce. When they finish, they can play in the basement playroom, while the adults converse.

Take the Feast Outdoors: A Picnic Thanksgiving

Dorothy Steinicke lives in Southern California and started a tradition about twenty years ago of celebrating the holiday in a local state park, which she finds not crowded at this time. Friends and family, about thirty people in all, attend and sit together at several picnic tables that have been pulled together and covered with tablecloths. It's potluck, and when the kids are done eating, instead of fidgeting at the table, they climb trees or explore the pond. "After a while, the adults rouse themselves and go for a hike," says Dorothy. "We go several miles and return before sunset for dessert."

Step-Family Alternate Outdoor Thanksgiving

Linda McKittrick was well aware that her stepdaughter, named J, who lives nearby in New Mexico, enjoyed celebrating a traditional Thanksgiving dinner at her mom's house with old friends and graciously suggested that she and her husband start a different tradition for the girl. So the second Thanksgiving feast each year, celebrated with J's dad and Linda, is held in the evening, outside, around a campfire, where they roast turkey dogs and make S'mores. "The sun sets and the mood cast by the fire leads to fun, storytelling, and deeper conversation," says Linda.

tech tip

A Great Website for History

The first English colony in Plymouth, Massachusetts, has been re-created near the original locale at a so-called living museum. There are period-appropriate buildings and people in costumes who reenact daily life in that place and time. This project is affiliated with the Smithsonian Institution and is well worth visiting. The fantastic website includes a wonderful section with resources for families: Plimoth.org/Learn (yes, that is correctly spelled as Plimoth.org).

Included is good information about the history of Thanksgiving and the first feast. One of the best features for kids is an interactive exercise called "You Are the Historian," in which kids can explore some historical items and documents, and read a letter written by someone who actually attended the first feast.

Sharing the Bounty of Thanksgiving

A great time to start philanthropic traditions and link gratitude for what we have with sharing.

Feast for the Animals

Nancy Mendez and her family share their feast with "the birds and beasts." Before they eat, her children and their cousins take a walk in the nearby woods (with a grown-up), carrying a bucket of seeds and food scraps. The bucket includes cranberries too mushed for the family's sauce, bread crumbs left over from the stuffing, and so on. They scatter the food for the birds and animals. On the way back home, the kids fill the bucket with twigs and kindling for the fireplace.

Feed the Poor

Some families try to work some part of the Thanksgiving weekend in a soup kitchen, but there are other ways you can help as well. One is to buy a duplicate feast: If you're having turkey, buy a second bird; if you're making mashed potatoes, buy a second bag. Pack this feast and deliver it to a local homeless shelter or agency that serves the poor. (Make this arrangement before buying the food.)

Make a Helping Others Jar

Take a used, clean coffee can and cut a slit in the plastic top. To decorate the can, cut white paper the height of the can, wrap this paper around the can and secure with glue or tape. To decorate, use crayons or markers, or paste magazine photos on the paper. Display the can in the kitchen, and put some money in while discussing a weekly plan of family giving. Talk about how that money could help others and discuss possible charities.

A Great Charity for Kids

Heifer Project International has over fifty years' experience in donating farm animals to the world's poor and has a great website, www.heifer.org. Also, the picture book *Beatrice's Goat*, by Page McBrier, about how a Heifer goat changed the life of a real African girl, makes a big impression on kids.

Hanukkah

Like other Jewish holidays, this features elements that can make for great celebrations, including appealing history, food, music, and rituals. Also, this is a holiday where kids get gifts.

Hanukkah, also spelled Chanukah, isn't nearly as big a deal within Jewish history and religion as Christmas is for Christians, but it has gotten built up a bit over the years. Some Jews feel that the gift-giving part of the holiday has gotten overemphasized, partly as a way for Jewish parents to compete with Christmas. So, just as many Christian families are trying to lessen the materialistic aspects of Christmas, many Jewish families stress the meaning of the holiday rather than gifts. Here are some Hanukkah celebration ideas:

Theme Nights

The Elkins of Boston used to give their kids a present on each of the eight nights of Hanukkah, just as they had been given nightly gifts as children. But Judy Elkin and her husband decided that with three kids, the practice was expensive and not sending the right message. Now, the kids get a gift from their parents every other night. On the first night, the kids only get gifts from each other; one night is "family fun night" featuring an activity like bowling; and one night is *tzedaka*, or charity, night. Every Friday throughout the year, before their Shabbat dinner, the family has put aside money for charity, and on the Friday night within Hanukkah, they decide on who should get the donation.

Focus on Food

Ellen Brosbe tries to emphasize the food, which is fried in honor of the miraculous oil that burned for eight days in the story celebrated by this holiday. Her kids take turns picking the menu: One night it's fish and chips, another night tempura, and so on. Instead of gifts, her kids get money, $1 multiplied by the number of candles lit each night.

How to Play Dreidel

A dreidel is a top with four sides, and each side has a Hebrew letter. Together, they stand for the phrase "A great miracle happened there." Some families play for pennies, whereas others use nuts or candy. First, the pennies or treats are divided evenly among the players. Each person puts one piece in a central pot or cup, perhaps two if the group is small. Players take turns spinning the dreidel and react according to what symbol is facing up:

ג **Gimel** Take all; then each player puts one more piece into the pot.

ה **Hey** Take half.

ש **Shin or Pey** Add one to the pot.

נ **Nun** Do nothing.

tech tip

Websites and Apps for Hanukkah

Produced by an organization of observant Jews, www.virtualchanukah.com is rich in history and activities. There are stories, prayers, and many videos, including several with directions on how to light candles in the menorah, the special candleholder, during the eight days of Hanukkah.

One of the most popular Jewish websites is Aish.com, maintained by a nonprofit organization based in Jerusalem. If you click on Holidays in the menu bar, you'll find a wealth of Hanukkah resources, including kid-friendly videos like one with an animated menorah.

An excellent website called Judaism 101 is maintained by a passionate Jewish individual who isn't affiliated with a specific organization but writes primarily from an Orthodox perspective. There is a great deal here about how to celebrate holidays like Hanukkah, and the history behind them. One of the pluses of this site is that much of the information is organized by the reader's level of knowledge of Judaism: The categories are "Basic, Intermediate, Advanced, and Gentile" (non-Jewish).

As expected, there are multitudes of apps for Hanukkah, ranging from the seriously religious to the seriously silly. For kids, there are a number of apps for iPhones and other gadgets, to play virtual versions of dreidel, a gambling game that is very popular during the holiday. One of them is called the iGevalt Dreidel Simulator (a playful take on the Yiddish expression "Oy, gevalt!" used to express surprise or alarm).

Winter Solstice

The shortest day of the year, which varies between December 21 and 22, has been celebrated for centuries by many diverse cultures. Traditional celebrations usually include fire and light and quiet contemplation.

Solstice Dinner

Jeanne Mollinger-Lewis's family has a special dinner emphasizing "food the sun grows," like nuts and fruit, and the kids get a major gift on this day. They line the walk to their front door with luminarias, candles inside paper bags weighted down with sand, and light sparklers and small fireworks they've saved since July 4.

Solstice Wreath

Rain Mako, who lives in a cabin in the Ozarks with her husband and children, made a wreath from a long, bare grapevine she found near their property. To decorate it for solstice, the family cuts evergreen boughs and inserts them in the twisted wreath, adding tiny white lights. Rain always felt her kids weren't grateful for all their gifts when they got a pile of them on Christmas, so her sons get one present a day between winter solstice and Christmas, left near the wreath.

Here Comes the Sun!

At our house, we sit down in the living room after dinner in total darkness. We talk about how the lengthening of the days would have seemed glorious to people before electricity and about the balance of light and darkness in our lives. Then we light a bunch of candles and throw open the front door, yelling "Come back, sun!" We make sun shakes of orange juice and ice cream in the blender, and play the Beatles song "Here Comes the Sun."

Solstice on the Beach

Stacy Louise Christopher lives with her family near the beach in Santa Barbara, California. Every year, they celebrate winter solstice on the beach, making a labyrinth in the sand near the shoreline, lining it with tea candles. The practice of walking a labyrinth is an ancient form of meditation, and they walk slowly while contemplating the year that is winding down. Then they have a potluck picnic and possibly some surfing, before a cozy bonfire.

Red for Letting Go, Green for New Beginnings

I have wholeheartedly adopted the solstice ritual that I read about in *Ode* magazine in December 2005. It is simple, powerful, and easy to do with young children. To prepare, just collect some twigs from your yard or a park. They don't have to be very thick, and about six inches is a good length (you will be snapping them in half, which will be hard if they are too small or too thick). Tie a red ribbon around one end of every twig, and a green ribbon around the other.

Editor Kim Ridley wrote that after enjoying a feast with friends, "We light a big bonfire in the backyard. Everyone gathers around it, each choosing a stick twined with red and green paper ribbon. Guests are invited to meditate silently on the solstice as a turning point, and then to think about something they want to let go of in their lives, as well as something new they want to see take root in their lives or in the world. When each person is ready, we raise our sticks above our heads. Then, in unison, we snap the sticks in half, throw the red-ribbon end into the fire, and shout 'good-bye and good riddance' to whatever we want to release. We keep the end wrapped with green ribbon throughout the year as a reminder of our new intention."

If it's not practical for you to make a bonfire, this can easily be done at a home fireplace, or even by burning the sticks (with parental supervision) in a kitchen cooking pan.

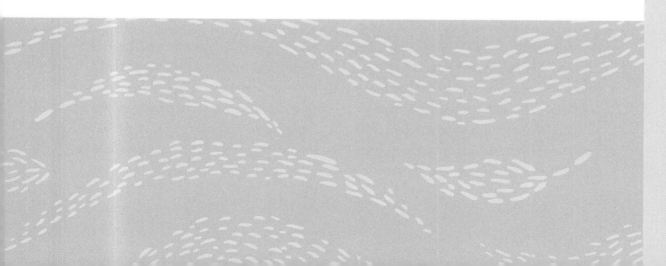

Pre-Christmas:
Celebrate the Whole Month

What changed my family's Christmas celebration most was the year I had food poisoning on Christmas morning and missed most of the fun. It finally sank in that Christmas should be a season, not a single day, and there are many positive results of that focus for kids. Putting so much weight on just one day can be crippling for kids and lead to big disappointments if it doesn't turn out just as they (or you) had hoped it would. We started really appreciating the daily things we did for Advent, including opening up a Lego Advent calendar every day in December and sitting quietly every evening to enjoy our tree after it was decorated.

Saint Nicholas Day Craft Kits

December 6 is the day many countries celebrate Saint Nicholas, a bishop who became a saint and was said to rescue children and help the poor. Many believe he was the real person who inspired the mythical Santa Claus, and they give their children small treats and gifts on the saint's day.

Once her kids were old enough, Teresa Schultz-Jones started the tradition that Saint Nicholas leaves craft kits for each of them, so they can make gifts for others. Teresa, who grew up with the Saint Nick tradition in Belgium, says, "This is just so much better than having all the excitement revolve around Christmas Day. Now they get very excited about what they'll get for S. Nicholas Day, and the prospect of what gifts they can make afterward."

Good Deed Paper Chain

Sara Tapley, a mother of six, hangs a multi-colored paper chain across the bay window in her dining room, after writing the name of one family member on each link. Every morning, each person has to break a link and do a good deed for the person whose name is written there; if you get your own name, you pass it on.

Make Your Own Advent Calendar

Make it!

There are hundreds of commercial versions, but it's easy to make your own.

Materials

Felt fabric, in black, red, green, and yellow. Buy a yard of black felt, and one-half yard each of red, green, and yellow.

Scissors

Fabric marker

Fabric glue

Dowel rod about half an inch in diameter, or less, cut to a length of twenty-four inches

Instructions

The black felt is the background. Cut it to be nineteen inches wide and thirty-five inches high. Cut the pockets three inches by three inches, and cut twelve pockets of red felt and twelve pockets of green. Cut three stars out of the yellow felt, one bigger than the other two. Next, lay all the pieces on the black background. There are six rows of four pockets, and they should alternate between red and green. There should be about an inch between the pockets. Number the pockets: 1 to 24. This can be done using a black marker (get one specifically for use on textiles) or by cutting out the numbers from the yellow felt. If using felt numbers, glue them on using fabric glue. Glue the pockets (or sew if you prefer) to the background—remember to just secure three edges and leave the top open! Attach the stars in a row at the top, with the big one in the middle. To hang, roll the top inch and a half of the black felt to the back, creating a sleeve through which you can insert the dowel rod. Glue or sew the edge to the back, to secure it. The rod will stick out at both ends, and you can hang the calendar on two nails, or if you wish, tie a ribbon to both ends of the rod, and hang using the ribbon, on one nail.

The Ritual

Starting on December 1, put something special in a pocket each day: It could be a piece of candy, a Bible verse, or a small toy, or a combination of these. With small children, you can buy something like an inexpensive set of farm animals or soldiers or cars and put one thing from the set in a pocket daily: By Christmas, your kid will have a complete barnyard, or a whole army, or entire car lot.

How to Make an Advent Wreath

Advent comes from the Latin word for *coming*, and many Christians find that using the full month before Christmas to concentrate on the religious meaning of this holiday helps to counteract the materialistic messages that bombard kids.

Materials

A simple Styrofoam wreath shape from the local crafts store (a donut shape)

Plastic pine boughs or live ones from your yard

Five candles, either three purple and one pink or four purple, plus one white (though in a pinch, any color will do)

A simple holder for one candle

Instructions

Stick the purple and pink candles into the Styrofoam, roughly at what would be the "corners" of the wreath. Then stick the pine boughs in all the way around, covering the white base. Decorate further, if you wish, with red ribbon, which can also be glued in a band around the base if the white Styrofoam shows through the greens. The fourth candle, the white one, goes into the holder, which is placed on your table inside the wreath. The greens are symbolic of new life and hope, while the flames stand for the light of Christ: The closer we get to his birth, the greater the light.

The Ritual

There are different views about what each candle stands for, but one common reading is that the first week's candle (purple) stands for hope; the second (purple) stands for love; the third (pink) stands for joy; and the fourth (purple) means peace. The fifth (white), which goes in the center and is lighted on Christmas Eve, is the Christ candle. On the first Sunday, light just the first candle: on the second light the first and the second, and so on. If you light candles each night, add a new candle on Sunday. Many families read a Bible passage after lighting candles.

Saint Nicholas Morning Surprise

Dorothy Steinicke's kids say Saint Nicholas Day is the best part of the winter holidays. After Thanksgiving, Dorothy did a lot of secret baking when her kids were small, often after they went to bed. Then, on Saint Nicholas Eve, she and her husband would stay up late and transform the downstairs. They strung her cookies on ribbons and draped them from the ceiling, arranged other cookies inside shoes lined up in the dining room, and set the table with their best linen, crystal, and china. On the table, they placed one of those holiday candleholders that rotates and chimes after candles are lit. The kids would wake to the sound of the chimes "and come out to find magnificence," says Dorothy. "Good silver glinting in candlelight in the winter morning darkness, festoons of cookies overhead. My children are now in high school and college, and this holiday has never lost its magic."

The Ultimate Saint Nicholas Website

The St. Nicholas Center is a charming, well-designed website, a true labor of love created by two people who are completely bonkers for this Catholic saint. Here you will find a great wealth of information and resources, including historical background, clip art, costumes, crafts, and activities. There are features on how Saint Nicholas Day is celebrated around the globe, as well as maps showing where the bishop lived before his posthumous sainthood. There's also an online store that stocks pretty much everything you can imagine: Saint Nicholas puppets, posters, cookie cutters, banners, buttons, screen-savers, ornaments, and napkins. You'll find all this at StNicholasCenter.org.

Manger Rituals

The Schroeder family has sixteen characters in its nativity set, and all except baby Jesus are wrapped up before the holidays begin. Each night after dinner, the kids take turns picking one wrapped character and setting it into the manger scene. That child then gets to pick which Christmas carol the family sings that night. Baby Jesus doesn't get put into the manger until Christmas morning, when the family sings "Happy Birthday, Jesus." Another family sets up its wise men across the room from the nativity scene, and every day of Advent moves them slightly closer.

Christmas Box

In the Gardiner family, the two daughters each have a pretty Christmas tin reserved for them, always kept on a certain windowsill during December. Every morning, they run to their tins to see what treat they got that day: It could be candy, a Christmas poem, a puzzle, or tickets to the *Nutcracker* ballet.

Just the Tree, the Dark, and Us

All the nights running up to Christmas, just before bed, we turn out all the lights in the living room except those on the tree and just quietly sit on the sofa together and enjoy it. This is a winding-down, smell-the-evergreen experience, where we each point to some of our favorite ornaments and talk about the vacation where we bought them or the person who made or gave us that beautiful or special object. Doni Boyd in Oregon does something like this with her family, but they take turns picking Christmas songs to sing as well.

tech tip

A good Christian website with background information on all the religious traditions of Advent, including the Advent wreath, and Bible verses to read during the weeks before Christmas is www.Crivoice.org/cyadvent.html.

More Family Christmas Celebrations

Camp Christmas

One winter when she had sixteen family members coming to visit her in Texas for the holidays and a limited amount of funds, Mary Kay Havens and her daughter created "Camp Christmas." They chose the word "camp" to suggest informality (sleeping bags and all) and fun, group activities. The highlight was a group carriage ride around Dallas, followed by a candlelight church service, but much of the time was spent at the Havens house, doing things in shifts. One small group would bake cookies while another sang carols and a third decorated Santa hats.

Candle Night

On Christmas Eve after church, the Straws light every candle they own. They read the Christmas story from the Bible and eat Christmas cookies with milk. The Taylor family of New Bedford, Massachusetts, has a different candle ritual that night: Sitting around the tree, each person is given an unlit candle. A lighted candle is on a table nearby. The first person lights his or her candle, tells about a prayer that God answered in the past year, then asks for help with something else. He or she lights the candle of the next person, who does the same, and so on. When all the candles are lit, the family sings carols and the youngest puts Jesus in the manger under the tree.

Journey to Bethlehem

In Nevada, the Hiltons pretend one night to follow in the footsteps of Mary and Joseph. They troop through the house and yard, as though on a journey, winding up at the foot of their Christmas tree. By candlelight, they have a picnic on a blanket, eating foods Mary and Joseph may have had, such as pita bread, fruit, and nuts.

Joy Balls

This charming idea was found within an annual e-mail list called Christmas Joys, which seems to be discontinued. A woman named Sally said her family had a tradition at Christmas parties of having something called a Joy Ball, which was like a piñata, but with toys, not candy. All year long, the parents would squirrel away little gifts costing $1 or less, wrapping each one in scraps of leftover Christmas wrap. Then they wrapped all of them in crepe paper strips, starting with one small gift, wrapping and adding gifts until there was one big ball. As the gifts were added, the crepe paper ends were just tucked in slightly: Only the last strip of crepe paper was secured with tape, so once the unwinding began, momentum would pull the ball apart. When all were ready to play, everyone got on the floor. The tape at the end was removed, and family members batted the ball around madly, grabbing gifts as they fell out.

Hay Foot, Straw Foot

Most of the Tilney family's holiday traditions have to do with "delayed gratification," insists Merritt Tilney. "We are not allowed to even look into the living room where the Christmas tree and presents are until we have completed the Hay Foot–Straw Foot ritual, opened our stockings, and eaten a complete breakfast," she says. Nobody dares cheat, she explains, because of the oft-told tale of a Tilney aunt who took a peek and saw the new bike she wanted so desperately. Her dad discovered the breach in protocol and removed the bike. She couldn't speak up, because she wasn't supposed to know about the bike. (It showed up for her birthday, in May.) In any case, the Hay Foot–Straw Foot ritual consists of the extended family lined up at the top of the stairs, oldest to youngest, hands on the shoulder of the person in front. As they troop down the steps, they all chant this old Revolutionary War rhyme that was designed to teach yokels how to march: They tied hay to the left foot and straw to the right, and since they knew hay from straw better than right from left, it worked for marching practice. Merritt says they do one verse standing still, then keep repeating the chant until everyone is downstairs, ready to enter the room with the Christmas stockings.

Hay foot, straw foot,
Belly full of bean soup,
January, February, March!

Christmas Reading Rituals

Literary Advent Calendar

When my son was little, every year around Thanksgiving, I would dig up every holiday-related book we had ever bought and wrap them all in Christmas paper. I laid them all out on the floor, so I could see which book falls on which day, and as I wrapped them, I taped a number between one and twenty-four on the front of the package. (If you don't have twenty-four books, use a few from the library before they're due, cut out a Christmas story from a magazine, or wrap a holiday DVD.) I always put the number 24 on *The Night Before Christmas*, so we could read that Christmas Eve, and if it's a longer than normal book, it would be scheduled on a weekend date. (Like J. R. R. Tolkien's wonderful *Letters from Father Christmas,* which is a storybook full of letters you take out of envelopes and read.)

Then, starting after supper on the first day of December, I would place a book under our felt Advent calendar (which hung on a doorknob in the playroom). The nightly ritual was that my son would take a felt ornament from a numbered pocket and put it on the felt tree, after which he was allowed to open the day's book. To preserve the sense that these books were only for special times, I packed them away in a box in the attic after the holiday.

For years, this was possibly my son's favorite holiday ritual outside of opening presents on Christmas morning. There was something so special about unwrapping a beloved book, such as *How the Grinch Stole Christmas,* then having him climb into my lap to hear the story. It actually seemed to mean more that he had heard most of the stories, because that is what tradition is all about: stoking the memories, and then reliving those favorite times.

I got this tradition from Nancy Giehl of Boulder, Colorado, who read it in *Family Fun* magazine, and I have since passed it along to many families. I know some families with more than one child who wrap their holiday books in different colored wrap. So if you had two kids, for example, you could wrap twelve books in red and twelve in green, and they could take turns opening them.

Night Tree

The Brock family loved this holiday book by Eve Bunting, which is based on an actual family's Christmas ritual. The family in *Night Tree* visits the same pine tree in the nearby woods each year on Christmas Eve, decorating it with treats for birds and other wildlife. The Brocks follow the ritual pretty closely, but they go to a wooded area on their property in Cheny, Washington. Beforehand, they make a garland of cranberry and breakfast cereal (popcorn works, too) and roll pinecones in birdseed after slathering them with peanut butter. After decorating the tree together, they sing carols and drink hot chocolate from a thermos.

More Great Christmas Books

There are classics like *The Night Before Christmas*, but here are some lesser-known books my son loved:

- *The Polar Express*, by Chris Van Allsburg
- *The Christmas Miracle of Jonathan Toomey*, by Susan Wojciechowski
- *December*, by Eve Bunting
- *Olive, the Other Reindeer*, by J. Otto Seibold and Vivian Walsh

Great Christmas Websites

There are hundreds of Christmas websites, a vast majority of them tacky or designed mostly to make a quick buck. Here are a few that provide excellent resources and have lasted longer than a nanosecond.

WhyChristmas.com was first launched in 2000 by James Cooper, a Christmas-loving web designer from the United Kingdom. It's clever and totally packed with resources such as Christmas customs from all over the world, recipes, and fun features like "Christmas Karaoke," which allows you to sing along to fifty popular Christmas carols. Unlike most of the big holiday sites, it doesn't sell ads, so there aren't constant pop-ups and other distractions.

MyMerryChristmas.com is an established mega site with an enormous quantity of content. It claims to be "The Internet's largest ongoing celebration of Christmas and the world's largest Christmas community." There are loads of resources, for instance, reviews of holiday-themed movies and television shows and fun regular features such as "Santa Speaks," an annual interview with the bearded one himself. This site is more of a community than most in that it includes an active message board and activities such as an ornament exchange, but you must become a member to do those more interactive things.

Northpole.com is arguably the cutest and most established Christmas site for kid-friendly content. It's been around since 1996, which is practically ancient for a website. The home page is set up like a village map, where you find yourself at the North Pole and have a choice of buildings to visit, such as the Toy Shop, Reindeer Barn, and Mrs. Claus' Kitchen. Kids can write and send letters to Santa and read stories about elves and reindeer and other North Pole occupants. A more recent addition is a wonderful educational feature called Elf Pal Academy that includes games, crafts, and activities for children.

Christmas Gift Rituals

One way to add meaning to the holiday is to give fewer gifts, but make the giving of them part of the ritual.

Three Gifts

Some families give each of their kids only three gifts, explaining that Jesus received three gifts from the wise men, and why should anyone else get more? The Suk family of Evanston, Illinois, follows this practice, but creatively. Each child gets one book, one game, and one toy, usually something major like a bicycle or electric guitar. The little things are wrapped and under the tree, but the major gifts are hidden, and the kids have to solve clues to find them. One year, the clues led to a garage-door opener, which led to a neighbor's garage and the hidden bike. The whole family troops around together as each child searches, youngest first.

Goofy Slippers

Pam Pinegar, a self-described "small woman with big feet," started a tradition with her two daughters that each year they buy one another the goofiest slippers they can find. Theme presents are fun, and many families give their kids new, Christmas-themed pajamas on Christmas Eve (at least no one looks ratty for the family photos).

The Gift of Ourselves

Each family member announces something he or she will do for the family in the coming year. Each person could write the planned gift on a slip of paper, with little ones getting help on that part. One idea is to slip the notes into stockings before the holiday. Read them aloud on Christmas morn. Kids could give the gift of a cheerful attitude about chores or homework. Or a child could offer to fix breakfast on Saturday, or walk the dog, or help carry in groceries. Parents can give the gift of their presence: spending one-on-one time with a kid every day at a certain time, or promising to take a child to the park weekly.

Gift Exchange

One way to limit excess is to pick names out of a hat, so extended family members have to shop for only one person. The Trieschman family of Baltimore picks names on Thanksgiving and adds to the fun by delivering a "joke gift" to the person between that holiday and Christmas. They try to do it anonymously and make it as silly as possible: Cindy Trieschman actually rented a donkey for a day and snuck it into her father's toolshed. On Christmas, the adults don't get to open their regular present until they accurately guess who picked their name.

Ornament Tradition

Many families give each child one ornament a year, often on a theme, like all doves or stars or angels. Michele Lynn gives her son an ornament related to something he was passionate about in the past year. One year, she gave him an ornament featuring Santa catching a Frisbee, because her son played on the school's Ultimate Frisbee team. She keeps all his ornament collection together, with slips of paper saying what year he got each. One day, when he grows up and makes a real home of his own, they will be his to take.

One Gift on Christmas Eve

Many families have a tradition of opening one present on Christmas Eve. In some households, that gift is holiday-themed pajamas: It's very sweet the next morning, when the kids come tumbling down the stairs dressed in matching jammies! Less common is the tradition Angie Karnoupakis grew up with in California: Her mother gave everyone a squirt gun on Christmas Eve. As she told *Real Simple* magazine in November 2004, "We'd run off to fill our new toys and ambush the rest of the family. I have great memories of us running around after one another and of Grandma hiding behind an open door to get each of us between the eyes as we ran past."

Gift Idea for Older Stepkids

Marveen Craig was wary of making elaborate new traditions as a stepmom. It wasn't only that the kids already had established rituals, but that they were grown when she joined the family. She came up with a terrific idea that everyone loves.

"I proposed that instead of giving each other Christmas gifts that might be too big/small, not the right color and all that, we should instead call our tradition Five Days of Christmas," says Marveen. The plan was for each one to create a special experience for all five, but keep it secret until right before it happened. These are Marveen's rules:

1. **Each family member chooses an activity they love and then treats the other members to it.**
2. **The recipients cannot decline or grumble. After all, it is a gift.**
3. **The "gift giving" must take place within two weeks of Christmas.**

And here are some of the gifts that were given based on this new tradition: An evening of bowling and dinner at a local steakhouse; front-row seats at a dinner-theater production; center seats on the ice at a pro hockey game; and a "Margarita Run," which consisted of a fully stocked limo picking everyone up and stopping at three different Mexican restaurants for appetizers. (From the appetizers, they voted on which restaurant they would go back to for dinner and dancing until midnight.)

Christmas Quilt: One Square Per Year

When my son was a toddler, his babysitter, Resa Veary, gave me a special gift: about twenty squares of plain, unbleached muslin fabric, nine inches by nine inches. The squares were placed inside a fabric drawstring bag, with two squeeze bottles of fabric paint: one red, one green. Resa said that every Christmas, I could have Max decorate one square, and someday, I would sew them all together into a quilt. What an inspired gift!

When he was very little, we would do simple things like have Max trace around a Pooh cookie cutter. When he learned to write his name, he just wrote his name over and over in red and green to decorate his square. Later, he would draw pictures of his favorite Pokemon or TV character, or a pet, like his leopard geckos, Dart and Chet.

I finally finished the quilt in 2011, after Max turned sixteen and made his fifteenth square. I decided to make the quilt four squares across and four rows down, and for the sixteenth square, on the bottom at the right, I wrote, "Max's Christmas Quilt" in red and green. This is my favorite type of tradition, because it celebrates the holiday each year but also showcases his growth, providing a snapshot of his passions and abilities year by year.

Most years, it probably took him less than thirty minutes to decorate his square, but cumulatively, this finished quilt amounts to a beautiful memento of his whole childhood. When I quilted it, instead of making lines or squiggles for my quilting pattern, I wrote words in script (using my sewing machine) describing some of our other holiday traditions like "Leaving Cookies for Santa." Now that it is done, we'll hang it every year on Christmas, but I'm really thinking about starting a new one as well. Maybe we will all work on squares!

From One Quilt, Many Gifts

Michele Isaacson took an old quilt her grandmother made that was falling to pieces and cut up the top to make heart- and star-shaped ornaments for her father, her siblings, and her kids, embellishing them with buttons she found in her grandmother's sewing basket.

Important Note to Non-Sewing Households

You can do this, too! Start decorating the squares, and when you have collected enough, contact a local quilt store or fabric shop in your community. They will give you contact information for a local quilter you can hire to stitch the quilt together and do the actual quilting of the top layer with a backing and batting. Better yet: When your kid, or kids, are almost done decorating their squares, sign up for a beginner quilt class, and finish it yourself.

Christmas Charity Traditions

Many families that want to raise compassionate kids have philanthropic traditions during Christmas. And it's also a solution to the age-old problem of what the grown-ups should give one another when they already have so much.

Family Charity Pick Rather Than Gifts

Members of Emily Sagor's extended family collect nominations in September or October of charities they would like to help. There are usually five or six nominated, and the person who nominated each gives some details about the organization and why he or she picked it. Before Christmas, they vote on the charity, and each family decides how much to send to her aunt, who bundles the payments and makes one check to the charity in the name of the entire family. Emily says they find it loads more gratifying than picking names and getting token gifts for the holiday. "Each year we end up not only learning about some new organizations that are worthy of our attention, but we also learn a bit more about each other as we learn what matters to each of us."

Giving Christmas to a Whole Family

Jennifer Grant's Episcopal church in Chicago allows parishioners to help an entire family. They get a packet with the names, ages, and requests for gifts. "My kids and I go to a big box store and get everything from canned yams to remote controlled cars to CD players to mittens and sheets," says Jennifer, a mother of four. "We come home, talk about each recipient, pray for each member of the family, wrap and label the gifts, and deliver everything to the church." What also makes the experience special, she says, is that the heads of household write a little about themselves on the forms, so "my kids get a sense of each person's story and dignity. They also sense that we're fortunate and that what we have belongs to God, not us. It makes for a less greedy Christmas and I don't find my kids begging for stuff around the holiday."

Local Scholarship from the Vogts

When the four Vogt kids graduated from high school, the family started a tradition in which everyone donates money for a scholarship to be awarded each year to the high school where most of the kids went, to help a needy kid with college costs. It isn't a vast amount of money, but it is helpful and a vote of confidence for someone who needs both. The guidance counselors help the family pick: Kids apply and write an essay and the family chooses who will receive the award.

Matching Allowance Funds to Make a Difference

For Sandy Graham's kids in Denver, her son and daughter each pick a local charity to help. They must donate a minimum of $10 from their allowance, which their parents match (up to $50). They talk about different causes, including the environment, soup kitchens, and so forth. One year, her son gave his money to a program to help underprivileged children, and her daughter gave hers for the homeless. The next year, both decided to support the local no-kill animal shelter, where they had gotten their own dog, Rascal. They went to the bank, where one withdrew $15 and the other $20, then went to Petco, where the family spent $70 on items from the shelter's wish list.

Christmas Bread

It isn't just money that makes a wonderful gift to others in your community. Dorothy Steinicke's family has a tradition of making "ridiculously huge batches of a complicated Christmas bread and giving it away to neighbors, old friends, and people who just happen to cross our path, such as homeless people and deliverymen." Dorothy says, "as my kids have gotten older they can participate more fully and now enlist some of their friends. It is pretty much an all-day endeavor, and then we have to rush to give it all away while the bread is still fresh!"

Kwanzaa

Introduced in 1966, Kwanzaa is a celebration of African culture that runs from the day after Christmas through New Year's Day. Each day is devoted to a different principle. More and more cities have public Kwanzaa celebrations, but many African American families also observe the holiday at home.

Candle Ceremony

A basic part of Kwanzaa is lighting candles each night and talking about the principle of the day. In Washington, D.C., Yvette Aidara, mother of a teenage son, celebrates with a group of friends, who take turns hosting on successive evenings. Among the children present, a different one is chosen each night to say the name of the day's principle in English and Swahili. Then, each person in the group says how he or she will put that principle into practice in the coming year.

History Game

Retelling history, particularly of one's ancestors, is another important part of Kwanzaa, and the Ruff family of Dublin, Ohio, always includes a history game in its annual New Year's Eve party. In one game, the names of famous Africans are pinned on the backs of some guests, and they ask questions of others until they guess the name pinned to them. Those who are able to celebrate Kwanzaa with much of their extended families favor oral history projects such as getting the children to tape-record interviews with their grandparents.

Creativity Party

Many families hold a party during the week of Kwanzaa around a particular theme. Angela Dodson and Michael Days in Trenton, New Jersey, usually choose the theme of creativity. Guests perform, tell stories, or read poems, and each brings a dish with African origins to the feast.

Magic Doll Brings Something Back from Africa

In Eugene, Oregon, Do Mi Stauber and her partner, Trisha Whitney, observe Kwanzaa with their adopted African American daughter, Alex. The day after Christmas, they always take down the Christmas tree and put up a Kwanzaa table. Every day, they try to do something related to the principle of that day: On collective responsibility day, they might all bring in firewood. On creativity day, they make one another a homemade gift.

But Do Mi and Trisha wanted to add a special magical element when Alex was young, so on the last night of Kwanzaa, which is also New Year's Eve, they would have her put her African doll, named Osa, on the Kwanzaa table. "In her lap, Alex would leave a traditional trading bead and a note Alex had written about something that makes her proud to be African American." The idea was that the doll would travel to Africa while the girl slept and trade her bead for a present. In the morning, Alex would find a gift, such as a drum or push toy made in Africa.

How to Make a Kinara, a Kwanzaa Candleholder

Materials

You can use any recipe for non-toxic clay. This one comes from Arts and Crafts Recipes, a Klutz guide.

You'll need:

2 cups baking soda

1 cup cornstarch

1¼ cups cold water

Paints

Paintbrush

Seven candles: three red, three green, and one black

Instructions

Mix the baking soda and cornstarch in a saucepan. Add water. Cook the mixture over medium-high heat, stirring constantly until it's the consistency of mashed potatoes. Spoon dough onto a plate and cover with a damp cloth to cool. When cool, roll the clay into seven balls and attach them side by side. Stick the candles into the balls, then pull them out to leave seven holes. The clay will take up to two days to dry, and then you can paint your kinara. You might want to use the Kwanzaa colors of red, green, and black.

The Ritual

Place the black candle, for the African people, in the center, with the three green candles (for young people) and the three red ones (for struggle), on either side of it. The first night, light just the black candle and discuss the first principle, unity. The next night, light the black candle and one other and discuss the second principle, and so on, as follows: Second night, self-determination. Third night, collective work and responsibility. Fourth night, cooperative economics. Fifth night, purpose. Sixth night, creativity. Final night, faith.

tech tip

Kwanzaa Website

You'll get the straight story on all the traditions and origins of Kwanzaa by going to a site maintained by the holiday's founder, African Studies professor Dr. Maulana Karenga, at OfficialKwanzaaWebsite.org. The site also sells books on the holiday and the wooden candleholder, called a kinara, used for the celebrations.

Fifty Questions for the Dinner-Table Conversation Basket

See instructions on page 40 for using the basket.

If there were a holiday named after you, how would people celebrate?

Describe the most wonderful animal you've ever known.

Tell us something you learned recently that surprised you.

What can you do better than your parents?

If you had one special power, what would it be?

Who was/is your favorite teacher and why?

Where would you like to live someday?

If you could bring any imaginary creature to life, what would it be?

Tell a story about what would happen if you got to meet your favorite fictional character, someone from a book or TV show you love. What would you say? What sort of adventure would you have together?

What would you teach that character to do?

If you could invent a new flavor of ice cream, what would it be?

If this family had a theme song, what would it be?

Who is your best friend?

What would you like to know more about?

Is there someone you can't stand (not in this family)? How would you change that person?

Which is your favorite season?

If you were a dog, what breed would you be and what would your name be?

If you won the golden ticket to Willy Wonka's chocolate factory, what sweet treat would you invent?

Name two countries you want to visit, and say why.

What is your favorite movie?

Who do you know who did something brave?

What's the best thing about a beach?

If there were a television sitcom or cartoon about your family, what would it be called?

How do you make people laugh?

What makes you mad?

If you were a new product or device, how would the ads describe you?

Name something that you really wanted but didn't get, and say how you feel about that now.

What do you do when you're bored?

Make up a nickname for everyone at the table, including yourself. (Nothing mean.)

What would your personal robot do for you?

What can you do now that you couldn't do a year ago?

What scares you?

What is your favorite movie pet?

Which character in Lord of the Rings (insert your favorite movie or book) is most like you?

Describe your dream house.

What do you like to smell?

What cheers you up when you are sad?

What is the best game ever invented?

If you could have dinner with any person in history, who would it be?

What or who makes you laugh?

Tell us about a dream you remember.

You just won the lottery—$1 million a year for life. What will change in your life? What will stay the same?

What is the single best thing about you?

How would you make the world better?

What do you love enough to save for your own children?

If you could relive any day of your life, which day would it be?

What bad habit do you wish you could break?

What stories do they tell about you as a baby?

What was the worst day of your life?

What is your definition of friendship?

If you could possess a talent or gift that you weren't born with, what would it be?

Who inspires you?

Gail Simpson's Open Adoption Ritual[1]

Read the family's story on page 146.

Giving and Receiving Ceremony Celebrating the Open Adoption of Sophie

Minister:

In our community we recognize life's major events through ceremony. John, Susan, Mary (Adopting Father, Mother, and Sister), and Karen (birthmother) invite you all to join with them in marking the Giving and Receiving of this child, Sophie (baby), in open adoption.

Karen, would you pass Sophie to John, Susan, and Mary as a symbol of your choice to have them adopt her and raise her as their daughter and sister.

John, Susan, Mary, Sophie, and Karen invite those of you who are part of the adoption triangle to join them in the reading below. Any person who has adopted a child is invited to rise now and join John and Susan in the reading by the Adopting Parents.

Adopting Parents, Speaking to Birthparent:

We solemnly receive this child, accepting the unfathomable responsibility of parenting her, committing ourselves to the daily renewal of spirit needed to raise children with faith, hope, courage, dignity, wisdom, and humor.

We humbly receive this child, awestruck by the mysterious forces which delivered this particular child into our care.

We joyfully receive this child, anticipating the tender pleasure of our journey with her.

Minister:

All adopted children, young and old, are invited to rise now and join Nancy (an Adult Adoptee in the congregation), who will read, for Mary and Sophie, the reading by the Adopted Child.

Adopted Child to Birthparents and Adopting Parents:

I bring you together in this mysterious intersection of nature and nurture which is adoption. I am the music to which you will dance of love and loss for a lifetime. Dance well. My melody is the sweet yearning for life. Teach me the language of love from which to compose my lyrics.

---

1   * Names have been changed.

Minister:

Any person who has given a child for adoption is invited to rise now and join Karen in the reading by the Birthparent.

Birthparents to Adopting Parents:

I give this child to be raised by you as your child.

She is a part of me

Whom I have nourished with my blood and spirit;

Whom I conceived in innocence of the awesome power her life would command;

Whom I have borne in the pain of fear, childbirth, and separation;

And in whom I rejoice, reveling in the miracle of my own creation and in the gift beyond measure which I now give to you.

Minister:

Will the rest of you please join me in reading the words of the Community?

Community to Adopting Parents:

Treasure this child's life as you treasure your own. Act in Karen's stead to provide the daily substance of nurture and love. In the fullness of time, let her know how love brought us together in this vulnerable moment of giving and receiving.

Community to Birthparents:

Go forth to fulfill the promise of your future, knowing that we celebrate your life and the story that you continue to create. We honor you as this child's proud heritage.

All Sing: "Every Night and Every Morn"

(words, William Blake, ca. 1803; music, Ralph Vaughan Williams, 1911)

Every night and every morn,

Some to misery are born.

Every morn and every night,

Some are born to sweet delight.

Joy and woe are woven fine,

Clothing for a soul divine,

And through every grief and pine

Runs a joy with silken twine.

It is right, it should be so.

We were made for joy and woe.

And when this we rightly know,

Safely through this world we go.

Acknowledgments

This revised edition reflects nearly a decade of additional research and personal experience since the first edition in 2003. Many of the 150-plus new rituals in this edition came from subscribers to my newsletter who have shared their traditions with me over the years. I'm so grateful for their continuing support, and for trusting me with their family stories.

I don't have space to list everyone I interviewed, but special thanks go to the mothers new for this edition who told me they were inspired to create their brilliant traditions after reading the earlier edition. That was a special thrill for me. These wonderful women include Stacy Louise Christopher, Jennifer Grant, and Karly Randolph Pitman. Thanks also to blogger Amanda Soule, whose SouleMama blog is a continuing source of inspiration.

Also, I circled back to some of the most creative mothers I interviewed for my two earlier books, and it turns out they had more rich rituals to share. These golden resources included Letitia Suk and Susan Vogt. As before, *Reunions* magazine editor Edith Wagner is the ultimate source on reunion rituals, and she continues to share her expertise freely. Thank you!

While researching the impact of technology on families, I came across the brilliant and generous Anne Collier, editor of NetFamilyNews.org, and a nationally known guru on Internet safety. She helped me find some of the awesome tech traditions in the book. Another person whose expertise affected me deeply is Laurie David, author of *The Family Dinner: Great Ways to Connect with Your Kids, One Meal at a Time*. I'm grateful she wrote this terrific book, and that she let me run an excerpt in my section on family dinners.

Thanks again to my agent and friend Geri Thoma, who has stood by me for many years (including literally, at my wedding). I'm grateful to all of my friends who keep a watch out for offbeat traditions, especially Liza Lucy and Wendy Kwitny, who steered me to some awesome rituals included here.

I am thankful for my editor at Running Press, Jennifer Kasius, who edited with a light hand but let me know when she thought I was running off the rails. Thanks to everyone at Running Press for believing enough in this book to let me make it bigger and better!

To Trina Dalziel, the illustrator for this new edition, thanks so much for interpreting my words and ideas through your utterly charming drawings. You've really captured the cozy, quirky heart of these traditions with vivid details and personal flourishes. And your illustrations fit beautifully within the pleasing architecture of sidebars, chapter headings, and all, created by the book's designer, Corinda Cook.

My deepest gratitude goes to my husband, Richard Leone, and our son, Max: I didn't start researching and writing about family traditions until you both came into my life.

How to Contact the Author & Get More on Rituals

Send e-mails to meg@megcox.com, and visit the author's website, megcox.com, for more information about her background and current activities. You can send regular mail to Meg through the publisher; Running Press will forward letters.

The author is always interested to hear about thoughtful and inventive traditions: maybe yours will be included in one of Meg Cox's newsletters, articles, or future books.

To keep getting fresh ideas about how to celebrate all of life's occasions, go to the Facebook page for this book, www.facebook.com/TraditionsBook.

For those who want to use this book as the basis for workshops on how to create fresh, powerful traditions, Cox has written a teacher's manual called *Got Traditions?* It can be purchased as an e-book and paperback at Amazon.com.